PEIRCE

AND PRAGMATISM

PEIRCE
AND PRAGMATISM

W. B. GALLIE

GREENWOOD PRESS, PUBLISHERS
WESTPORT, CONNECTICUT

Library of Congress Cataloging in Publication Data

Gallie, W   B   1912-
    Peirce and pragmatism.

        Reprint of the ed. published by Dover Publica-
    tions, New York.
        Includes bibliographical references and index.
        1.   Peirce, Charles Santiago Sanders, 1839-1914.
    2.   Pragmatism.   I.   Title.
    B945.P44G3 1975   191   75-25534
    ISBN 0-8371-8342-1

This edition originally published in 1966 by Dover Publications, Inc., New York

Reprinted with the permission of W. B. Gallie

Reprinted in 1975 by Greenwood Press,
a division of Williamhouse-Regency Inc.

Library of Congress Catalog Card Number 75-25534

ISBN 0-8371-8342-1

Printed in the United States of America

PREFACE TO THE DOVER EDITION

THIS book is intended as an introduction, for the general reader of philosophy, to a philosopher who has a certain fame as the founder of Pragmatism, but whose work as a whole is not as widely known as it deserves to be. Peirce has won the admiration of many of the most distinguished philosophers of this century both in America and Great Britain, but chiefly as a forerunner of recent and contemporary philosophical interests and methods. It is also important, however, that Peirce's work should be appreciated on its own account and because of its connection with a number of classic issues in the history of philosophy. This book has been written with that aim in view. In particular I have tried to re-state in fairly simple language a number of Peirce's ideas and doctrines which are brilliantly original as well as central to his philosophical position, but which he never succeeded in presenting in a form suited to the general reader.

Peirce's philosophical writings are now available in a number of forms. First, there is *The Collected Papers of Charles Sanders Peirce*, Vols. I to VI edited by Charles Hartshorne and Paul Weiss, Vols. VII and VIII edited by Arthur W. Burks (Harvard University Press, 1931–1958). This is essential reading for any detailed study of Peirce, but the general reader can neither be expected nor advised to make his acquaintance with Peirce through *The Collected Papers*. Luckily, various excellent selections from Peirce's writings are available, and a list of these is given in the Bibliographical Notes on page 243. One of these selections, *The Philosophy of Peirce*, Selected Writings, edited by Justus Buchler (London and New York, 1940 and later editions), seems to me particularly well suited to the needs of university students; and I have therefore indicated, with regard to the main theme of each of my own chapters, where support for or amplification of it can be found in *The Philosophy of Peirce*. On the other hand, in the interest of completeness and to assist more advanced students of Peirce, I have referred in the case of all actual quotations and of a number of key arguments to *The Collected Papers*.

I should like to record again here my debt of gratitude to the late Perry Miller and to Professor Charles Hartshorne for their kind advice in connection with the material in Chapter II. And I must repeat my thanks to the Harvard University Press for their permission to quote from *The Collected Papers of Charles Sanders Peirce*.

W. B. GALLIE

The Queen's University of Belfast
Belfast, Northern Ireland
August, 1965

CONTENTS

CHAPTER ONE

INTRODUCTORY

Pragmatism and the Pragmatists

*

THE word Pragmatism was introduced into philosophy as the name of a principle or method of logic, 'a method of ascertaining the meaning of hard words and abstract conceptions,'* and again 'a method of determining the meanings of intellectual concepts, that is, of those upon which reasoning may hinge.' †
The specific purpose of this method, according to its inventor Charles Sanders Peirce (1839–1914), was to clarify – and in some cases to eliminate as meaningless – traditional metaphysical questions;‡ but, when developed in Peirce's most mature writings, his Pragmatism forms part of a highly systematized theory of logic, and as such has important bearings on every other department of philosophy.

Peirce's teachings, however, had little effect on other philosophers of the late nineteenth and early twentieth centuries, and it is chiefly through the writings of the psychologist William James (1842–1910) that one aspect – and only one aspect – of Peirce's Pragmatism has become widely known among students of philosophy. This, its emphasis on the so-called practical character of all genuine thinking, was suggested in Peirce's original formulation of his Pragmatist maxim (1878): 'Consider what effects, that might conceivably have practical bearings, we conceive the object of our conception to have. Then, our conception of these effects is the whole of our conception of the

---

* 5·464. All quotations, unless otherwise indicated, are from the *Collected Papers of Charles Sanders Peirce* (Vols. I to VI). Following the practice of Peirce's editors I give first the number of the volume, and then, after a decimal point, the number of the paragraph in that volume. Thus in the case of this first quotation 5·464 means Vol. V, numbered paragraph 464 of the *Collected Papers*.

† 5·467.   ‡ 5·2.

object.'* Partly because of this original – and unfortunately cumbrous – statement, partly because later Pragmatists have continued to emphasize (though with varying intentions) the importance of practical considerations, of actual or possible physical operations, in even the most strictly intellectual pursuits, there has been a tendency in this country to associate Pragmatism with that anti-intellectualist wave which broke over western philosophy towards the end of the last century and of which Nietzsche's gospel of Will-to-Power and Bergson's philosophy of Life-force are the other most famous examples. Moreover, in this connection, Pragmatism has often been regarded, at any rate by British philosophers during the first half of this century, as an all too American product; with the implication, sometimes explicitly asserted, that it is a raw, almost a backwoods doctrine, such as would naturally arise in a new country where material interest and opportunities are paramount and the refinements and austerities of pure theory are little appreciated.

Whatever be the justice of this general estimate of Pragmatism, a grosser misrepresentation of its intellectual background could scarcely be imagined. Harvard, the nursing ground of the movement, was in the second half of the last century a cultural centre at least the equal of Oxford and Cambridge; it had long and deep, if somewhat narrow, intellectual traditions of its own, and in the opinion of Charles Darwin it contained enough brilliant minds in the 1860s to staff all the universities in England. Nor were the founders of Pragmatism in any sense intellectual backwoodsmen: Peirce and James – and the same can be said of the best of their Pragmatist successors – thought and wrote as men profoundly steeped in European culture and with a lively awareness of the best contemporary movements in European thought. Peirce in the 1870s and 1880s was teaching logic on lines which were eventually to reach Oxford some sixty years later, while James, as professor of psychology, was facing the main philosophical problems that

* 5.2.

arise from that subject with a freshness of vision and a mastery of all relevant detail which no British philosopher has ever commanded. But – to be done with these inexcusable misunderstandings – it should be noticed that British critics of Pragmatism have concentrated their attacks mainly on the writings of James and his disciples, neglecting, or treating only at second hand, Peirce's original statement and later developments of his Pragmatist principle.

In the present study we shall be concerned almost exclusively with Pragmatism in its original meaning as a 'method of logic' and as one facet of the general philosophy of Peirce. The reason for this choice is very simple; it is that Peirce, in the opinion or the present author and of most of those who are well acquainted with his writings, is the one unquestionably great figure in the Pragmatist movement, and that his general philosophy, of which his Pragmatism is an essential facet, seems likely to prove of more lasting value than the philosophical movement to which he gave an initial impetus and a name. This being so, it is important that we should at the outset get an adequate grasp of the main difference between Peirce's original Pragmatism – what he intended his 'method of logic' to be and do – and the Pragmatism of James. This task will involve us at once in somewhat technical discussion; but it should have the effect of dispelling a number of unfortunate associations of ideas, and will at the same time serve to remind us of some of the salient features of the spirit of the age in which Peirce's Pragmatism and the rest of his philosophy came into being.

Most discussions of Peirce's Pragmatism take as their starting-point the above quoted maxim: 'Consider what effects ...' Later we shall find good grounds for maintaining that, despite its verbal clumsiness – its heavy reiteration of the words 'conception', 'conceivable', 'conceive', and its abrupt introduction of the phrase 'practical bearings' – this maxim was evidently formulated with great care; only – and this is all too typical of its author – his efforts were directed at bringing out the essentials of his own thought rather than at introducing the idea of

Pragmatism, helpfully if somewhat superficially, to the general reader. Rather than attempt to unravel here the complexities of the maxim, we can best begin to suggest its aim and scope by citing a number of simpler formulations and descriptions of Pragmatism which are to be found in other parts of Peirce's writings.

One of these, a rough adumbration of the fully developed maxim, occurs in Peirce's review (1871) of Fraser's edition of Berkeley's Works. In the course of this review Peirce criticizes Berkeley's opinion that the only way of deciding what distinctive meaning – if any – an abstract term or formula possesses, is to ask: Can we frame an idea (by which Berkeley seems always to have meant an image or mental picture) corresponding to it? If we cannot, Berkeley maintained, then the term or formula in question is without meaning, and whatever usefulness it may appear to possess is spurious. It was in this vein that Berkeley criticized, for example, certain key terms in Newtonian mechanics. Peirce rounds on this view by remarking that if it had 'prevailed in mathematics (and Berkeley was equally strenuous in advocating it there), and if everything about negative quantities, the square root of minus terms, and infinitesimals, had been excluded from the subject on this ground that we can form no idea of such things, the science would have been simplified no doubt, simplified by never advancing to more difficult matters.' He then adds, 'A better rule for avoiding the deceits of language is this: Do things fulfil the same purpose practically? Then let them be signified by the same word. Do they not? Then let them be distinguished. If I have learnt a formula in gibberish which in any way jogs my memory so as to enable me in each single case to act as though I had a general idea, what possible utility is there in distinguishing between such a gibberish formula and an idea? Why use the term *a general idea* in such a sense as to separate things which, for all experiential purposes, are the same?'[*]

It is important to see as clearly as we can what is here at stake

* *North American Review*, vol. 113 (1871), pp. 449–72. Cf. 8.33.

between Peirce and Berkeley. As against the view that an abstract formula has meaning if and in so far as we can frame a definite idea or image corresponding to it, Peirce is maintaining that an abstract formula has meaning if, and only if, we can *use* it, – or can act under its influence in a distinctive and appropriate way. Whether anything – an idea – corresponding to the formula can be found among the furniture of our mind is, on his view, altogether irrelevant to the question whether that formula means anything. Our answer to this question depends solely upon how we answer the prior questions: How does one use the formula, or what distinctive things must one do in employing it, or interpreting it correctly? Here is the clue to Peirce's choice of such phrases as 'fulfil the same purpose practically' and 'effects that might conceivably have practical bearings.' Two or more things or situations differ practically, for Peirce, in so far as we find ourselves compelled in the course of experience to *treat* them differently, which involves expecting different reactions from them, and thereupon preparing ourselves to react to them again with suitable differences in our turn. To put virtually the same point in other terms, we commonly say that words stand for objects; but the word is nothing, Peirce maintains, apart from the actual occasions of its use, and the object is nothing (for us) except in so far as we can act on it and/or adjust ourselves to its reactions on us. We would therefore do better to say, as the Pragmatists' maxim virtually bids us say, that a given word means its distinctive object only through expressing or communicating a distinctive method or technique of action, expectation, and adjustment with regard to that object. Now if this could be granted, it would seem to follow that the meaning of any word, sentence, or other symbol essentially requires a succession of experiences – actions, expectations, and adjustments, real or imagined – to articulate it; or, in other words and as against Berkeley and those who think with him, that the distinctive meaning of a word or other symbol cannot be contained in or equated with a single mental image or picture. To ask what a person means by a word or formula is not to ask him what is in his mind when he utters or accepts it; it is, rather, to ask him what he is prepared to do when he utters or accepts it.

In this criticism of Berkeley, Peirce rests his argument on the case of somewhat abstruse mathematical symbols; but his general conception of the way words and other symbols mean can probably be best illustrated by examples drawn from the vocabulary and practice of the natural sciences. Here is an instance of the latter kind. 'If', Peirce writes, 'you look into a textbook of chemistry for a definition of *lithium*, you may be told that it is that element whose atomic weight is 7 very nearly. But if the author has a more logical mind he will tell you that if you search among minerals that are vitreous, translucent, grey or white, very hard, brittle and insoluble, for one which imparts a crimson tinge to an unluminous flame, this mineral being triturated with lime of witherite rat's-bane, and then fused, can be partly dissolved in muriatic acid; and if this solution be evaporated, and the residue be extracted with sulphuric acid, and duly purified, it can be converted by ordinary methods into a chloride, which being obtained in the solid state, fused, and electrolyzed with half a dozen powerful cells, will yield a globule of a pinkish silvery metal that will float on gasolene; and the material of *that* is a specimen of lithium. The peculiarity of this definition – or rather this precept that is more serviceable than a definition – is that it tells you what the word "lithium" denotes by prescribing what you are to *do* in order to gain a perceptual acquaintance with the object of the word.'*

On this account to say of a bit of metal 'This is lithium' is to say that it is of a kind that will result from or can be got from the performance of the above prescribed operations. Now it would, at first sight, accord better with Peirce's Pragmatism to define lithium in terms, not of any conditions that suffice to produce it, but of its characteristic effects, physical and chemical: and, again at first sight, it would accord better with ordinary usage to equate a chemist's knowledge of lithium, or what the word 'lithium' means to *him*, with the sum of his information as

* 2·330.

to how bits of lithium behave, rather than with his knowledge of how to obtain lithium in a relatively pure state. The fact is, however, that the chemist's knowledge of lithium – exemplified in any informative statement he may make about it – depends on his capacity to obtain specimens of lithium (and of course of a vast number of other chemical substances besides) under a variety of physical conditions. Indeed in any science of a highly systematic character, our knowledge of – and hence our informative statements about – the behaviour and effects of a given agent are inconceivable save in relation to generally accepted procedures for isolating and identifying, combining and separating, the agent in question. If this were not so, then any information we might receive, e.g. about the behaviour of *lithium*, would not be live information – we would not know how to begin to use it. But further, the precept which shows us the meaning of 'lithium' serves to illuminate something which lies latent in all our vaguer, more workaday conceptions: viz. that genuine understanding of any of these includes or presupposes a capacity to make 'operational contact' with its object; otherwise we could not set about verifying any alleged informative statement that is made about it. Now this is only a more specific form of our previous suggestion that a given word means its distinctive object only through expressing a distinctive procedure of action, expectation, and adjustment: and this in turn was simply a more elaborate form of expressing what Peirce meant when he said that words should be distinguished when they differ practically, or that the meaning of any word, or conception, consists in those 'effects that might conceivably have practical bearings.' If one conception does not in this sense differ practically from a second, then acceptance of it adds nothing to our acceptance of that second conception; and if it has no assignable practical effects whatsoever, then the words that express it are so much meaningless verbiage.

Let us now try, in the light of the foregoing examples, to assess the broad character and purpose of Peirce's maxim. In the first place, it is an instrument of logical clarification and analysis:

its aim is to help us distinguish as clearly as possible the different functions of different verbal and other symbolic expressions. But in the second place it is pretty clearly the product of a mind 'saturated through and through with the spirit of the physical sciences.'* This is most obvious, perhaps, in Peirce's insistence that, save in relation to physical actions (real or imagined), no word, symbol, or conception has any definite meaning. We might reasonably say, then, that the general conception of human knowledge which underlies Peirce's maxim is an essentially experimentalist one. But does this mean that his Pragmatism is simply a generalization of the conditions under which the highly specialized terms of the natural sciences come to possess their distinctive meanings? There are a number of passages in Peirce which strongly suggest this interpretation. In one of these he begins by remarking that the habits of mind of every experimental scientist – he himself had been one for some thirty years – are moulded to a surprising degree by life in the laboratory: and he then proceeds as follows: 'Every statement you make to him (*sc.* the experimentalist), he will either understand as meaning that if a given prescription for an experiment ever can be given and ever is carried out in act, an experience of a given description will result, or else he will see no sense at all in what you say.'† Here indeed is something very like the Pragmatist maxim expressed in terms of the characteristic habits of mind of the experimentalist; and, in view of such passages as this, it is by no means surprising that some people should have imagined Peirce's Pragmatism to be nothing more than a generalization of laboratory methods and meanings.

But before we accept this interpretation we shall do well to remember that laboratory methods, being complex and many-sided, do not admit of one and only one 'natural' or 'obvious' generalization. On the contrary a number of philosophies of the last three hundred years have consisted in attempts to generalize the essential methods, standards, and presuppositions of the experimental sciences, yet most of these philosophies succeed in differing considerably one from another. Broadly speaking, the generalization of scientific methods and meanings which any philosopher offers us will reflect his opinions – whether or not they are consciously formulated – as to the most general conditions to which *all* intelligent activity must conform. This is certainly true of Peirce's Pragmatism, which owes its originality not to what he saw in his laboratory life – for that was there for others to see – but to the framework of general philosophical ideas which he brought to bear on what he saw and did in the laboratory. Or, to urge the same point from a slightly different angle, Peirce's Pragmatism, like many other philosophical theories, *selects* certain features of experimental science for generalization: the only important claim that can be made for it, therefore, is that the features which it selects are capable of suggesting a body of generalizations which hold true of other forms of human knowledge; for example, mathematics, history, metaphysical speculation, and indeed our everyday practical judgements of fact. Whether this claim is wholly justified in connection with Peirce's maxim is one of the main questions with which we shall be concerned in the chapters that follow. Here it is sufficient to point out that Peirce spared no pains in trying to show how far his maxim is applicable to these other fields of knowledge: certainly he was not the kind of philosopher who simply *assumes* that the methods and standards of the natural sciences provide a model for the expression and advancement of other parts of our knowledge. We may therefore conclude that while Peirce's experience as a laboratory scientist strongly influenced the forms in which he expressed his Pragmatism, and while they provided him with his favourite illustrations of how his Pragmatist maxim should be used, yet they in no sense *made* it or were, in his opinion, sufficient to justify it as a general principle of logic.

Probably the clearest proof of Peirce's width of vision and critical caution in this respect is provided by his attitude to metaphysical questions; for example, 'Has every event a cause?', 'Do history and science suggest the operation of a single purposive intelligence in nature?', 'Can mind act on matter, and conversely?,' and so on. How does Peirce envisage the clearing up of such questions as these through the application of his maxim? Some of his statements on this issue read like an anticipation of Logical Positivist teachings, as when he claims that Pragmatism has the effect of showing that 'almost every proposition of ontological metaphysics is ... meaningless gibberish – one word being defined by other words, and they by still others, without any real conception ever being reached,' * or where he urges that the 'demonstrations of the metaphysicians are all moonshine.' † On the other hand, Peirce at all stages in his career believed in the possibility of – and himself made signal contributions to – what he describes as 'purified metaphysics.‡ This would consist of a number of highly general questions having a definite bearing on matters of fact or existence, but not falling under the purview of any of the special sciences, and not amenable to any of their special methods. Nevertheless these questions, Peirce believed, do admit of reasoned, if inevitably tentative, answers: and these answers are meaningful, by Pragmatist standards, because, while not themselves figuring as part of our experimental knowledge of particular facts or general laws, they can help in a unique way to make such knowledge possible: for example, by suggesting new and more fruitful approaches to notoriously difficult, or – as some would too easily maintain – essentially insoluble, problems.

To sum up this introductory discussion of Peirce's Pragmatism: it is a method of logic, suggested partly by the characteristic methods of the mathematical and natural sciences, but also grounded in a number of much more general considerations which we shall discuss below under the title of Peirce's *Theory of Knowledge*. All successful scientific work, Peirce would have maintained, embodies a kind of 'unconscious Pragmatism', but this does not mean that his Pragmatism could have been conceived, or can be understood, simply through observa-

* 5·423.   † 1·7.   ‡ 5·423.

tion of scientific procedures; for these procedures themselves rest on certain presuppositions common to all purposive thought and discourse. Pragmatism, in Peirce's hands, is a logician's tool; and because of this Peirce tends to approach the traditional questions of philosophy primarily as a logician. He is, indeed, fully appreciative of the intellectually vaguer though practically more pressing implications of traditional metaphysical issues; only, he felt that it was his job as a philosopher to deal with these problems as intellectual problems, unaffected, as far as possible, by personal feelings and loyalties, no matter how important and necessary these might seem to him to be for the conduct of life. Hence, we may say that Peirce's intellectual character – as opposed to his somewhat eccentric personal traits – was a thoroughly orthodox one, in the very best sense of the word. And in this respect he stands in marked contrast to his friend and would-be expositor James, to whose treatment of Pragmatism we must now turn.

In his immensely readable book, *Pragmatism, a New Name for Old Ways of Thinking*, James endeavours to apply Peirce's method to a number of philosophical questions, some metaphysical, some ethical: but the most interesting – and least satisfactory – chapters of his book are concerned with the meaning of the word 'truth', with its 'cash value', when it is subjected to the test of Peirce's Pragmatist maxim. As every reader of modern philosophy knows, James's broad answer to the question is that 'truth' is 'what pays' or 'what works'; or, more precisely, that if the results of accepting any belief are 'good' or 'satisfactory' that belief is to be counted 'so far forth' true. Closely bound up with this account of truth – which embodies what most students of philosophy take the word Pragmatism to mean – are James's contentions, first, that most of our intellectual beliefs can be justified only on grounds of their social, moral, and biological utility, and second, that on issues in which purely intellectual considerations afford virtually no guidance to our beliefs, the claims of our 'passional and volitional' nature should be allowed to decide what we shall believe. It is not difficult to see that these openly anti-intellectualist teachings stand in definite opposition to the intellectual temper of Peirce. Even before James's book *Pragmatism* had appeared, Peirce had seen clearly which way the wind was blowing, and with a gesture in which chivalry and irony were curiously blended, he had surrendered to James and his disciples the right to the name Pragmatism, choosing as a new title for his own original principle 'Pragmaticism', a coinage 'ugly enough to be safe from kidnappers'.*

How did James succeed in using Peirce's principle to defend the conclusions – or rather the general attitude to philosophical questions – which ever since have been associated with the name of Pragmatism? To explain this it is necessary to say something of James's highly individual intellectual character, and something too of his quite unusual approach to philosophy.

Like Peirce, James was by training a scientist. He qualified as a medical doctor, and then turned to psychology which he taught as professor at Harvard from 1873 to 1898 – a period during which experimental methods were rapidly being applied to psychological questions. But, unlike Peirce, James was never greatly influenced by the spirit of the laboratory and was never drawn to reflect closely on its methods. He encouraged the development of laboratory psychology, but himself contributed little to it, confessing himself an 'arm-chair psychologist'. Moreover – and here again he stands in marked contrast to Peirce – James confessed himself 'mathematically imbecile' and 'a-logical if not illogical', and in one of his last books he publicly and solemnly 'renounced logic'. But, as against these defects, which would almost certainly have proved fatal to any other man attempting to philosophize, James possessed two assets of a quite unusual kind. Besides immense native intelligence, he had an unusually developed sensitivity to the predicaments – moral, political, and religious, as well as philosophical – of his age; and he could make his listeners and readers alive to these predicaments, and make them share something of his own

* 5·414.

courageous attitude towards them. Few if any philosophers since Plato have equalled James in his capacity to present to ordinary people the kind of facts – new, unfamiliar, puzzling or alarming facts – in the face of which philosophical wonder is most commonly reborn. Moreover, James believed that the philosophical perplexities of his age were highly relevant to its other more practical predicaments; and for the last fifteen years of his life (1895–1910) he devoted his strength unsparingly to the task of creating what it seemed to him his age so sorely needed, a new metaphysics. If James failed in this task – and in view of the defects in his philosophical equipment it was almost inevitable that he should fail in it – he at least succeeded in communicating to other thinkers, better equipped than himself, something of the enthusiasm, the unacademic freshness, and all-round sanity with which he approached the traditional problems of philosophy.

From his undergraduate days onwards, James was much disturbed by the allegedly 'materialistic' implications of certain recent scientific discoveries, in particular the laws of energy and Darwin's theory of natural selection. To many sincere thinkers during the latter decades of the nineteenth century these doctrines seemed to imply that the human mind is nothing but an impotent register of physical forces, whose most important properties had now (as it seemed) been described by physics and whose special applications to life on the earth's surface had at last been sketched in Darwin's account of evolution. And this picture of mind as an automaton – which stood in such painful contradiction to the otherwise excessively optimistic and assertive spirit of the age – was set within an equally grim and ghastly framework: the conception of the universe as a single mechanical system throughout which entropy, the numerical expression of the non-availability of energy, is constantly increasing. Taken together, the automaton theory of mind, the conception of evolution as due to a struggle for existence, and the doctrine of the running-down, or heat-death, of the universe, made up the so-called nineteenth-century nightmare, a curious complex of theoretical beliefs and emotional reactions, without reference to which little of the philosophy of the late nineteenth and early twentieth centuries can be adequately understood.

Quite early in his career James became convinced that this nightmarish world-picture was not necessitated by the actual doctrines (assuming these to be true) of the sciences in question; he was convinced that the mechanistic materialism in general, and the automaton theory of mind in particular, went far further than the established facts of science either required or warranted. But though he felt this to be so, he lacked the logical power to see and say clearly *why* it was so: and the main thread in his philosophical development consists in his persistent efforts to find philosophical justifications for his initial feeling or hunch against current materialistic doctrines. To this end he welcomed aid from the most diverse quarters. Psychical research, the psychological study of mystical experiences, new theories of the 'unconscious', the sturdy commonsensism of the French philosopher Renouvier and the intoxicating 'vitalist' philosophy of Bergson, the suggestion (first elaborated by Peirce) that some parts of physics admit of an indeterminist interpretation, and the suggestion of Ernst Mach that the ultimate subject-matter of physics consists in our elementary sensations – all these were grist to James's mill, and took their respective (or successive) places in the various versions of the 'new metaphysics' which James poured out in popular books and lectures during the first decade of this century. What James looked for, and indeed found partial proof of, in these various doctrines, was support for his own native conviction that the universe is an infinitely richer, warmer, more varied and indeed more 'jumpy' place than nineteenth-century materialist doctrines would have us believe: and, above all, that it is a place in which human thoughts, choices, and aspirations count for something, make a real difference, and can have values and justifications of a sort that the 'nineteenth-century nightmare' either neglects or denies.

But how – to return to our central question – did Peirce's

Pragmatism afford assistance to this project? Or, rather, how did James seek to apply his friend's logical doctrine in the interests of his own 'new metaphysics'? There are two quite distinct parts to this story, for all that James himself never clearly distinguished them. His earliest applications, or developments, of Peirce's Pragmatism culminated in his doctrine of the Will-to-Believe; his later developments of it form one facet of his Radical Empiricism. Both parts of the story have their origin and explanation in the fact that James was, first and foremost, a psychologist – and probably the most gifted descriptive or literary (as opposed to experimental) psychologist that has ever lived.

*

In his psychological writings, James consistently presents the facts of mental life, not indeed in terms of, but always in the most intimate relations to, men's biological needs and functions, and the constant task of adaptation with which every organism is faced. When he turned from psychology to philosophy he proceeded to sharpen this view of mental life in two very peculiar ways. First, from the plausible thesis that certain biological interests underlie, or provide some of the necessary conditions of, all our thinking, he passed to the more exciting (and more ambiguous) thesis that the sole function of thought is to satisfy certain interests of the organism, and that truth consists in such thinking as satisfies these interests. But secondly, James urged that whenever these interests – now conceived as personal and subjective rather than as strictly biological – are faced with issues which cannot be settled on strictly intellectual grounds, or on the evidence of actual experience, other factors, deriving from the 'passional and volitional' side of our nature, should be allowed to determine our opinions. The issues James was thinking of were those in which traditional moral and religious beliefs appear to be in irresolvable conflict with the findings, or alleged implications, of natural science; so that, in effect, what we have here is simply a biologically-minded psychologist's restatement of the view that in fields where proof is impossible, faith is the one alternative which it is *reasonable* to embrace. This was the doctrine – described by Peirce as the 'suicidal'* doctrine – of the Will-to-Believe.

What affinity has this doctrine to Peirce's Pragmatism? The correct and simple answer is: none whatsoever. Peirce's Pragmatism, as we have seen, is a method of clarifying conceptions, or of getting at the distinctive meanings of words and statements, and contains no direct reference to tests of the *truth* or *reasonableness* of statements or beliefs. Certainly, it would seem to follow, from Peirce's doctrine, that no statement or belief can be true unless its meaning can be articulated by means of the Pragmatist maxim, that is, unless it has 'effects that might conceivably have practical bearings.' But the fact that a given belief has such bearings (in Peirce's sense of that term) is no evidence of its being true or even of its being such as to be reasonably accepted. James's doctrine of the Will-to-Believe – his first *application* of Peirce's Pragmatism and one which he never entirely succeeded in discarding – results in fact from one elementary misunderstanding of Peirce's doctrine and from one wholly unwarranted extension of it. First, as to the misunderstanding: the answer which a man comes to accept to a question that cannot be settled on intellectual or experiential grounds may certainly have, in one sense of that phrase, very definite practical bearings on that man's life and conduct; on his inward happiness and moral well-being, for example. But this perfectly natural and familiar sense of the phrase 'practical bearings' is definitely not the one that Peirce intended. This brings us to James's unwarranted extension of Peirce's doctrine. The 'effects having practical bearings' of an unreasoned, or logically non-defensible belief may well turn out to be beneficial and, by some other than intellectual tests and standards, justifiable. But since Peirce's Pragmatism has no direct bearing on the question of truth or justifiability – except that our conception of truth and justifiability are among those that require to be articulated by means of the Pragmatist maxim – it is hard to see that it can

* See *The Thought and Character of William James*, vol. ii, p. 438.

give support to the view that some *un*reasoned beliefs are, in some sense or other, justifiable. This view may be true: it may be that we ought to believe certain things for which there can be no logical justification. But if this is so, then such beliefs ought to be distinguished in the clearest possible manner from those beliefs whose consequences can be tested, by acknowledged intellectual and experiential methods, for truth or falsity. Quite apart from its total misapplication of Peirce's principles, the 'suicidal' doctrine of the Will-to-Believe has the unfortunate effect of blurring this all-important distinction.

But this was not the end of James's misunderstanding of Peirce. A second vital strand in James's Pragmatism is supplied by what he called his Radical Empiricism, the central tenet of which is that in describing any particular thought as true, or capable of being true, or even in calling it a thought in someone's mind, we are always, basically, referring to certain possible and directly experienceable transitions between this particular 'bit' of experience and other bits with which, in the continued course of experience, it can be brought into relation. Truth and falsity – like the other values and dis-values which we attribute to different parts of our thought and conduct – essentially belong *within* experience: they do not refer to any congruence or matching of any part of experience with something 'outside' or 'above' it. There was nothing very original in this suggestion, the germ of which, at the very least, can be found in the writings of Hume and of Kant. But James did have the merit of re-stating it with great vigour, and of applying it very suggestively to the traditional problem of body and mind.

Now at first sight James's Radical Empiricism has a marked affinity to Peirce's Pragmatism as expressed in the formula of 1878. According to that formula the whole meaning of any conception is to be found in such of its effects as 'might conceivably have practical bearings' – for instance such reactions as we should be prepared for in carrying out, in action, a particular experimental procedure. According to James, the meaning of any thought, or that which renders it capable of truth or falsity, is a possible (cf. Peirce's conceivable) sequence of further experiences. This last statement is certainly looser than Peirce's formula, but that is because James's Radical Empiricism was not intended simply as a logical doctrine; it was to be the basis of – and in fact proved to be the one philosophically valuable element in – James's 'new metaphysics'. Nevertheless the apparent resemblance between the two doctrines is undeniable; and it is hardly surprising that James should have come to think of Peirce's Pragmatism as simply the logical expression of his own Radical Empiricism.

Where then, it may be asked, lies James's second misinterpretation of Peirce's Pragmatism? Our full answer to this question must wait till Chapter VI, when we shall have seen some of the wider implications of Peirce's Pragmatism conceived as a principle of logic, as well as the general conception of human knowledge which underlies it. What can be suggested here, however, is the way in which James's Radical Empiricism – no less than his earlier doctrine of the Will-to-Believe – reflects his essentially psychological approach to philosophical questions. As a psychologist James was interested in thoughts in so far as they are (or are alleged to be) *describable* and *predictable*; that is to say, he is interested in thoughts as elements or phases in the life-history of this or that particular individual. The weakness of this approach is that it tends to neglect – certainly it does not begin to explain – the essential generality of all our thinking: a facet of our thoughts which we can perhaps most easily appreciate by reflecting that we usually think of things which are, to some degree, of common or public interest – things whose relevance is certainly not confined to their impact on some particular phase of some particular person's experience or life-history. Peirce, by contrast, continually emphasizes this facet of our thinking, both in his Pragmatism and in other parts of his philosophy. 'It is not "my" experience,' he asserts, 'but "our" experience that has to be thought of.'* And he finds the clearest proof of this thesis in the way that language guides and

* 5·402, note.

controls the greater part of our thinking: for language is essentially a vehicle whereby one expresses those parts of one's experience that *are* general, that must be 'ours' rather than 'mine' if they are to be communicated at all.

This difference between the two thinkers is interestingly brought out in a letter which Peirce wrote to James after he had received his copy of *Pragmatism, a New Name for Old Ways of Thinking*. Old, in poor health, and as it happened a pensioner on James's generosity, Peirce pathetically beseeches his friend 'to try to learn to think with more exactitude.' He goes on to admit that James has a wonderful gift of imparting to audiences 'as near the exact truth as they are capable of apprehending.' That faculty, he says, makes James of great use to the world; whereas he himself 'is like a miser, who picks up things that *might be* useful to the right person at the right time, but which, in fact, are utterly useless to anybody else and almost so to himself.' Then the letter ends abruptly, 'What is utility, if it is confined to a single person? Truth is public.' *

Here, as we shall find, is one of the clues to Peirce's profound originality and relative isolation. James, for all his anti-intellectualist waywardness, was a typical product of the main stream of western thought since the Reformation; he was an individualist, interested in the experiences, perplexities, and satisfactions of individual souls, and anything claiming to be more-than-individual he distrusted from the depths of his own Protestant and American soul. Peirce in this respect resists the main great stream of modern philosophy. Ideas, ideals, movements of thought and feeling, traditional wisdoms, life-tendencies, and above all the life which is inherent in symbols – these were to him every bit as real as the individuals who apply them or, rather, as the individual occasions, the actions and reactions, in which they are applied. Quite apart from differences in the quality of their respective philosophical equipments, Peirce and James were antithetical intellects. Hence the irony of the fact that James was to make Peirce's neglected Prag-

* See *The Thought and Character of William James*, vol. ii, p. 437.

matist principle known to a wide public; and hence the truth of
Professor R. B. Perry's dictum that 'the philosophical movement known as Pragmatism is largely the result of James's misunderstanding of Peirce.'

★

But why, we may ask, did James's version of Pragmatism win
immediate fame, while the original doctrine of Peirce remained
for many years virtually ignored? Perhaps one could as well ask:
why does an inspired lay preacher draw better audiences than
an inspired professor of logic? But in the present case there were
other more personal causes involved. James, as we have seen,
came into philosophy with an established reputation as a psychologist: indeed his *Principles* is probably the best textbook of
psychology ever written. Peirce, by contrast, was practically an
unknown man, esteemed only in a few circles of experts in logic
and physical science. His writings of more general philosophical
interest were scattered in various periodicals over a period of
forty years, and none of them were brought together in a single
volume until long after his death. Moreover, Peirce's peculiar
literary gifts had worked against his popular recognition. He
was a master of the short philosophical paper in which, as in its
model the scientific paper, a few relatively isolable issues are
dealt with explicitly, while their general relevance to other
parts of philosophy is left to the (relatively expert) philosophical
reader to discern. But Peirce lacked both the inclination and the
special capacity – partly that of the artist, partly that of the
teacher – to present his ideas in a sufficiently inviting and
rounded form to win the interest and understanding of the
general public. On the contrary, his favourite method is to
return to his own earlier (often earliest) treatments of the topic
at issue, and to correct or amend these in the light of later
development of his ideas, sometimes with wonderfully clarifying effect but sometimes hiding his own genius for self-correc-
tion in a cloud of garrulousness.

History, however, has slowly begun to make amends for

this situation. James has remained, to be sure, the most widely known and influential philosopher that America has produced; and so long as he is reckoned an intellectual liberator and inspirer, rather than a great constructive thinker or pioneer, no sane judge will question his importance among philosophers of the last hundred years. On the other hand, it is remarkable how little of the positive content of his 'new metaphysics' has remained alive or has even seeded itself effectively in recent British or American philosophy. To confine our attention to the two greatest names among latter-day Pragmatists: John Dewey and G. H. Mead were both Pragmatist philosophers inasmuch as they emphasized – indeed more strongly than James did – the relevance of actual physical operations to all live knowledge; they were both empiricist thinkers, perhaps more radically empiricist than James, in their insistence that philosophers should take seriously the specific observational procedures of those (chiefly scientists) who actually make discoveries; they were both profoundly influenced by new methods in psychology and the social sciences, and they both carried out admirably James's precept that philosophy should be kept 'in touch with facts'. Nevertheless, although in all these respects Dewey and Mead might well be counted among James's spiritual god-children, it is hard to see in any of their distinctive contributions to philosophy – Dewey's instrumentalist conception of thinking, or Mead's analysis of gestures and their relation to significant symbols – any definite imprint of the philosophical teachings of James. By contrast the debt – or where there is no debt, the marked affinity – of Dewey, Mead, and their followers to Peirce becomes steadily clearer. In their close studies of the methods of the mathematical and natural sciences, their speculations on the part played by language and other symbols in the advancement of knowledge, and in their trenchant criticisms of all 'intuitionist' theories of knowledge, the strongest Pragmatist writers of recent years have been following, consciously or unconsciously, in the steps of Peirce.

Nor has the recent influence of Peirce been confined to thinkers of the Pragmatist school. It is today widely recognized, even by those who have given his writings but cursory attention, that Peirce's anticipations of many recent philosophical developments were astonishing. Many of his interests, and many of his characteristic methods of approach to philosophical questions, which to his contemporaries must have seemed freakish to a degree, are today commonly regarded as parts of the technique of every competent philosopher. This accounts for the somewhat naïve self-satisfaction which underlies much recent appreciation of Peirce: as though recognition of his posthumous up-to-dateness were the highest possible praise that he could receive. Without wishing to deny that Peirce's anticipation of much recent work, especially in the fields of logic and the philosophy of language, is evidence of his strength and originality as a thinker, we may, nevertheless, reasonably ask: are these anticipations the best things that can be found in Peirce, or are they rather symptoms of a more general philosophical originality and power? The answer which we shall give to this latter question is an emphatic Yes. In the chapters that follow we shall try to show that Peirce was much more than a lucky pioneer, a discoverer of odd seams which later researches have proved to be fruitful. The greatness of Peirce, we shall argue, lies rather in the organic unity of his thinking, a unity which has been obscured by his own failure to present his teachings during his lifetime in unified literary form, but partly also by the fact that he sought to test out his central doctrines on a wide variety of clearly defined issues. More than this, it may reasonably be urged that, whatever the oddities of his personal temperament, Peirce's general philosophical attitude is one from which contemporary philosophy, in all its branches, has a great deal to learn. Behind a certain amount of superficial eccentricity, Peirce's writings display an intellectual balance and integrity and gifts of critical penetration and constructive suggestion which make him all but unrivalled as an expositor of his central theme, 'the scientific intelligence'.

Why the unity and strength of Peirce's thought have remained so long neglected will be made clear in our next chapter, where we shall consider the strange and unhappy history of his outward life and the even stranger history of his writings.

CHAPTER TWO

PEIRCE'S LIFE AND WRITINGS

*

THE main facts of Peirce's life can be told in a few paragraphs. He was born in Cambridge, Massachusetts, in 1839, the second son of Benjamin Peirce, professor of mathematics and astronomy at Harvard, and in his day America's foremost mathematician. After receiving a high school education Peirce went on to Harvard where he graduated, not with great distinction, in 1859; but his real education he owed to his father, who encouraged him with his precocious laboratory experiments and, more important, taught him mathematics. Benjamin Peirce was primarily an applied mathematician, but the originality of his mind was perhaps best shown in his *Linear Associative Algebra*, the opening sentence of which, 'Mathematics is the science which draws necessary conclusions', shows an approach far in advance of current conceptions in America, and indeed in Europe. The main lines of Peirce's intellectual development were laid down by his father's teaching.

Many passages in Peirce's writings reveal the depth of his affection, as well as his sense of intellectual debt, to his father; and there seems, in fact, to have been something almost idyllic in the relations between the two men. While Peirce was still an undergraduate, they were often to be seen walking and talking together, hour after hour, after lectures; and strangely enough, it would be Benjamin Peirce's mathematical projects and problems, not the problems of Charles Peirce the student, that they were discussing. On the other hand, Benjamin Peirce's influence on his son was not entirely beneficial. He appears to have forced him excessively during his boyhood, and in later years would frequently refer in the course of lectures to his son's scientific promise and achievements, prophesying that they would far surpass his own. This can hardly have increased

Peirce's popularity with his university teachers, and almost certainly aggravated certain traits in his character which help to explain his later misfortunes. Peirce seems never to have been able to get on with anyone whom he did not greatly admire and who did not reciprocally admire him and treat him as an intellectual equal: in particular he found it hard to get along with university presidents and professors.

It was thanks to his father's influence that Peirce became associated with the United States Coastal and Geodesic Survey, with which he held a number of posts from 1861 to 1891. His work with the survey left him, luckily, with considerable time to pursue his own scientific and philosophical researches. (His philosophical reading had begun, oddly enough, with Schiller's *Aesthetic Letters*: from this he passed on to Whately's *Logic* and Kant's *Critic of the Pure Reason*, the latter of which he claims – in this like another great mathematician-philosopher – to have known at one period almost by heart.) During the 1860s he found time to give a number of lecture courses at Harvard on logic and the history of science, and for one spell of five years he held a lectureship in logic at Johns Hopkins. On the receipt of a small legacy in 1891 Peirce relinquished his post with the survey; and, apart from a short spell of tutoring in New York and occasional lecture courses at Harvard, he spent the rest of his life in almost complete seclusion in the small township of Milford. Peirce's aim, when he retired, was to work up into a single comprehensive system the four or five immensely important philosophical discoveries which he had made during the previous thirty-odd years. But for one reason or another the great books which he planned failed to appear. Financial difficulties drove him, after a few years, to devote much of his time to writing popular reviews of philosophical and scientific books; and during his last years, when illness prevented him from any sustained work, he subsisted on the charity of a few friends, of whom the most eminent and the most generous was William James. He died in April 1914.

★

To his fellow citizens in Milford, Peirce, in his later years, was known only as a hopeless eccentric: a solitary, careless of his appearance, irregular in his habits, and a debtor who tried to escape his creditors by working in a loft the ladder to which he would pull up behind him. In academic circles, however, Peirce had throughout his life enjoyed a certain fame. The most influential American philosophers of the time, James and Royce, frequently and generously acknowledged their debts to him. He had published, if we include his contributions to J. M. Baldwin's *Dictionary*, nearly eighty original philosophical papers, chiefly on logic and metaphysics, and some twenty papers and one small volume entitled *Photometric Researches* embodying his work in physics, astronomy, and the theory of measurement. In addition, between the years 1891 and 1906, he contributed approximately a hundred and eighty reviews, chiefly of philosophical and scientific books, to the New York *Nation*. But this output did not match up with the expectations of his friends, to whom he wrote, during the 1890s, of volumes on logic and metaphysics, either completed or in an advanced stage of preparation. And the question inevitably arises: why did the promised volumes – which all his friends knew Peirce had it in him to produce – fail to appear?

What has sometimes been taken to be a closely related question arises over Peirce's choice of a career. On a number of occasions between 1865 and 1895 he made efforts to obtain a permanent teaching post in a university; but, though he had the backing of powerful friends and admirers, he never succeeded. Why was this? More by implication than by overt statement the impression has been widely conveyed that the same answer must be·returned to both the above questions: namely, that Peirce's loose and wayward character prevented him from carrying through work commensurate with his unquestioned gifts. On the very scanty evidence available, it seems clear that Peirce's temperament was an unusually difficult one, both for himself and for other people: on the other hand, the suggestion that this explains his failure to do the work he had it in him to do, seems to have been based on ignorance of the facts (Peirce did complete one book for the press, though he never succeeded in finding a publisher) and on a very strange view of what real work in philosophy means.

Discussion of Peirce's character is rendered particularly difficult by the fact that, both during his lifetime and up to the present, those who knew him best seem to have sought deliberately to shield his name. The feelings which have prompted this policy deserve respect; but it would be most regrettable if, as a result of it, the mystery of Peirce's character is to remain for ever unsolved. There was certainly something – and probably a great deal – that was queer about Peirce. Reports (including his own) present him as having been highly emotional, vain, snobbish, morose, quarrelsome, intellectually arrogant, and quick to take offence, and, at the same time, as easily duped, hopelessly unpractical about money matters, and with a remarkable capacity for forgetting appointments. A number of these unfortunate traits are presented in the following brilliantly cruel piece of self-portraiture. 'I insensibly put on a sort of swagger here, which is designed to say: "You are a very good fellow in your way; who you are I don't know and I don't care, but I, you know, am Mr Peirce, distinguished for my varied scientific acquirements, but above all for my extreme modesty in which respect I challenge the world."'* These traits were easily noticed in Peirce as a young man, and they do not seem to have been much softened as he aged. On the other hand, in company which he liked, Peirce could be charming and witty, and he was capable of inspiring deep affection in those who knew him well. William James in his letters always writes of Peirce with affection and understanding; but in reading these letters – as published – one gets the impression that a good deal is being withheld. For example, while still an undergraduate, James writes: 'In last year's class there is a son of Professor Peirce, whom I suspect to be a very "smart" fellow with a great deal of character, pretty independent and violent thought. ...' Some

* See *The Thought and Character of William James*, vol. i, p. 538.

fourteen years later he writes to his brother Henry in Paris: 'I am amused that you should have fallen into the arms of C. S. Peirce ... but the way to treat him is after the famous "nettle" receipt; grasp firmly, contradict, push hard, make fun of him, and he is as pleasant as anyone, but be overawed by his sententious manner and his paradoxical and obscure statements ... and you will never get a feeling of ease with him any more than I did for years, until I changed my course and treated him more or less jokingly. I confess I like him very much in spite of all his peculiarities, for he is a man of genius, and there is always something in that to compel one's sympathy.' Then, after an interval of nearly twenty years, 'As for Charles Peirce, it is the most curious instance of talents not making a career. He dished himself at Harvard by inspiring dislike in Eliot. ... He is now so mature in character, with rather fixed half-bohemian habits, and no habit of teaching, that it would be risky to appoint him. I yield to no one in admiration of his genius, but he is paradoxical and unsociable of intellect, and hates to *make connection* with anyone he is with. ...'*

Despite the opinion expressed in the last of these passages, James made valiant efforts during the 1890s to obtain for Peirce a permanent teaching post at Harvard. But these efforts were unavailing. Peirce's notorious 'uncomfortableness' may have partly accounted for this; but the main reason was, undoubtedly, that by this stage in his career Peirce had, deservedly or undeservedly, gained the reputation of being a heavy drinker and a loose-living man. The first of these charges was almost certainly exaggerated, though it is known that Peirce prided himself as a connoisseur of claret. The second charge was no doubt bound up in some way with the divorce case which terminated Peirce's first marriage. He had married, at the age of twenty-three, a Miss Melusina Fay, a society lady who in her latter years was very well thought of in Harvard circles. But, for whatever reasons, the marriage proved an unhappy one;

* All these excerpts are from letters published in *The Thought and Character of William James*, vols. i and ii.

Peirce's wife deserted him in 1876, and he divorced her on grounds of desertion seven years later. There seems to be little doubt, however, that, although legally the wronged party, Peirce was himself much to blame in this unfortunate affair; the divorce caused a permanent rift between him and his own brothers and almost certainly affected his chances of obtaining later in life the kind of teaching post which he desired and deserved. In 1884 Peirce married again; and his second wife, a French lady, survived him. He had no children.

Peirce's failure to obtain a permanent university post accounts in some measure for his failure to win during his lifetime the recognition which his philosophical achievements deserved. Publishers and research endowment trusts showed themselves indifferent to an author who, without official university backing and the assured if small public which this usually brings, offered or promised lengthy books on recondite, specialist topics. But even if publishers had clamoured for his books, it is doubtful whether Peirce could ever have presented in systematic and popularly assimilable form the wealth of philosophical ideas which his papers and lectures severally contain. He was essentially a philosopher's philosopher, an inventor and deepener of ideas, theories, and methods but with neither the gift nor the ability to be an effective expositor of his own discoveries. Peirce's failure to produce books is therefore largely the result of a more basic failure on his part: possessed though he was to a quite prodigious degree by the will to learn, he had very little of the will to teach or instruct. This is shown in the style and manner of his papers, which, as was previously mentioned, suggest a scientist setting out his results for the scrutiny of fellow enquirers rather than a teacher seeking to impart difficult ideas by easy doses to students and disciples.

Nevertheless, this lack of any easily recognized pattern in Peirce's philosophical writings does not betoken any lack of underlying unity, either of aim or of method, in his thinking. On the contrary, the longer Peirce is studied, the clearer does it become that his thought is unusually close-knit; and that his grouping of philosophical questions remained remarkably constant throughout his life, for all that he was persistently trying out, and persistently testing and rejecting or trying to improve upon, particular methods of dealing with them. Moreover, Peirce's ideal of philosophy, and the way in which he practised it, called for quite unusual intellectual preparation and for creative effort of the most varied kinds. He expressed this ideal in a somewhat hackneyed way by saying that he wished to make philosophy a science: but what he meant was something far from hackneyed. This was, that philosophy should imitate the sciences by making its premisses and methods more explicit; by establishing generally acceptable standards of correct usage and sufficient proof (with the proviso that no given expression of these standards should be taken as perennially adequate); and by adapting to its own peculiar problems methods of reasoning and analysis which have proved fruitful in other better-developed branches of knowledge. The value of results which Peirce obtained in his service of this ideal is not relevant to the issue under discussion; what is relevant is that Peirce certainly went about philosophy in a very hard way, and that even if the results he obtained had been disappointing, his lifelong devotion to his ideal would provide sufficient proof of his inward integrity. Finally, in this connection, it should be remembered in Peirce's favour that his most original and impressive contributions to philosophy were carried through – conceived, applied, criticized, reformulated again and again and continually deepened – over a period of nearly fifty years, entirely without the stimulus of popular recognition and reward. (Even his work in symbolic logic – a field in which he was recognized as an expert by his contemporaries – could not be adequately appreciated until many years after his death.) If Peirce did fail to utilize his own brilliant gifts and opportunities, it was certainly not from want of trying.

Peirce's actual writings, then, provide an answer to the worst charges that have been levelled against Peirce the man. But they do more than this: they are bound to make any sympathetic reader feel very doubtful about the justice, or at any rate about the depth and the completeness, of these charges. For, by a strange paradox, the personality disclosed in Peirce's writings is an almost wholly attractive one; perhaps it is a slightly eccentric personality, but it is pre-eminently sunny, high-spirited, generous, and robustly self-confident. Throughout his writings Peirce shows himself entirely free from academic jealousy and from personal assertiveness; in controversy he is always the fairest, indeed most chivalrous, of opponents; and although his best writings contain plenty of punch, they show not the slightest trace of swagger. Witty, arch, enthusiastic, magnanimous, occasionally fanatical in pursuit of his own most difficult ideas or in his assaults on the doctrines of others, but in the main sanely and even severely self-critical, Peirce the writer stands in most extraordinary contrast to what is generally reported of Peirce the man in society.

Here is a psychological riddle which, it may be hoped, future biographical researchers will help to unravel. But perhaps one important clue to its solution is to be found in a passage which closes one of Peirce's earliest philosophical essays. He there censures the habit of thought which identifies a man's essential life, his humanity, with either the ebb and flow of his animal vitality or else with his will. As against this view, Peirce himself urges that a man's essential life is made up of his communings – speech and listening, questioning and answering – whether with himself or with other members of the community to which he belongs. Man is essentially a sign-maker and a sign-reader; and his life as a whole is in the nature of a word, a sign, a message. Thus Peirce writes, 'The word or sign which man uses *is* the man himself,' and again, 'my language is the sum total of myself.'* This is no doubt a very one-sided account of the matter, the expression of a quite unusual – excessively intellectual – temperament and outlook; it may even seem like a piece of special pleading on the part of a man who foresees his own incapacity to cope with the pressures and responsibilities of practical life. On the other hand, it suggests very forcibly what was of most value in Peirce's own life. This consisted in his com-

* 5·314.

munings and conversings with himself and with others: in his youth, with his father, and later, when he became a solitary, with the great thinkers of the past. With them he not only felt but *knew* himself to be one of a community of equals. Out of his lifelong communings with their works he was in fact to succeed, despite every appearance of failure, in doing the one thing which he really cared about doing; in the simple but telling words of his expositor, Dr Buchler, he succeeded in advancing philosophy.

*

At Peirce's death his unpublished manuscripts, numbering several hundreds, were purchased from his widow by the Department of Philosophy at Harvard. They were found to be in a state of almost total disorder, but by 1931, thanks to the efforts of many American scholars, in particular Professors Charles Hartshorne and Paul Weiss, these manuscripts had been thoroughly sifted and collated, and a selection from them, together with almost all Peirce's published work in philosophy, appeared between 1931 and 1935 in the first six volumes of his *Collected Papers*. In 1957 two further – and final – volumes appeared, edited by Professor A. W. Burke. These volumes contain papers on the philosophy of science and selections from Peirce's scientific writings and from his reviews and correspondence, as well as a bibliography.

Meanwhile, in the years that had intervened since his death, interest in Peirce's writings had slowly increased. In 1915 John Dewey published an important article, *The Pragmatism of Peirce*, in which he expressed the opinion that 'Peirce was more of a Pragmatist than James.' In 1916 C. I. Lewis published his *Survey of Symbolic Logic* which made clear Peirce's pre-eminence among the nineteenth-century founders of that science. Six years later a selection of Peirce's writings appeared in book form under the title *Chance, Love and Logic*. The title was perhaps unfortunate, but everything else about the book, including the introduction by its editor, Morris Cohen, made it an admirable introduction to Peirce's thought. *Chance, Love and Logic* made Peirce for the first time an easily accessible author. In Great Britain it exercised an important influence on one philosopher of the first rank: the young Cambridge logician F. P. Ramsey.

By 1931, therefore, when the *Collected Papers* began to appear, Peirce was by no means a forgotten man. But if any of his admirers had hoped that the publication of this authoritative edition of his works would at once widen his fame, they were to be disappointed. The *Collected Papers* are an impressive work of scholarship; they largely meet the needs of the advanced student of philosophy who can quickly find in them Peirce's leading ideas on almost every topic of philosophical interest; but they do not make the reading of Peirce either easy or attractive. Peirce's editors have sought to give to his best unpublished writings equal pride of place with his published work; and with regard to some of Peirce's unpublished papers on formal logic and the philosophy of mathematics, and a number of his unpublished lectures – especially his Pragmatism lectures of 1903 – this policy was undoubtedly the correct one. It has its disadvantages, however; it creates an impression of Peirce as a philosopher of threads and patches – and one who needs to be threaded and patched by outside hands. Further, although by publishing a number of incomplete essays and drafts, which Peirce himself discarded, his editors have succeeded in throwing light on some of his most difficult ideas, their policy has also had the effect of laying him open to the charge of inconsistency on many fundamental issues. Peirce, like a number of other solitaries, used writing as a method of thinking; and any man who does this is likely to 'ride' a theory – perhaps for twenty-odd pages to see where it leads him – which he would not dream of submitting to the public.

These criticisms apply in particular to Volumes I, IV and VI of the *Collected Papers*, in which unpublished materials predominate: Volumes VII and VIII invite criticisms of a different character: they leave the reader wishing that he could have much more of Peirce writing, as he does in his letters and reviews, in so fluent and popular a style; and while the selections from Peirce's scientific writings are judicious, they fail to convey the penetrating quality, and indeed the historical significance, of Peirce's best work in physical science.

On the other hand, it must be remembered that an editor's job is to edit, not to expound or justify or advertise; and in giving Peirce – or so much of the best of Peirce – to the world, the editors of the *Collected Papers* have performed an immense service to philosophy. The difficulties which they have met point to the continuing need of expository and critical studies of different aspects of Peirce and of his work as a whole. A number of such studies have appeared in the last two decades, and others – some of them of the first importance philosophically and historically – are now in progress. In the present study, as in a number of recent books on Peirce, the discussion is centered on his Pragmatism, which is considered in relation both to his theory of knowledge and to his attempts at 'purified' metaphysics; and an attempt has been made to show the relevance of Peirce's most original ideas, not only to current philosophical interests, but to some of the main streams of philosophical discussion from Plato to the present day. This approach means that we must neglect much of what is most original in Peirce: for example, his contributions to symbolic logic, his applications of probability theory to the problem of induction, his general theory of values – logical, ethical and aesthetic – and of the mutual relations of different philosophical disciplines. Of these omissions, the first is perhaps the most serious, since it could be claimed that, without some acquaintance with Peirce's work as a symbolic logician, it is impossible to appreciate his most characteristic method of approach to traditional philosophical problems. But modern symbolic logic is a highly technical subject, and its early developments are particularly difficult to describe, or even to suggest, in non-technical language. In this situation a compromise course seems justified: we shall therefore attempt, in the paragraphs which immediately follow, to indicate in the simplest possible way those features of Peirce's work in symbolic logic which have most obviously affected his work in other parts of philosophy. Inevitably, this description will be superficial as well as being highly selective; but not, it is hoped, to the point of being positively misleading.

*

Peirce created a number of what were known in the nineteenth century as Logical Algebras. Every such algebra has for its basis a set of symbols to which, as to the letters used in ordinary algebra, no specific meanings or values are attached. Certain rules are then stated as to how these symbols may be manipulated, i.e. combined, separated, and substituted one for another: these are usually described as the translation or transformation rules of the algebra. The algebra is designated *logical* because, by operating the symbols in accordance with the prescribed rules, one can 'generate' a set of further symbols whose relations to one another are analogous to, and therefore capable of representing, the relations which hold between certain principles of traditional logic. What is the purpose of this complicated if ingenious procedure? We find at least three different justifications of it given by different logicians. First, it may be said that a logical algebra simply exhibits more clearly than any other method can the mutual relations between traditional logical principles, and that this is its sufficient justification. Secondly, a logical algebra may be counted important on the ground that it helps us to discover the *simplest* logical principles, that is to say those from which other (and this means as a rule the ordinary, familiar) logical principles can be shown to follow as special cases. Thirdly, a logical algebra may be prized because – or so it is often claimed – the correct operation of it enables us to 'generate', not only the traditional principles of logic, but other formal systems as well, for instance the system of cardinal arithmetic. Peirce's *Collected Papers* contain passages which lend support to each of these three views; but it is clear that in his opinion the first of the functions of symbolic logic which we have mentioned is the most important one. Radical in most philosophical matters, Peirce shows himself somewhat conservative in maintaining, again and again, that deductive logic is essentially a *normative* science. It is not the science that, *par excellence*, draws deductive conclusions: that science, he maintains, is pure mathematics. The function of deductive logic is, rather, to display how we ought to proceed in deductive arguments; and it does this by classifying the various types of deductive argument and setting out, in the most lucid and articulate way possible, models of every such type. It is thus the science that *studies*, largely for the purposes of self-criticism and correction, what pure mathematics *does*. Whether in maintaining this view Peirce was altogether justified is a question on which we need not here embark; our concern is simply with the way in which Peirce's long experience as an originator, critic, and interpreter of logical algebras was to affect his thinking in other less highly specialized branches of philosophy.

In the first place this experience finally confirmed in Peirce's mind, if it did not originate, what is perhaps his most characteristic and fundamental philosophical insight: namely, that every symbol – be it a word, a sentence, or a scientific formula – is essentially something *to be developed*, something that requires or calls for development if it is to fulfil its proper function of expressing and communicating intelligent thought. That this is true of the symbols of every algebra – its a's and b's, x's and y's – is fairly obvious: the only point in writing down and manipulating such symbols is to get something further – some further equation or conclusion – out of them. Peirce, however, maintains that the same can be seen to be true, on reflection, of all signs and symbols, or at any rate of all such as are used for the purposes of intelligent thought. Not only does every such sign require to be interpreted if it is to be understood – and therefore to be *interpretable* if it is to be intelligible or meaningful; interpretation of any sign used for the purposes of thought means, Peirce claims, its interpretation in terms of, or by means of, some further sign, which may confirm, amplify, qualify, or correct the original sign but which will, in some way or other, *develop* it. This thesis of Peirce, which will greatly concern us in later chapters, we may here sum up by the cliché: No interpretation – and hence no meaning – without development.

It will be useful, however, to mention here two important corollaries of this central thesis of Peirce, the first of which easily commends itself to common sense, though the second certainly has an appearance of paradox. It is an obvious consequence of our cliché that there could not possibly be such a thing as a single isolated sign: on the contrary, any sign is essentially an element in a working system of signs – for instance, a language, however elementary, in actual use. But Peirce's point is perhaps best illustrated by the case of someone who possesses, or knows how to use, only one general symbol – for instance a child who uses the word 'dinner' to refer to every type of food. Peirce would maintain that such a child could not. use the word 'dinner' significantly or intelligently unless he could use certain other signs, especially gestures of pointing, of acceptance and rejection, and so on, in conjunction with, and in amplification of, his uses of the word. This exemplifies the general fact that there can be no such thing as *the* (one and only) sign, or *the* (one and only) substitute, for a given object: such a conception, Peirce maintains, is utterly meaningless. Or, to put the same point affirmatively, a sign is essentially the kind of thing that can, at the very least, be repeated, and that must, if it is to be repeated effectively in a world that does not stand still, admit of expansion, qualification, corroboration, correction – in a word, development.

The second corollary which we should notice here, is that since there can be no one (and only) sign of a given object, so there can be no one (and only) interpretation of any given sign: hence the meaning of a sign, or the conception answering to it, cannot be of a simple, single, 'one and only' nature. That is to say, there is no such thing as an absolutely simple, self-sufficient conception: our apparently simplest conceptions – say our conception of a given shade of colour – are not absolutely simple, or unitary, or self-sufficient: and just the same must be true of certain conceptions, e.g. that of the soul, or of matter, or of

God, or of knowledge, or of a substance, or of quality, or of mere being, which various philosophers have asserted to be absolutely simple, ultimate, unitary, self-sufficient conceptions. On the contrary, Peirce maintains, every genuine conception is essentially related to other conceptions, just as every sign requires, if it is to signify, other signs that can express, by developing, its meaning; and one of his ways of expressing this point is by affirming that every genuine conception can be defined. Now it might be objected that, if this were so, then all definition must in the end be circular, and therefore useless: Peirce, however, maintains – and on this score his experience as a symbolic logician simply confirms in the clearest possible way what reflection on other less purely formal sciences would suggest – that, in fact, all definitions are, in a sense, circular. A definition is *viciously* circular only when it involves reference to the very term which it claims to define; for example, the definition of man as 'offspring of man' or 'member of the species *homo sapiens*'. On the other hand, we find an inevitable and quite innocent circularity in the definition of all relational terms: e.g. father and son, above and below, greater and less, etc., no one of which can be defined save in terms of its correlate and conversely. Now Peirce's long experience as a formal logician had shown him that all the allegedly ultimate conceptions and principles of logic (and indeed of mathematics) are in this sense circular, because essentially relational; they can be understood and expressed only in terms of their mutual implications. To give two instances. The notion of a given quality is distinct from the notion of the corresponding class of things (those that have this quality), yet each of these notions requires the other to elucidate it. Again, although it is easy to understand Peirce's contention that the implication relation is fundamental in logic, yet for certain purposes this relation too can be, and needs to be, defined. Peirce himself introduced into symbolic logic the conventions whereby 'p implies q' can be defined as 'either p or else not q' (what is referred to commonly as 'material implications'), or as 'not (p and not q)' where the relation of implication is defined in terms of the notions of negation and double negation. From this lesson – to which, as Peirce was quick to see, the definitions employed in all the most developed sciences clearly conform – he drew the conclusion that, despite the apparent paradox, there are no genuine conceptions, no matter how scientific or how elevated they may appear to be, that are in fact ultimate, self-sufficient, essentially indefinable.

*

We may usefully consider two further ways in which Peirce's work as a symbolic logician has left its mark on the rest of his philosophy. In the first place it helped to make him an unusually powerful critic. We may recall, in this connection, that whenever a symbolic logician manipulates his symbols he must have clearly in mind (until they become habitual to him) all the translation rules to which his symbols are subject: indeed, if he neglects these rules, he will not be using his symbols in any definite way, since, apart from the rules that govern their combinations, separations, etc., his symbols have no distinctive meanings. When therefore a thinker, trained in the procedures of symbolic logic, comes to analyse and criticize an argument from everyday discussion or from general philosophy, we should naturally expect him to demand two things: first that all the premisses of the argument in question shall be explicitly stated, and second that the rule or model (corresponding to transformation rules in symbolic logic) to which his argument and *any other similar argument* conforms shall also admit of explicit statement. To concentrate on this last point: a critic who has been trained in symbolic logic will tend to consider any given argument as, in Peirce's words, 'a member of a *genus* of arguments all constructed in the same way and all claiming that when their premisses are real facts, their conclusions are also.' *
More commonly Peirce writes of *classes* of arguments or inferences or reasonings, and maintains that it is essential to any piece of reasoning that it should carry with it the 'side-thought' that

* 2·649.

it belongs to such a class. The defining principle of any class of arguments (or inferences or reasonings) – the principle in accordance with which each member of the class is 'constructed' – Peirce calls the 'leading principle' of that class.

Now it is altogether characteristic of Peirce that, when presented with any philosophical argument, he immediately asks for a clear statement not only of the premisses from which it is derived, but of the leading principle to which it conforms. To ask for this last is, however, easier than to get it, for, as Peirce himself fully realized, leading principles are in fact very seldom stated, and for this reason are best conceived as 'habits of mind, constitutional or acquired' which govern different classes of inference. Nevertheless, every piece of reasoning, however vague the terms in which it is couched, conforms to and exemplifies some leading principle or other; and one of Peirce's greatest services to philosophy was to urge that we should drag into the daylight the leading principles on which every piece of philosophical argument relies. And once they are explicitly stated, what sorry things the leading principles of the philosophers are often found to be! One great favourite is that a conclusion of inference should be accepted if, irrespective of any specific consequences, it seems 'agreeable to reason'; another is that a conclusion should be accepted because its contraries (seldom specified in any detail) 'seem inconceivable', or because thought or expression (seldom analysed or sampled with any great care) 'would be impossible without it'. It is chiefly through his exposure of the extreme weakness of their 'leading principles' that Peirce proves himself so devastating a critic of, for example, Descartes, Berkeley, Kant, and William James, and of almost every writer on logic since the Middle Ages.

Finally, Peirce's work as a symbolic logician also profoundly affected his manner of expressing some of the central ideas of his theory of knowledge. He frequently describes the thinking process as though it consists simply in the 'development' of one symbol – say a sentence asserting some matter of fact – out of another, or of the 'translation' of one symbol by another. Now it may naturally be objected that our everyday thoughts are to be distinguished from the operation of an algebra precisely by the fact that whereas the latter may be a mere matter of 'developing' and 'translating', the former clearly are not. The natural development of our thoughts about the actual world is always being interrupted, redirected, qualified, or proved false by facts that are *forced* upon us by the course of experience, facts which we are compelled to see, to react to, or, in some less direct manner, to take account of. And of course all this is true: and Peirce was quite well aware of the difference in question. Only, he insists, when we are engaged in any continuous and purposive thinking about the actual world, the facts which this world forces upon our attention must be taken account of in the special way that thought requires; that is, they must be accepted as new premises to be developed in accordance with the principles that have guided our thought so far. The great distinction, as Peirce sees it, between our purely formal thinking (as in pure mathematics and deductive logic) and our experiential or factual thinking, lies in this: that in the former the development of our thought is constrained *only* by certain conditions which we ourselves have laid down – either explicitly, in the statement of the hypotheses we select for the purposes of deductive development, or else implicitly, in so far as they are necessarily involved by the symbolism we elect to use; whereas in the latter our thought is constrained by factors that are in no sense of our own choosing.

Peirce's preoccupation with logical algebras (and with his highly elaborate 'graphs' of deductive procedure) by no means blinds him, then, to the obvious fact that the greater part of our thinking is constrained by the demands and intrusions of experienced fact. On the contrary, – and in this he may be compared with Leibniz before him – his powerful grasp of the peculiarities of purely formal thinking enables him to set out in high relief, and to articulate with unusual exactness, hitherto obscure or confused features of our experiential, factual thinking. In this respect, Peirce's work as a formal logician parallels and supplements, in its effects on his general philosophy, his experience as an experimental scientist: each of these contributes in striking fashion to his general philosophical equipment, but neither of them dominates or restricts, or renders in any way pedantic, his approach to the broader problems of philosophy.

*

Peirce's intellectual character, as we have said, is primarily that of a logician: but it also contains features not commonly found in conjunction with logical penetration and precision. Quite the most notable of these is his speculative daring, which shows itself not only in the number of altogether original ideas which he threw up and developed in the course of his work, but in the almost 'shameless' way in which he would brush past time-honoured (and often not threadbare) approaches to traditional philosophical problems. He does not try to solve such problems by producing last-minute knock-down evidence in favour of one side or the other in the traditional dispute. His method is always to review the unquestioned facts from which the dispute is said to arise, and to show that it arises either through unadmitted ignorance of some of the relevant facts or because of the presence, among the alleged facts, of certain unrecognized and as a rule distorting elements of theory. These elements he removes and proceeds to interpret the facts within a different framework of general ideas of his own devising. But this revision or rearrangement of traditional schemes of ideas is never with Peirce a mere matter of intellectual virtuosity; he has no desire to put up *ad hoc* theories or fairy tales to 'save the appearances'. His revisions or rearrangements are always such as will recommend themselves to informed students of the history of logic and of the sciences, whereas the theories or schemes of ideas which they replace usually betray narrow or downright mistaken conceptions of scientific reasoning. Peirce could well have claimed that, in comparison with himself, most of his philosophical contemporaries were philosophically, because scientifically, uneducated – no matter how brilliant their natural gifts of reasoning and constructive imagination. Few if any of them had learnt, as he had, the main logical lessons of the seventeenth-century scientific revolution, still less the logical lessons to be learnt from the nineteenth-century revolution in mathematics (one outcrop of which was the new science of symbolic logic) and from what seemed to Peirce the most significant scientific development of his own day – the application of statistical methods to physics, biology, and the historical sciences.

A most useful and necessary brake on Peirce's speculative daring is provided by his great erudition. That he should have possessed a thorough knowledge of the history of philosophy and of the physical sciences since the Renaissance is not surprising; but Peirce was also a close student of Aristotle, of the Stoic logicians, and of the philosophers of the Middle Ages. To the great philosophers of the past he is never tired of expressing his indebtedness; but his admiration of their single-mindedness and exactness of thought is sanely tempered by his recognition of their barbarously narrow conceptions of reasoning. Peirce's historical knowledge was as accurate as it was extensive, and he displays considerable insight into the social forces that have helped to mould philosophical thought in different ages. Indeed it is quite probable that his reputation will be enhanced when a more representative selection of his writings on the history of science and philosophy has been made available.

A third admirable feature of Peirce's thought, distinguishing it from that of almost all his contemporaries, is his almost total freedom from partisan bias of any kind. This is a quality which the ordinary man no doubt expects in every great philosopher; but in fact it is very seldom found, which largely explains why philosophers are so easily grouped into camps or sides or schools. Peirce is a thinker who cannot be confined to the bounds of any camp or school. He is of course usually known as a Pragmatist; but as we have seen, he modestly resigned his right to that name. In his youth he counted himself an 'idealist' but, as we shall discover, his thought is in certain important respects supremely realistic. His freedom from partisan bias, however, is best displayed in connection with some of his own distinctive doctrines. Thus, although a lifelong theist, he shows no desire to 'redress the balance' of philosophical thought in favour of religious experience as against the findings of science. On the contrary, he did not believe in 'mixing up Religion and Philosophy',* and it is notable that the kind of pan-psychistic cosmology which he endeavoured to work out during one period of his career gives no particular support to his own theistic beliefs. Again, within the cosmological scheme which Peirce himself favoured, mechanical laws play a quite subordinate rôle: they are presented as regularities which themselves require explanation. But, in his methodological writings, Peirce insists again and again that in every field of research we should begin by trying out hypotheses modelled as closely as possible on those which have proved so fruitful in mechanics. Thus, although opposed on metaphysical grounds to any form of mechanistic philosophy, Peirce is fully aware of the significance – for philosophy as well as for practical life – of the 'mechanical genius of man'.

*

Not only was Peirce, at his best, a thinker of outstanding vigour, daring, and many-sidedness, he was also, if more intermittently, a writer of remarkable force and charm. To be sure, he has often been charged with obscurity; and his editors go so far as to maintain that his thought is at its best when he writes least well. But this highly uninviting judgement is far from justified. On the whole, Peirce's style, like that of most writers, lifts perceptibly when he is on top of his subject: at such times it will crystallize into memorable incisive statements or flower out in imagery that is at once firm and suggestive. On the other hand, it must be admitted that the level of writing in the *Collected Papers* is extremely uneven. This is due partly to the fact that uncorrected drafts and fragments stand side by side with finished papers, and partly to the fact that Peirce, when dealing with entirely novel

* 5·107.

subject-matters, is often forced to make use of cumbrous coinages which jar harshly on the literary ear. But this is not the whole explanation. Peirce's style differs perceptibly at different periods of his life. In his first important group of papers (1867–1868) he writes with immense vigour, but very cryptically. He has not yet developed his own philosophical vocabulary, and one can well sympathize with the young William James who found these articles 'exceedingly bold, subtle and incomprehensible'. The series of articles which he published in 1878, and some of the logical papers of the next decade, show Peirce at his best as a writer. He is now master of his own thought and his own vocabulary. He writes with evident care; every sentence is elegantly turned, every paragraph opens out his thought unhurriedly but decisively. But even in these articles Peirce's literary gifts are not easily appreciated at a first reading. Every paragraph is so packed with meaning, every key phrase so suggestive of other doctrines which Peirce is not at the moment propounding, that the reader may easily get an impression of 'cloudiness', or may feel that the writer is holding back too much of what he would really like to say. That was always Peirce's trouble. His thought, so far from being chaotic (as is sometimes alleged), was in fact too closely interconnected over too wide a field to admit easily of effective literary expression.

The year 1891, when Peirce retired to Milford, may be said to open a third phase in his literary development. From now on he was to write for a number of years with a greater freedom and often with a more brilliant suggestiveness than he had ever before achieved. But during this period his writing, like his thought, becomes looser: sometimes it rambles, at other times it becomes excessively disjointed. These tendencies are even plainer in some of the great papers which Peirce wrote, chiefly to elucidate and defend his own version of Pragmatism, after the turn of the century. In these, sense of shape, sense of proportion, and sustained unity of direction are often entirely lost. There are still powerfully developed paragraphs and pregnant dicta; but now Peirce rambles persistently, repeats himself, and employs expressions and arguments which, except for those fully acquainted with his thought, are obscure to a degree. At this last stage Peirce seems like a tired journeyman, weighed down by the number of unwieldy packages on his back – packages which he stops to rearrange periodically, but never with complete success. Nevertheless, the packages contain some of Peirce's most brilliant findings, and the rearrangements he attempts usually deserve the most sympathetic attention.

At every stage in his career Peirce is liable to break out into delightful passages of 'intellectual larking'; and though he never wrote to wound, he knew how to make fun of his intellectual opponents. For example: 'I am a man of whom critics have never found anything good to say. When they could see no opportunity to injure me, they have held their peace. Only once, as far as I remember, in all my lifetime have I experienced the pleasure of praise – not for what it might bring but in itself. That pleasure was beatific; and the praise that conferred it was meant for blame. It was that a critic said of me that I did not seem to be *absolutely sure of my own conclusions*. Never, if I can help it, shall that critic's eyes ever rest on what I am now writing; for I owe a great pleasure to him; and, such was his evident animus, that should he find that out, I fear the fires of hell would be fed with new fuel in his breast. ... My book will have no instruction to impart to anybody. Like a mathematical treatise, it will suggest certain ideas and certain reasons for holding them true; but then, if you accept them, it must be because you like my reasons, and the responsibility lies with you. Man is essentially a social animal: but to be social is one thing, to be gregarious is another: I decline to serve as bellwether. My book is meant for people who *want to find out*; and people who want philosophy ladled out to them can go elsewhere. There are philosophical soup shops at every corner, thank God!' *

Peirce certainly wrote for those 'who want to find out', and because of this his writing is not aimed at making philosophy easy or attractive, and is not likely to do so. But it does reflect

* 1·10 and 11.

admirably his intellectual singleness of purpose, his submergence of any personal considerations to the task he has in hand. His best pages are certain to reproduce in any sincere student of philosophy something very like the admiration which William James expressed after hearing one of Peirce's lectures on logic, 'I never saw a man go into things so intensely and thoroughly.' On the other hand, Peirce often succeeds in revealing indirectly the happier side of that half-bohemian eccentricity which steady academic men of his time must have found unpardonable. How many philosophers, for instance, would dare to give the following as an illustration of the way in which muscular effort may bring about a change of habit? 'If I wish to acquire the habit of speaking of "speaking, writing, thinking", etc., instead of "speakin', writin', thinkin' "', as I suspect I now do (though I am not sure) – all I have to do is to make the desired enunciations a good many times; and to do this as thoughtlessly as possible, since it is an inattentive habit that I am trying to create.' *
Again, how many philosophers would – or could – have chosen the following illustration of the hidden intellectual import of even our most casual sensations? 'A lady's favourite perfume seems to me somehow to agree with that of her spiritual being. If she uses none at all her nature will lack perfume. If she wears violet she herself will have the very same delicate fineness. Of the only two I have known to use rose, one was an artistic old virgin, a grande dame; and the other a noisy young matron and very ignorant; but they were strangely alike. As for those who use heliotrope, frangipanni, etc., I know them as well as I desire to know them. ...' †

Moreover, Peirce could, on occasion, give wonderfully eloquent expression to his own deepest feelings. To give two strikingly contrasting examples. The first, contained in a ramblingly reminiscent comparison of his own intellectual character with that of William James, is probably the bitterest 'philosophers' epitaph' ever penned. 'Who, for example, could be of a nature so different from his as I? He so concrete, so living; I a mere

* 5·479. † 1·313.

table of contents, so abstract, a very snarl of twine.' * But what a contrast to this bitterness is provided by these sentences on the great medieval artists and thinkers – sentences in which Peirce, albeit unwittingly, has succeeded in expressing something surprisingly close to his own intellectual ideal. 'The men of that time did fully believe [sc. in God, the authority of the Church, etc.] and did think that, for the sake of giving themselves up absolutely to their great task of building or of writing, it was well worth while to resign all the joys of life. Think of the spirit in which Duns Scotus must have worked, who wrote his thirteen volumes in folio, in a style as condensed as the most condensed parts of Aristotle, before the age of thirty-four. Nothing is more striking in either of the great intellectual products of that age, than the complete absence of self-conceit on the part of artist or philosopher. That anything of value can be added to his sacred and catholic work by its having the smack of individuality about it, is what he has never conceived. His work is not designed to embody *his* ideas, but the universal truth; there will not be one thing in it, however minute, for which you will not find that he has his authority: and whatever originality emerges is of that inborn kind which so saturates a man that he cannot himself perceive it. The individual feels his own worthlessness in comparison with his task, and does not dare to introduce his vanity into the doing of it. Then there is no machine-work, no unthinking repetition about the thing. Every part is worked out for itself as a separate problem, no matter how analogous it may be in general to another part. And no matter how small and hidden a detail may be, it has been conscientiously studied, as though it were intended for the eye of God.' †

* 6·184.
† From Peirce's review of Fraser's *Berkeley, North American Review*, vol. 113 (1871), pp. 449–72. Cf. 8·7 ff.

CHAPTER THREE

PEIRCE'S THEORY OF KNOWLEDGE

1. *The Assault on Cartesianism*

*

THE 'theories of knowledge' that have been advanced by different philosophers differ strikingly, not only in their conclusions, but in the styles of argument they employ and the terms in which they are conducted. What is common to them is this: that they one and all result in a certain kind of elucidation of such verbs as 'to know', 'to think', to 'understand', 'to doubt', and so on, a kind of elucidation which is entirely different in purpose and methods from those attempted, for example, by lexicographers and other linguistic scholars. Philosophical elucidations of the kind of words ('cognitive words') which we have just instanced are intended to establish the correct or most convenient uses of these words from the point of view of clarity and consistency. And this requires that we must give careful attention to the logical connections between them: for instance, the way in which 'A knows that *p* is true' involves 'A understands what *p* means' and excludes 'A doubts whether *p* is true'. At any rate we can say with confidence that philosophical elucidation of 'cognitive words' – which is what all theories of knowledge result in – are most obviously needed when, as a result of sudden advances in knowledge or any other great shift in human interest, certain traditional uses of them cease to be convenient and new uses come into being which conflict, sometimes strikingly, sometimes less obviously, with the old. In such a situation a philosopher will seek to justify the new use against the old, or vice versa, or he may recommend certain uses which neither side in the conflict has thought of but which may well satisfy the interests of both. This kind of situation has recurred again and again in the history of European philosophy; and since the Renaissance the main (though by no means the sole) cause of its recurrence has been the rapid development of the mathematical and natural sciences. Scientists, since the time of Copernicus, have claimed to know very strange things by what seemed to ordinary men very strange methods; and they have also claimed to doubt very strange things, such as to ordinary men seem obvious or indisputable. It is largely because of this that theories of knowledge have bulked so large in philosophy from the time of Descartes onwards, and that these theories of knowledge should have been aimed primarily at helping intelligent, reflective people to make sense of the more surprising claims of the new sciences, and of the new uses of cognitive verbs which the making of these claims seemed to require.

Most modern theories of knowledge have a further feature in common: they presume – rather than explicitly argue or assert – that those uses of cognitive verbs which seem most serviceable for the expression of scientific argument provide the model for the correct use of these verbs in every other field of discourse. This is but one expression of a tendency, perhaps the most characteristic tendency of modern philosophy, to assimilate all human knowledge, and in particular all expressions of human knowledge, to the model of scientific statements. This tendency first appears clearly in the work of Descartes who, for this reason alone, would deserve the title of the 'father of modern philosophy'. But 'father' in philosophy is not simply an honorific title; for either subsequent philosophers have been bad sons of their father, revilers and destroyers of his characteristic doctrines, or else Descartes was a veritable father Adam, whose sins of omission and commission were to be visited on every succeeding generation of philosophers. If the latter account be true – and there is truth in it, for Descartes, like most great men, was great also in his sins – then every descendant who has rounded on him in one generation after another, may be thought of as a would-be redeemer of philosophy from Cartesian errors. But, and here is the proof of Descartes' greatness and lasting power, every such would-be redeemer seems fated to be accused in his turn of unwitting subservience to some more insidious doctrine or presupposition, some deeper layer in the legacy, of 'that French cavalier who set forth with so bold a stride.'

Peirce is no exception to this rule. His criticisms of Descartes are historically as important as those made by Spinoza or Leibniz, Hume or Kant; and, in respect of logical force and simplicity, are vastly superior to any of theirs. Like all great philosophical criticisms they are essentially simple, and, once they are made, they seem to be the 'obvious' criticisms, such as we should have expected from any competent philosopher. More important is the fact that they are the criticisms of a man who has fully understood the inspired hope that lies behind Descartes' philosophy: namely, to get the whole of human knowledge 'under control' in the kind of way that scientists have got under control their own highly specialized methods of investigation. In rejecting Descartes' recipes for realizing this aim, Peirce has of course the advantage of writing after a lapse of two centuries, during which the rapidly developing methods of science had been interpreted and analysed by a succession of great philosophers. But this advantage – which other nineteenth-century philosophers shared with him – does not account for the force and thoroughness of Peirce's criticisms. These are due, rather, to the fact that Peirce, thanks to his superior logical equipment, goes to the very root of the matter: to the first premisses and guiding principles – and behind these, to the un-criticized presuppositions – of the Cartesian philosophy.

Peirce's criticisms of Descartes provide, both logically and historically, the best possible introduction to his own developed theory of knowledge. They are to be found in two papers which he published in 1868, and which bear the quaint titles *Concerning Certain Faculties Claimed for Man* and *Some Consequences of Four Incapacities*. These papers were to remain virtually ignored by other philosophers for at least sixty years, partly, no doubt, because they are so cryptically expressed, but chiefly because of their profound originality. It is no exaggeration to say that they foreshadow the most important developments in the theory of knowledge which have been made in the present century; and if Peirce had died in the year in which he completed them – he was then less than thirty years of age – they would have been sufficient to establish him as a philosopher of genius.

In order to straighten out and bring into full relief the main tenets of these early articles of Peirce, it will be useful to distinguish three aspects of Descartes' theory of knowledge, and then set out Peirce's criticisms of each of these aspects in turn. We shall therefore consider: first, Descartes' conception of *Intuition* as the fundamental activity of mind; second, certain rules of method which seem to be required by this conception of Intuition; and third, the kinds of fact or object which, according to Descartes, can be most completely and certainly known.

*

Descartes took over the traditional and familiar distinction between two sorts of knowledge, direct and indirect, or immediate and inferential. His account of inference, which has since met with much criticism, need not greatly concern us: the one thing we should notice about it is that it virtually reduces inference to a succession of those direct acts of knowledge which he termed Intuitions. Thus, according to Descartes, we intuit or see *all together* the truth of a certain directly known premiss, the way that premiss necessitates a certain conclusion, and thereupon the truth of that conclusion. (This illustrates what is meant by saying that Intuition, or direct knowledge of primary, uninferred truths, is for Descartes the fundamental activity of mind.) His account of Intuition may be set out in three logically successive stages as follows:

1. Every Intuition is of an essentially indubitable or self-evident truth: i.e. a truth such that one has only to understand the meaning of the words used to express it to see that it must be true. Examples would be the statement 'I am thinking, therefore I exist,' or the principle 'If equals be added to equals, their sums will be equal.'

2. Every Intuition, in virtue of (1) above, must be an abso-

lutely simple two-term relation between knowing mind and known fact or truth. It is as though the truth in question were waiting to reveal itself directly to the 'natural light' (one of Descartes' favourite metaphors) which will pick out the whole of that truth and nothing but it. (For if an Intuition passed, as it were, beyond its proper object so as to include anything in the nature of a conjecture or an untested assumption, it would immediately lose its distinctive intuitive character.)

3. Certain preliminaries may have to be gone through before we actually achieve a particular Intuition; but once it is achieved it is in no way dependent on any other thought. It is therefore useless to ask for an explanation of why any fact, revealed to Intuition, is as it is: unless, to apply Peirce's words, 'God makes it so' is regarded as an explanation. (It is only in this way that Descartes explains, for instance, why Thought should be the intuitable 'essence' of one class of existing things, viz. minds, and extension in three dimensions should be the intuitable 'essence' of another, viz. material things.)

Of these three stages or moments in his account of Intuition, Descartes lays most emphasis on the first; but the second, as expressed in proposition (2) above, is probably of the greater importance, since it is in terms of proposition (2) that the remaining feature of Intuition presented in proposition (3) is most naturally expressed.

Let us now look back at the traditional view of direct knowledge of which Descartes' theory of Intuition is evidently intended as a refinement. This traditional view, which appears to be supported by everyday uses and experience, is that, if there is to be inference or derivative knowledge, there must first be some direct knowledge on which inference can be based. Thus, the ordinary man knows what it is to reach a conclusion by an explicit process of inference; he knows too that in at least some cases of this kind the premisses he employs were not themselves reached by a similar process of inference: on the contrary, they express something which he had learnt, let us say, by using his eyes and looking, or something which it would seem to him impossible, or at least absurd, to question. The ordinary man un-questionably believes what his senses seem to 'tell him directly' and never doubts, for example, the familiar principles of logic and arithmetic about which, as it seems to him, his intellect 'tells him directly'. On the other hand, the ordinary man has no theory whatsoever about the exact nature, or the defining conditions, of such knowledge. In particular, he has no theory about its *absolute* directness or simplicity or essentially 'two-term' character. He will affirm, to be sure, that some parts of his knowledge are direct, simple, non-derivative relatively to other parts of it; but that is as far as his common-sense logic takes him. Again, he will maintain that some of the things he knows directly (in this homespun sense) are indubitable; but the idea of essential indubitability and self-evidence, in the sense of self-dependence, is something that has never occurred to him. It would therefore be a mistake to accept Descartes' account of Intuition on the grounds that it agrees with everyday experience and usage. It was certainly suggested by – and itself suggests – such usage: it claims to agree with it but also to refine it and render it more precise. In other words the Cartesian account of Intuition is in the nature of a *theory* about certain facts, and as such stands in need of proof or justification; for it is all too easy, in attempting to render a vague view more precise, to strip it of such truth as its original vagueness contained.

What test, then, should we apply to the Cartesian account of Intuition; or what evidence can be produced in favour of it? Is the fact (or alleged fact) that we have intuitions in Descartes' sense supposed to be itself known by Intuition? Or, on the other hand, is it supposed to be known by means of inference – for instance, from the fact that unless there *were* intuitions there could be no knowledge of any other kind whatsoever? These are the questions which we find Peirce putting in the first of his papers of 1868; and the really amazing thing is that no previous philosopher had put them with this – as it now seems to us – obvious and compelling simplicity. In the two hundred odd years that had elapsed since Descartes wrote, the doctrine of

Intuition had lived on, occupying a steadily decreasing area in successive maps of knowledge, but reappearing persistently and sometimes in new and unexpected places. Hume and Kant, for example, no doubt both thought that they had dealt the doctrine its death-blow; but it remains, in fact, practically unaltered in Hume's account of our knowledge of arithmetic and algebra, and (if we eliminate certain subjectivist trimmings) in Kant's account of our knowledge of geometry; and it was to enjoy new life in the present century under the name of 'Knowledge by Acquaintance'. Let us see, then, how Peirce criticizes this doctrine, which gives us, in the most general form possible, the core of all Cartesian theories of knowledge.*

Suppose that the first of the alternatives proposed above were the true one, viz. that the fact that we have intuitions is itself intuitively known. If this were so, we might expect, at any rate among trained thinkers, virtually unanimous agreement as to which sorts of knowledge are intuitive and which are not; but it is notorious that nothing like such agreement is to be found. Nor, if we reflect, should this surprise us; for experience in the law courts, psychological laboratories, and elsewhere shows us that, even in terms of the familiar common-sense distinction between immediate and inferential knowledge, it is extremely difficult to distinguish what we have directly seen or heard from the inferences and interpretations we put upon it. How much more difficult should this task be when the quality to be distinguished – that of being an Intuition in Descartes' sense – is one which calls for careful discrimination and exact definition. The most that can plausibly be claimed is that there are certain specially privileged cases in which we can tell directly – i.e. by Intuition – that a given piece of knowledge is intuitive: in other, for some reason obscurer, cases of intuitions, this, it will have to be argued, is not possible. Peirce proceeds therefore to consider three of these allegedly privileged cases. But the result of his examination is that the question: Can we tell intuitively that our knowledge in these cases is intuitive? turns out to be

* 5·213 ff.

premature, if not wholly gratuitous. For in all three cases Peirce succeeds in showing that the original specimens of knowledge chosen are, in all probability, not intuitive at all.

He first examines the allegedly privileged case of the knowledge which each one of us has of himself as a unique 'thinking subject'.* Such knowledge, it has sometimes been claimed, is 'obviously' intuitive; but observation of young children, and especially of their speech-habits, suggests a total absence of such knowledge in them. Children appear to come by the idea of themselves as unique individuals having thoughts of their own (a) through interpreting the speech which others (adults) address to them ('That is what *you* think, Tommy, not what Peter thinks'), and (b) as a hypothesis to account for, or provide a locus for, their own errors, dreams, etc. A plausible conclusion from these facts is that our self-knowledge is always in fact inferential, although the inferences on which it is based have become for the most part so habitual to us, and as a result of this habituation so 'telescoped', that we very easily come to regard our self-knowledge as immediate or intuitive. This conclusion is of course not a necessary one. It is possible that Peirce's account of how we *come* by our self-knowledge is correct, and yet that at some point in our lives our self-knowledge, which had hitherto been inferential, suddenly – or perhaps gradually – becomes direct or intuitive. This is a possible view; but it sounds suspiciously like special pleading. As a hypothesis it compares, in respect of simplicity and cohesion, very unfavourably with the account of the facts which Peirce offers. We may therefore reasonably conclude that the case for the intuitive character of self-knowledge is not proven; and hence that the claim, that we can recognize this intuitively, hardly merits consideration.

Peirce next considers the allegedly intuitive character of our knowledge of our different mental states, in particular our capacity to distinguish a state of belief from a state of mere supposition or a state of doubt.† Here it will suffice to say, for this is a subject we shall deal with in more detail in our next chapter,

* 5·225 ff.   † 5·238 ff.

that Peirce has little difficulty in showing, at the very least, the plausibility of the contrary thesis: viz. that we distinguish such states, not by direct intuition, but by inference from certain of their observed concomitants and effects. Thus Peirce argues, taking over the suggestion of the Scottish psychologist Bain, that we know *when* we are believing because of our readiness to *act* on what we believe, whereas, when we merely entertain a supposition, no such readiness to act can be discovered. In this field again, therefore, the claim that we can tell intuitively that certain parts of our knowledge are intuitive in character turns out to rest on prior claims which the Intuitionist has yet to establish.

In his articles of 1868 Peirce touches very briefly on a third of these allegedly privileged cases: our knowledge of the simplest 'data of consciousness', or 'sense data' as many contemporary philosophers describe them. Broadly – and we are here filling out his early treatment of this issue in the light of his maturer writings – he rejects the claim that we have direct intuitive knowledge of such elementary data on the ground that whenever we know something we know it *as* something – as being of such and such a character, or as standing in such and such relations. In other words, to know something, we must classify it or relate it; and this, Peirce maintains, is something that cannot be done without the use of signs or symbols of one kind or another. To give an example, the redness of a flower is something that, if actually presented to a person with normal vision, he certainly *sees* directly in the sense that he cannot see the flower as other than red. Again, if for any reason he attends to the colour, and if he possesses normal powers of abstraction and classification, he can hardly avoid *thinking* of it as red – no matter whether he uses the English word 'red' or some other word or sign to denote it. On the other hand, that what he then thinks of is not something simple and directly given, and that it requires the use of symbols to hold it steady 'in the thinker's mind', may be suggested as follows. People of normal vision sometimes disagree about the colour of a presented object; and when this happens there are ways of deciding which of the disputants is right – for instance by fetching a colour chart, whose correctness both parties will admit, and laying a shade or range of shades on the chart over against the object about whose colour there is disagreement. Hence it would appear that one's knowledge, or the correctness of one's classification, of a given colour is not so simple and direct after all; it is something whose hidden complexity can be suggested by some such formula as, 'If one were to apply certain standard tests, one would find that the colour falls within a certain range of shades, those referred to in ordinary English as "red".' To know that the colour of an object is red means then, at the very least, to know that it shows a resemblance in greater or less degree to one wide class of objects (other red objects) and a contrast in greater or less degree to a second, wider class of objects (those whose colours are other than red); and the use of the word 'red' or of any logically equivalent symbol presupposes the capacity to perform this, admittedly very simple, piece of comparison and contrasting. But whether one really possesses this capacity is something that can only be shown by one's later actions and statements with regard to the object in question. If, for instance, after pronouncing the colour of a flower to be red one proceeded to group it with blue flowers, or if one went on to say, 'Yes, its shade is of a redness that is almost olive-green', one would naturally be suspected either of being unable to discriminate colours in the way people of normal vision do, or of not knowing how to use colour words correctly. Now incapacities of both these kinds are sometimes found; and this fact helps us to see that our allegedly direct and intuitive *knowledge* of, say, a given colour is something that admits of testing by evidence – or, in the language of Peirce's Pragmatism, by certain of its later practical effects.

This brings us to Peirce's own, at first sight, somewhat paradoxical suggestion that every piece of apparently direct intuitive knowledge – including our knowledge of the most elementary 'data of consciousness' – is in fact of the nature of a hypothesis; since every claim to knowledge involves the *assumption* that a certain method of classification or systematization will in fact apply to a particular object or set of objects in a particular way. Now of course the *truth* of a hypothesis is something that has to be tested, by its consequences or effects. Just which, or how many, of these effects must be considered and found to hold good if a hypothesis is to count as true, is a question to which no over-all answer can be given; but it is difficult to believe that all possible relevant tests of the truth of *any* hypothesis can be enumerated and checked over *in a single act of Intuition*. Unless this can be done, however, it would seem that recognition of even the simplest quality must rest on the *assumption* that certain relevant necessary consequences are in fact realized in the case in question. And such an assumption is something which the Cartesian doctrine of Intuition cannot possibly allow.

If this argument of Peirce's could be accepted, then it seems clear that the very existence of Intuitions – let alone the claim that their existence can be intuitively known – would be very dubious indeed. It is therefore important to consider a third line of defence to which believers in Intuitions (or in 'knowledge by acquaintance') may resort. This defence, which depends entirely on general considerations and requires no reference to any specific instances (or alleged instances) of Intuition, may be stated briefly as follows. Suppose that Peirce is right, and that any judgement we care to examine, no matter how simple and direct it may at first appear to be, turns out to rest on certain assumptions, i.e. to be such that in making it we are *ipso facto* accepting certain prior premises as true. Then we may ask: What is the logical status of these premises themselves? Were they, in their turn, established by some prior process of inference? And if so, what about the premises of this prior process? Were these also derived from certain still remoter premises? Evidently this line of questioning can be pushed back and back: but ultimately (so the present argument maintains) we must come to some piece of knowledge which was not derived from any prior knowledge; for how, otherwise, since the life of each one of us goes back for only a finite time, could our knowledge conceivably have *begun*? There must, then, this argument concludes, have been at least *one* first piece of knowledge which was wholly direct and self-evident, i.e. an Intuition. But of course, once this is granted with regard to one Intuition, there seems to be no good reason for denying the existence of others. If the facts seem to require a plurality of first premisses – and, in view of the varied types of knowledge that we possess, this seems likely – then we are perfectly justified in inferring the existence of Intuitions of facts or truths of many different types. It is no doubt extremely difficult to decide just what these absolutely first premisses of our knowledge are: and this accounts for the variety of opinions which philosophers offer on the subject. But neither this variety in the opinions of philosophers, nor for that matter their inability to provide in any single specific case conclusive proof of the intuitive character of a given piece of knowledge, in any way invalidates the general conclusion that there must have been, in the life of every one of us, at least one cognition which was purely intuitive.

What is Peirce's reply to this argument? In his papers of 1868 he seems content to show that it is not a conclusive argument. Thus he points out that if the series of inference-depending-upon-inference-depending-upon-inference were a continuous or compact one in the mathematical sense, then no absolutely first term to the series would be required, or indeed would be possible; for between the limit to which such a series converges and any member of it you care to mention there is always at least one further member. The argument under consideration presupposes, therefore, that the series of our thoughts is not a continuous one in the strict sense.*

The obvious weakness of this retort is that it offers no positive grounds for holding that our thought-sequences are continuous in the strict sense, or that they possess any other property which would require that they cannot depend on intuitive logically

* 5·263.

self-dependent premisses. But if we accept Peirce's contention that all knowledge involves the use of signs and symbols, it is fairly easy to appreciate the positive point that he here has in mind. For we have all had to learn how to use symbols correctly in order to make even the most elementary classifications correctly. For instance, when asked to name the colours of different objects, a young child has – visibly – to stop and think: he tries to recall certain instructions which he has previously received and which are, for him, the only possible justification of whatever answer he tentatively and hopefully puts forward. (His thoughts might be expressed by saying: 'If Mother *did* say red for this object yesterday – and I *think* she did – then red it is!') Generalizing from this, we may say that every piece of knowing depends, not simply causally but logically, on what one has previously learnt, since all knowledge rests on the assumption that certain methods of classification and systematization, which have been learnt in connection with other earlier situations, can be applied, in a particular way, to a given situation. Once this is admitted, the great error of Descartes and of all later Cartesians becomes plain: it is the assumption that we cannot learn *until* we know. If this assumption were warranted, then it would be senseless to say of any two thought-sequences, neither of which develops or builds on a basis of self-evident first premisses, that one is performed better or more intelligently than the other. But to common sense it seems obvious that in most processes of learning we simply must build upon – with a view to testing, improving, or rejecting – whatever prior beliefs or conjectures we can bring to bear on the problem facing us. We must build on what we have; and we quite obviously build better or more intelligently in some cases than we do in others.

Development of this line of thought would lead us to an alternative conception of knowledge as the claim that we have learnt to apply certain methods of classification and systematization ideally well; this claim, however, being always open to possible questioning and testing. Peirce calls this general conception of knowledge 'fallibilism' because of its frank admission that there is an element of untested assumption in all our claims to knowledge, and hence that the correctness of any such claim depends on the correctness of the premises or prior beliefs on which it is based. But, agreeable though it is to common sense in many respects, this conception still leaves us with the paradox that, if there are no absolutely first premises to any sequence of thought, then the thinking life of each one of us can have had no definitely assignable beginning. Let us therefore try to see whether this paradox really rests on an absurdity, or whether it arises because we are here facing a question which genuinely requires some drastic revision of our habitual ways of thinking.

Certainly it would be absurd to maintain, with regard to the life-history of any individual, that it contains no time *before* he had begun to think. On the other hand, it is perhaps not altogether absurd to claim, with regard to any one of his articulate thoughts, that that thought must have depended logically on some previous thought or previously established tendency-to-think. What this suggestion really amounts to is that it may be impossible *in principle* – not simply because of our lack of observational or experimental or imaginative skill – to 'pin-point' the origins of thought, or of intellectual life, in any given individual. And should the reader feel a strong disinclination to accept this suggestion, then let him put the following question to himself. Does he really believe that, given ideal conditions of observation, he would be able to 'pin-point' the exact moment at which a child can be said to have begun to *talk*, or to have become able to *follow a story*, or to have begun to *understand a foreign language*, or begun to *enjoy music*? In each of these cases we meet with a difficulty which is partially parallel to that which meets us when we ask: Has the mental life of every individual a definite beginning in time? Common sense has no difficulty about accepting the suggestion that in all these cases capacity to think, to speak, to understand or what not, depends, at any mentionable stage, on the exercise of a previously formed capacity. It is only the necessary conclusion from this suggestion

– namely that, in a sense which does no violence to the known facts, our thinking life has no definitely assignable beginning in time – that common sense finds unpalatable.

Suppose, then, that we were to re-state the paradox in conditional – and therefore apparently milder – form as follows. So long as we are talking about a person's *thoughts* we must assume that these are intelligible in the sense of being at the very least attempts to apply previously learnt methods of classifying, relating, and so on. This statement must be taken to allow that if we were to probe back imaginatively in the attempt to understand any particular thought, we should find prior thoughts (premisses) giving place to habitual and in the end to purely instinctive responses, adapted to the course of experience by means that are entirely beyond intelligent control. But so long as the process, which we might thus imaginatively reconstruct, remained a genuine thinking or learning process, its successive advances would depend logically as well as causally on previous conjectures, beliefs, suppositions, etc., which would enable us to understand them, though they would not of course in all cases fully justify them.

*

Can we now attempt an assessment of Peirce's criticisms of the doctrine of Intuition? Certainly they would appear to rob it of all its immediate plausibility, so that it can at best be maintained as a hypothesis, claiming assent because it helps to explain certain facts which no other theory can. Now Descartes himself would certainly have claimed that his doctrine explains why certain methods of investigation give us results of a uniquely high degree of certainty and exactitude. Before attempting any final assessment of Peirce's criticisms, therefore, let us see what, according to Descartes, the main methodological consequences of the doctrine of Intuition are. These may be summarized very briefly, since they are among the most famous theses of modern philosophy.

1. Since all genuine knowledge consists in, or is derived from, Intuitions, the possibility that we may continue to harbour

opinions not so constituted or derived must be deliberately excluded. This means that, for the purpose of purely intellectual
inquiry, we must subject all our beliefs, especially those which
seem most direct and fundamental, to the strictest possible
scrutiny. Hence the celebrated Cartesian method of doubt: the
recommendation that every man of serious intellectual aims
should, at least once in his life, make the experiment of doubting
everything that he has believed hitherto.

2. But any simple belief, which survives the test of the
severest doubt, will thereby prove itself an Intuition: that is,
prove itself an instance of direct, simple, self-sufficient knowledge of truth. And no other test of this intuitive character can
be conceived than that some individual mind shall find, after
applying the test of doubt, that he clearly and distinctly perceives
that some fact or truth *must* be precisely as he asserts it to be.

3. Increase in general knowledge consists in a step-by-step
advance from the simplest intuitions. But it is essential to success
that we should start with the simplest intuitions, and that in our
advance we should follow the right (the one and only right)
order. Mathematics, for example the geometry of Euclid, provides a model on both these scores.

4. Explanation, or the understanding of complex facts, results
from showing how a certain fairly 'advanced' conclusion is
derived from the simplest intuitions. But to ask for an explanation of what explains – for example, to ask for the justification
of Euclid's axioms – would be absurd. In all investigation we
depend on certain ultimates, which admit of no explanation,
unless, to repeat Peirce's tart observation, 'God made it so' is
to be regarded as an explanation.

Peirce rejects these methodological rules and recommenda-
tions on the following grounds:

1. 'We cannot begin with complete doubt. We must begin
with all the prejudices which we actually have when we enter
into the study of philosophy. These prejudices are not to be
dispelled by a maxim, for they are things which it does not
occur to us *can* be questioned. ... A person may, it is true, in the

course of his studies, find reason to doubt what he began by believing; but in that case he doubts because he has a positive reason for it, and not on account of the Cartesian maxim. Let us not pretend to doubt in philosophy what we do not doubt in our hearts.' *

The nerve of Peirce's criticism here is that we cannot doubt without a *positive* reason: genuine doubt arises only when two or more beliefs appear to conflict with one another. Doubt has, as it were, the effect of suspending belief; but it would be impossible for this to happen unless one believed – or knew – that there is something incompatible between certain beliefs which he had previously held. In fine, one can never doubt except on a positive basis of belief or knowledge.

2. Why cannot the individual consciousness be taken as the ultimate criterion of knowledge? What is wrong with asserting with Descartes, 'Whatever I clearly and distinctly perceive is true'? The history of philosophy supplies one fairly obvious reason. It shows us that metaphysicians 'will all agree that metaphysics has reached a pitch of certainty far beyond that of the physical sciences; – only they can agree on nothing else.' He then proceeds: 'In sciences in which men come to agreement, when a theory has been broached, it is considered to be on probation until this agreement is reached. After it is reached, the question of certainty becomes an idle one, because there is no one left who doubts it. We individually cannot reasonably hope to obtain the ultimate philosophy which we pursue; we can only seek it, therefore, for the *community* of philosophers. Hence, if disciplined and candid minds carefully examine a theory and refuse to accept it, this ought to create doubts in the mind of the author of the theory himself.' †

Here the observable practice and authority of the *community* of scientists is contrasted with the excessive individualism which we find in philosophy. We should notice, however, that the authority of the community of scientists derives entirely from the fact that agreement tends to be reached (if we except the

* 5·265.   † 5·265.

most elementary questions) *only by those who inquire*. Why is this? Partly because, by tradition within the several sciences, every new result for which attention is claimed is accompanied by a full account of the problems that gave rise to it and of the methods by which it was reached, as well as an adequate indication of the background of theory which it assumes to be true. Thus every contribution to science is an appeal to *other* scientists to go over the same ground for themselves: and this is in practice the scientist's substitute for Cartesian doubt. But Peirce's conception of the community of inquirers means more than the observable fact that co-operation and mutual criticism are of the first importance in science; it also embodies his understanding of the first article of faith of every scientist, namely the belief and hope that if investigation into any given problem be carried sufficiently far, one solution will always establish itself as logically superior to all its rivals. This hope, which binds together successive generations of scientists, is all that Truth means, Peirce claims, in science. Wherever that opinion is reached – as it no doubt is reached on many questions in both science and history – agreement *among those who inquire* is automatically reached. Everyone concerned with the truth will have put the suggested solution to the test by the best methods available to the community; and therefore no one concerned with the truth 'is left to doubt it.'

3. 'Philosophy', Peirce goes on to tell us, 'ought to imitate the successful sciences in its methods, so far as to proceed only from tangible premisses which can be subjected to careful scrutiny, and to trust rather to the multitude and variety of its arguments than to the conclusiveness of any one. Its reasoning should not form a chain which is no stronger than its weakest link, but a cable whose fibres may be ever so slender, provided they are sufficiently numerous and intimately connected.' *

Why did Descartes seek to erect a comprehensive system of knowledge on the basis of a single factual premiss ('I exist as a thinking being') with the aid of a small number of allegedly

* 5·265.

self-evident, though in fact never clearly enunciated, principles of reasoning? Chiefly, as we have suggested, and indeed as he himself tells us, because of the example of geometry. In Euclid's geometry a large number of theorems are deduced from a surprisingly small number of axioms and definitions. Now quite obviously the truth of the different theorems in Euclid's ten books was not originally suggested to their separate discoverers in the exact order in which we find these theorems presented by Euclid. Descartes of course knew this; but he would have claimed that what matters in Euclid, namely the demonstrative or proven character of his theorems, does depend on this order: more generally, he would have claimed that there is one, and only one, order in which any system of progressively more complex truths can be properly demonstrated. Modern mathematicians, however, would reject this claim. They would maintain that whenever a subject-matter admits of demonstrative or deductive presentation, there are a variety of ways in which this can be done. In other words, the theorems we find deduced in any one system can as a rule be deduced from any one of a number of different sets of axioms, and the only reasons for preferring one of these axiom sets to another are those of economy, elegance, and pedagogic efficiency. The general importance of this view, however, is perhaps most clearly seen in the case of the physical science, whose truths are quite obviously gained in piecemeal fashion and therefore always subject to subsequent corrections, but are nevertheless in the end presented (for instance, in most textbooks) in deductive or semi-deductive form. Let the reader glance through three or four textbooks of mechanics, and he will quickly discover that their different writers, although agreeing entirely in all their conclusions, i.e. the proved general principles of mechanics, nevertheless differ considerably as regards the nature of their proofs and the order in which they present them, and may well also differ in their definitions of the key terms of the science.

It turns out therefore that the third of Descartes' methodological rules combines three important errors. Descartes wrongly assumes that, to achieve knowledge of any given subject-matter, we must commence from some piece of direct, indubitable knowledge: largely because of this, he has greatly exaggerated the part which deduction from first premisses plays in any branch of knowledge; and finally he has misconceived the characteristic function, or service, of deduction itself. These errors are particularly insidious in the case of philosophy which is concerned with wide, and in the main vaguely expressed issues – the very last issues to admit of 'knock-down' demonstrative solution.

4. Both in his 1868 papers and in later writings Peirce consistently urges that science knows nothing of 'absolutely inexplicable' facts. In general, science aims at rendering facts intelligible or manageable by discovering the laws which, in the appropriate sense, explain them. It may be, of course, that these explanations will involve the hypothesis of further facts whose existence and character remain (thus far) wholly unexplained: but where this is so, the suggestion that these further facts should be counted absolutely inexplicable is one which no scientist will allow. The suggestion of 'ultimates' and 'inexplicables' smacks to the scientist of dogmatism or mysticism or both. In Peirce's judgement, it commits the supreme sin against the scientific spirit: 'It blocks the road of inquiry.'

*

It would be difficult to find, in the whole history of philosophy, a battery of criticisms more devastating and complete than those which we have just cited from the second of Peirce's papers of 1868. If the doctrine of Intuition is to be judged by its methodological consequences, then the case against it is here decided once for all. There are, however, certain further consequences of the doctrine which, although of a less general character than those just considered, have perhaps exercised an even stronger hold on subsequent philosophers; and it will be useful before we close the present chapter to notice Peirce's reaction to these more specific tenets of the Cartesian philosophy.

According to Descartes, our fundamental intuitions relate to facts of two basically different kinds: on the one hand the simplest truths of mathematics and logic, on the other hand our own thinking processes or attitudes. Now Descartes recognized clearly that truths of the former kind are purely hypothetical, they do not relate to matters of fact or existence: the consequence is, therefore, that in his philosophy all our knowledge of fact is based ultimately on our knowledge of our own thinking processes, and hence of ourselves as essentially 'thinking substances'. In its completed form, to be sure, his philosophy allows that we possess real knowledge of the material world; but he insists that this knowledge is essentially derivative. Indeed he goes so far as to claim that, whenever we know some material fact, we *ipso facto* know – and know more clearly, directly, and certainly – of our own existence as thinking beings.

By no means all philosophers who maintain an intuitionist theory of knowledge would agree to these markedly subjective conclusions of Descartes. For example, most contemporary adherents to the doctrine of 'knowledge by acquaintance' would affirm that the most typical objects of direct acquaintance – those often described as 'sense data' – are of a neutral status, neither mental nor material. Nevertheless, it may be doubted whether any of these latter-day Intuitionists have succeeded in wholly sloughing off that subjectivism which, to the general reader, is one of the most striking features of western philosophy since Descartes; and we shall therefore be resurrecting no outmoded 'guy' if we turn, for the remainder of the present chapter, to Peirce's strenuous rejection of this subjectivist tendency, whether it be manifested in the obviously paradoxical form which Descartes gave to it, or in other forms, apparently milder but basically no less wrong-headed.

As we have already seen, Peirce denies in his 1868 papers that we have direct intuitive knowledge either of ourselves as unique individuals or of our own inner states and attitudes. He does not deny that we *know*, in some way or other, these important facts about ourselves; nor does he wish to deny that such knowledge may be as certain, as well-attested, as any other knowledge we possess: all he denies is that such knowledge is wholly intuitive, i.e. non-derivative, non-inferential. In this spirit he points out, for instance, that we cannot know that we are angry unless we believe in the objective existence of some person or situation which, as it were, 'deserves' our anger.* And similarly, he argues, we cannot recognize the quality of one of our sensations save as the result of a complex process of inference from the fact (or presumed fact) that some object, which we claim to perceive, appears to have that very quality. Again, we may recall his suggestion that we first form a definite idea of ourselves as a *hypothesis* to account for the existence of, or provide a locus for, our own errors – the fact that we claim to see or remember or in some other way to know of the existence of things which other people, to judge by their speech and actions, do not see or remember or believe in. Now on all these scores ordinary common-sense reflection – unless and until it is affected by the Cartesian philosophy – will almost certainly agree with Peirce. But in the next step he takes common sense will have more difficulty in following him. For he argues that it is only a generalization of this last suggestion to maintain that *all* our knowledge of minds and their workings – our own minds or other people's – is derived from our knowledge of certain 'outward' physical facts: namely those parts or results of our own and other people's behaviour which we call *signs*.† Signs – most of the sounds we utter and many of the other bodily movements we make – are, in their actual occurrence, perfectly good physical things or happenings; but the relations in which one physical thing must stand to others if it is to work as a sign are of a kind that we should not expect in things or processes that are, as we say, purely physical or material. Now we shall find Peirce claiming that to know, with regard to a succession of physical events, that they make up a sign or series of signs, is to know of the existence and operation of a mind (or number of minds); and that to be engaged in making or manifesting or

* 5·247.　　　　　† 5·249 ff.

reacting to a series of signs is to be engaged in 'being a mind' or, more simply and naturally, to be engaged in thinking intelligently.

At first sight this view seems highly paradoxical: chiefly perhaps because it seems to put our knowledge of our own minds, thoughts, attitudes, etc., on all-fours with our knowledge of the minds, thoughts, and attitudes of their people. And this is something that common sense cannot easily accept. On the contrary it seems, at any rate on first reflection, that everyone's thoughts are in a quite unique and peculiarly intimate way his own; his own private and in large measure secret possession. But Peirce has no wish to deny the obvious fact that every man's thoughts and feelings – in this like his incipient words and actions – are in some way private to him: indeed, in a *sense*, are him and therefore quite uniquely his.* What has to be denied, on Peirce's view, is that this immediacy and privacy of a man's thoughts, feelings, and incipient actions in any way serve to account for his *knowledge* of them. (Still more must it be denied that such immediacy and privacy can be taken as a criterion of *all* genuine knowledge.) And on this score common sense can perhaps be won round to agree with Peirce. For in ordinary life we all know very well how difficult it is to be sure how we have come to think as we do – as opposed to being able to reiterate our formed opinion and offer reasons, that is to issue statements, in defence of them. On the other hand, it is in some cases relatively easy to 'read' other people's thoughts, as disclosed in their overt speech and actions; and it is no exaggeration to say that we learn to read our own minds with skill largely as a result of practice in reading the minds (or descriptions of the minds) of other people. This suggests that we should be unable to 'know ourselves', or to know what we are thinking, unless our thoughts got expressed in words and other signs such as we find other people using in appropriate situations and ourselves learn to apply to *their* actions, in just those situations. Is it then so very paradoxical to say, as Peirce virtually does in a number

* 5·310 ff.

of passages,* that we know what we have been thinking only in so far as we find ourselves asserting, by words or other suitable means, some conclusion which we have come to, and find further that we are capable of defending this conclusion, or of providing reasons for it – and always in this latter case by means of words or other symbols? And is it not perfectly obvious that words, or signs of whatever description, are things whose function is not confined to expressing our own private thoughts; i.e. that 'sign-reading' is essentially of the same kind, whether the signs we read are made by ourselves or made by other people?

But, while urging this, we may agree that we never succeed in 'seeing ourselves' *exactly* 'as others see us', or in seeing others exactly as they see themselves; nevertheless we do – if Peirce's view is correct – see ourselves, as others do, through our own speech and the rest of our interpretable behaviour; and we see others (as they see themselves) through *their* speech and other interpretable behaviour. The important consequence is, that our knowledge of our own thoughts, and hence the possibility of our controlling, developing, and criticizing them, is not essentially different from our knowledge of, and hence our power to influence, the thoughts of others. In other words, whenever we think we are in effect communicating – seeking to persuade or instruct or perhaps simply questioning – either covertly with ourselves or overtly with other people. 'All thinking', Peirce writes, 'is dialogic in form. Your self of one instant appeals to your deeper self for his assent'; † and again, 'One's thoughts are what he is "saying to himself", that is, is saying to that other self that is just coming into life in the flow of time. When one reasons, it is that critical self that one is trying to persuade; and all thought whatsoever is a sign, and is mostly in the nature of language.' ‡ What a man says to himself, he (or his later self) understands: and just as we have to *learn* the meanings of the words which other people address to us, so we have to learn the meanings of the things we say, or think, to ourselves.

* 2·26 ff.   † 6·338.   ‡ 5·421, cf. 4·6.

Peirce's contention that thoughts are signs, or that every knowledge-situation is essentially a sign-situation, will be considered in more detail in later chapters. Here, however, we may notice that it signalizes, in the clearest possible manner, Peirce's break with the Cartesian tradition. Whereas that tradition sees knowledge as essentially direct and dyadic, a two-term relation between knowing mind and known fact, Peirce sees it as essentially triadic, that is, as involving in all cases the three terms, sign, object signified, and interpreter – or, as he prefers to say, interpretant. The formal contrast between the two views is striking. Other critics of Cartesianism have rightly pointed out that the knowledge-situation is always a much more complex affair than the Cartesian view, epitomized in the image or model of 'the natural light', will allow. But it is one thing to make such a general criticism; quite another thing to set out an alternative so striking in its simplicity and at the same time admitting, as we shall find Peirce's to do, of such surprisingly fruitful developments.

CHAPTER FOUR

PEIRCE'S THEORY OF KNOWLEDGE

II. *Critical Commonsensism*

*

PEIRCE nowhere gives us a unified official exposition of his own theory of knowledge. Its central tenets, powerfully illustrated in his elucidations of certain 'cognitive verbs', have to be brought together from writings of widely different dates, in some of which his primary purpose is to refute *other* theories of knowledge, in some to expound his Pragmatism, in some again to defend his own metaphysical theories. Largely for this reason we are faced with what at first seems a formidable difficulty: we find the main tenets of Peirce's theory of knowledge expressed in three different terminologies, with the result that its underlying unity is obscured. On closer inspection, however, each of these terminologies is seen to have a merit of its own: each enables Peirce to bring out certain facets of his own thought which neither of the others is so well suited to express. Therefore, at the risk of some repetition, we shall in this and the following chapter present Peirce's theory of knowledge in three successive versions or stages, indicating the importance – and indeed the necessity – of his shifts in terminology, as we pass from stage to stage. Our first version, which we shall call Peirce's *Conception of Inquiry*, is couched in terms which at first sight appear to be psychological, or at any rate to be simply descriptive, in nature. Our second version, Peirce's *Conception of Inference*, is couched, roughly speaking, in the terms of traditional logic: our aim at this stage will be to clarify Peirce's view of inference as the 'essential function of the cognitive mind' and his conception of 'habits of inference'. Our third version (Chapter V) will consist in a fairly detailed exposition of Peirce's doctrine of *Thought-signs* – broadly the consequences which he draws from his claim that every thought-situation, like every sign-situation, is essentially triadic in structure.

Throughout our first two versions we shall emphasize Peirce's 'critical commonsensism', his contention – already adumbrated in his criticisms of Descartes – that we must commence philosophy, like every other branch of inquiry, from an examination of our relevant common-sense beliefs, and then subject these to that general line of criticism – 'fallibilism' Peirce calls it – which the example of the most successful sciences suggests. Peirce's critical commonsensism, we shall find, expresses an attitude of mind as valuable as it is rare; that of a man of profound scientific culture who nevertheless retains an almost reverent appreciation of the vague matrix of practical beliefs from which all science springs.

Peirce's conception of Inquiry

In what is perhaps his most famous paper, *The Fixation of Belief* (published in 1878 as the first of that series of papers in which his original formulation of the 'Pragmatist maxim' appeared), Peirce gives a careful elucidation of some of the most important mutual relations of the words 'belief', 'doubt', 'thought', 'knowledge', and 'experience'; and it is to achieve this elucidation that he introduces, in a technical sense of his own, the word 'inquiry'.

Belief, Peirce tells us, is the natural or most common condition of the intelligent mind: it is a 'self-satisfied' condition, and this is due to its apparent adequacy to the needs of action. Different beliefs, in fact, are best distinguished by the different modes of action to which they give rise; hence a given belief may be conveniently described as 'the establishment of a rule of action, or, say for short, a habit.' * We should also remark that a belief does not necessarily make us act at once, but rather 'puts us into such a condition that we should behave in such a way when the occasion arises.' † Hence the most accurate way of expressing any belief will contain a hypothetical element; since it will tell

* 5·398. † 5·373.

us that *if* a situation of such and such a character ever arises, the person, or perhaps any person holding that belief, will regard that kind of situation, and will be inclined to react to it, in a characteristic way.

'While belief lasts', Peirce tells us, 'it is a strong habit, and as such, forces a man to believe until surprise breaks up the habit. The breaking of a belief can only be done to some novel experience, whether external or internal....' * What is the precise force of the word 'experience' in this connection? Peirce does well to remind us, in one passage, that 'experience which could be summoned up at pleasure would not be experience': † on the contrary, experience is the main thing that constrains our thinking, and, at any rate on some occasions, compels us to a 'forcible modification of our ways of thinking.' ‡ In a word, belief, like action, must accommodate itself to that which it finds thrust upon it: that is, to the broad course of experience.

Once we are constrained to abandon a given belief, however, a new condition of mind, Doubt, ensues, which provides in almost every aspect the sharpest possible contrast to belief. Doubt is an 'uneasy and dissatisfied state' from which we 'at once struggle to free ourselves and pass into the state of belief.' § Peirce compares it to the irritation of a nerve and the reflex action produced thereby, whereas the physiological analogue of belief would be provided by nervous associations. The struggle to *re*-fix belief, by removing the irritation of doubt, Peirce names Inquiry: and the sole purpose of inquiry, he tells us in his 1878 paper, is the settlement of belief. 'We may fancy that this is not enough for us, and that we seek, not merely an opinion, but a true opinion. But put this fancy to the test, and it proves groundless; for as soon as a firm belief is reached we are entirely satisfied, whether the belief be (*sc.* in fact) true or false. ... The most that can be maintained is, that we seek for a belief that we shall *think* to be true ... But we think each one of our beliefs to be true, and, indeed, it is a mere tautology to say so.' ‖ He makes the same point in the neat epigram, 'Thought in action

* 5.524.   † 5.524.   ‡ 1.321.   § 5.372.   ‖ 5.375.

has for its only possible motive the attainment of Thought at rest.'*

Thus far it might seem that the function of Inquiry is a purely instrumental one – to produce fixed or firm beliefs – and that, so long as it achieves this end, it matters not what particular methods or canons it employs. Peirce mentions three methods of fixing belief which have in fact been commonly employed by the great mass of men, by their rulers and by philosophers: the method of Tenacity, the method of Authority, and the method of 'Agreeableness to Reason'. But none of these methods wholly succeeds in fulfilling its function. For Inquiry has as its aim the attainment of *that* belief, on any particular question, which shall prove satisfactory under every conceivable relevant circumstance; and circumstances inevitably arise in which purely traditional beliefs, maintained by the method of Tenacity, and beliefs imposed by Authority or suited to the intellectual pre-dilection of particular thinkers, are either questioned by some rebellious thinker or discredited by their manifest conflict with the facts of experience. It thus turns out that there is only one genuine or trustworthy method of Inquiry, namely the method of science. The central tenet of this method is that there is *one* discoverable answer to every genuine question, one answer, that is to say, to which all who seek to fix opinion on a given question – not for today or tomorrow or in subservience to any practical interest, but having regard to every conceivable cir-cumstance in which the question might be raised – would agree. But now, whenever this tenet takes full possession of a man's mind he is driven to devote himself to the ideal – or hope – of approaching *towards* the one true opinion on some subject, no matter whether he himself is likely ever to reach it. Men of this type may be said to be possessed by the 'will to learn'; and it is only such men, Peirce tells us, who have any real success in scientific research. By contrast with them, the rest of us tend to employ the scientific method on any given question, Mondays, Tuesdays, and Wednesdays, and one or more of the alternative,

* 5·396.

less efficient but less arduous methods of fixing opinion on Thursdays, Fridays, and Saturdays.

This line of thought, which came to mean more and more to Peirce as he aged, is powerfully illustrated in the following passage: 'In all its progress science vaguely feels that it is only learning a lesson. The value of *Facts* to *it*, lies only in this, that they belong to Nature; and Nature is something great, and beautiful, and sacred, and eternal, and real – the object of its worship and its aspiration. It herein takes an entirely different attitude towards facts from that which Practice takes. For **Practice**, facts are the arbitrary forces with which it has to reckon and to wrestle. Science, when it comes to understand itself, regards facts as merely the vehicle of eternal truth, while for Practice they remain the obstacles which it has to turn, the enemy of which it is determined to get the better. Science, feeling that there is an arbitrary element in its theories, still continues its studies, confident that so it will gradually become more and more purified from the dross of subjectivity; but practice requires something to go upon, and it will be no consolation to it to know that it is on the path to objective truth – the actual truth it must have, or when it cannot attain certainty, must at least have high probability, that is, must know that, though a few of its ventures may fail, the bulk of them will succeed.' *

Here we seemed to have moved a long way from Peirce's earlier conception of Inquiry as an activity possessing purely instrumental value. And this apparent inconsistency in Peirce's thought might seem to be underlined by his contention, with which we shall presently be concerned, that scientific inquiry is essentially an endless undertaking, and that 'Thought without development is nothing. ... Thought must live and grow in incessant new and higher translations or it proves itself not to be genuine thought.' † But if there is apparent inconsistency here, it is of a kind that is forced on us by the facts and that points the way to a deeper understanding of the relation between science

* 5·589.   † 5·594.

and practice and between inquiry and belief. On the one hand, scientific inquiry *is* grounded, both logically and causally, in a number of pre-scientific beliefs, which have been reached and maintained by one or other of the three alternative methods of fixing belief which Peirce describes: moreover, Peirce fully recognizes that even in its most developed phases science remains hedged about, and is to some extent directed by, the needs and interests of practical life. On the other hand, the ends and standards of scientific inquiry cannot be equated with those of practice – whether conceived in terms of immediate economic utility, personal well-being, or social cohesion. For if once science is directed to fixing belief in subservience to the interim needs of practice, it thereby ceases to be genuine science. Any adequate account of the position must do justice to both these sides of it. Science, the free spirit of inquiry, the will to learn, have their roots in our practical beliefs, and have as their initial motive simply the 'fixation' of these beliefs. Nevertheless, by the cunning or dialectic of Nature, inquiry can only fulfil its proper function, the settlement of belief, if it abjures all thought of an immediate or temporarily useful settlement: in hitching its waggon to the star of the one true opinion that *may* be discovered, or at least approached, if only the scientific method be employed, inquiry establishes itself as a partially autonomous activity, with ends, standards, and indeed interests of its own.

But what, besides the inspired hope of attaining the one unquestionable opinion, is the peculiar genius of the scientific method? Peirce's answer is at first sight surprisingly simple: conformity to the laws of inference. But behind the apparently naïve simplicity, and indeed at first sight obvious inadequacy, of this answer, lies a revolutionary innovation on Peirce's part. For by 'the laws of inference' he does not mean, as does the traditional Aristotelian logic, simply those standards by which the *demonstrative* character of certain arguments can be judged: nor does he simply add to this conception, in the manner of many nineteenth-century logicians, the considerations of those standards by which inductive arguments can be assessed. Among the laws of inference Peirce places one which relates to the *admissibility of hypotheses* – this law, we shall find, turns out to be equivalent to his Pragmatism – and the effects of the extension of the traditional conception of inference are considerable. But even if this innovation be acceptable, the assertion that the scientific method is to be distinguished from other than scientific habits of thought simply by its conformity to logical laws, seems at first blush very odd. Logical principles are, roughly speaking, principles of appraisal and criticism, principles for judging whether certain arguments *really* establish the conclusions which they claim to establish. As such, logic seems to play an entirely critical, uncreative rôle. How then can strict or conscientious conformity to logical principles – even if these are taken to include Peirce's principle of Pragmatism or the logic of hypothesis – account for the positive virtue, the power of discovery which we ordinarily attribute to the methods of science?

Peirce has, in effect, two answers to this objection. In the first place we find him maintaining that, just because the scientific method is the one method which genuinely fulfils the task of inquiry, we all do in fact use it in connection with many of our everyday problems; indeed, whenever we think *in order to find out*, we set about employing it, if only in a very rudimentary fashion. Failure to adhere to it may be due to mere laziness, as when we lapse back on to habitual, uncriticized beliefs; or it may be due to the exigencies of practical life, as when we cannot afford to wait for the hypothetical achievement of the one true opinion; or it may be due to the inherent vagueness or clumsiness of the symbols we employ in our everyday thinking. But whatever the cause, the manifest fact of such failure indicates part of the answer to the above objection; namely, that even if logical principles are themselves purely critical and uncreative in character, resolute adherence to them may well prove creative. In the second place, we must not forget the inspired hope, that there *is* one opinion to be reached on every significant question, with which scientific inquiry begins. Possibly not all scientists share Peirce's conception of Nature as 'something great, and beautiful, and sacred, and eternal and real – the object of worship and aspiration'; but all must share his faith that there is one real answer to every definite question, that is to say, one answer which is destined to be reached if only the scientific method is pursued far enough.

An obvious objection to this way of putting the matter, however, is that it is unnecessarily oblique. Why should we not say simply that science or inquiry is that activity whose aim is truth? We have already suggested Peirce's answer to this objection: *all* our beliefs, whatever their nature and methods of origination, embody in a sense a claim to truth. Savages, bigots, drunkards, and morons, all claim truth for their beliefs; but they very rarely, if ever, *seek* truth – because they do not know how to. A scientific thinker, by contrast, is one who does know how to seek truth; and he makes his claims, not so much for the truth of this or that belief, as for the fact that his conclusions, as reached so far, conform to the standards and ideals of inquiry, i.e. if Peirce be right, to the laws of inference when these are adequately conceived. 'Strictly speaking,' Peirce tells us, '*belief* is out of place in pure theoretical science,'* which gives us, in place of beliefs, hypotheses confirmed to a certain degree or provisionally established truths 'into which the economy of endeavour prescribes that, for the time being, further inquiry shall cease.' † This is only another way of making Peirce's point that the conception of truth enters into science only as an ideal, i.e. as the 'inspired hope' that inquiry into any problem will, if sufficiently far pursued, terminate in that opinion 'in which the community settles down.'‡

Evidently, however, this whole way of thinking depends on Peirce's unusually extended conception of inference and the laws of logic. Hence the need for a closer examination of Peirce's account of these matters, in particular his account of that law of inference which determines what hypotheses are admissible as hypotheses. But before we turn to this task, it is important that we should appreciate the following general

* 5·60. † 5·589. ‡ 6·610.

point. Because Peirce introduces the conception of inquiry in connection with the words 'doubt', 'belief', 'experience', etc. – words which are usually taken to stand for different states of mind – it would be natural to regard inquiry as a certain kind of *thinking*. Peirce, however, would wish the word 'inquiry' to be used to cover any activity, physical as well as mental, which we engage in to 'remove the irritation of doubt'. The actual physical operations which are involved in experiment are therefore quite as much a part of inquiry as are the doubts and purposes that prompt them. The same may be said of the physical signs and symbols by means of which the aims and results of physical experiment are communicated from mind to mind, and indeed from day to day, from minute to minute, within one and the same mind. And in fact, as Peirce is never tired of pointing out, it is not to private processes of thought, but to arguments, statements, and terms which figure in public discourse, that logical principles are, at any rate in the first instance, applied.

Inquiry, then, is Peirce's name, less for some describable mental process, than for the fact that *somehow* a wide variety of our activities have come to be initiated and guided by signs which admit of logical criticism and correction; and it is only when men find themselves in this situation that they can set themselves conscientiously to conform to those intellectual standards and ideals which it is the function of logic to formalize. (Inquiry depends on the fact that man is a sign-using animal, and that the sign-systems which he employs include signs for the questioning, correction, and qualification of other signs.) How this situation has come about, Peirce does not seek to explain, at any rate in detail. Like almost every other philosopher of the western tradition, he lacked the kind of historical imagination which this task would require: on the other hand, he does concern himself greatly with the wider implications of the fact that such a situation could arise, and has in fact arisen, in the world. In particular he is concerned to emphasize that the ideals which characterize inquiry are as real, as unquestionable facts as any other facts we care to mention. And this is a point of the very first importance. It means that inquiry – for all that its history, and the laws of its development, are perfectly legitimate objects of study – can never wholly be appreciated in descriptive or causal terms. Inquiry is an activity directed by its own standards on to its own ideal ends; and to recognize its operation in any given situation involves an element of evaluation – an evaluation of the *rightness*, as judged by logical standards, of a given phase of a particular investigation. For the same reason, to practise inquiry can never be equated with the mere producing of certain characteristic effects; to practise Inquiry is also, to make manifest, to oneself or to others, one's acceptance of certain logical standards and ideals, and one's *claim* to be acting and thinking in conformity with them. For this reason we can never understand what a man is looking for, or is thinking, unless we to some extent share his aims and intellectual standards. Of course it frequently happens that we find another person's aims and standards hopelessly inadequate or confused: in that case we try to get him to share *our* aims and standards, that is, to recommence his thinking or searching in a new and better way. We are thus brought back to the conception of Inquiry as that activity to which *logical* considerations apply.

Peirce's conception of Inference

Peirce, as we have seen, distinguished three main types of Inference – deduction, induction, and hypothesis (or, as he often prefers to call it, abduction). On the characteristics of the first two types he says many original and important things. Notably, while assenting to the view that the conclusion of every deductive inference is 'already contained' in the premises, he insists that there is nevertheless an observational, and even in an extended sense an experimental, element in all deductive procedures; and this is a matter on which most contemporary logicians still have much to learn from him. He also has the merit of seeing that induction is primarily an inferential method of *testing*, rather than of advancing or originating, knowledge;

and it is in this light that we should understand his preoccupation with the *rationale* of sampling, and his claim that the
'justification of induction' amounts simply to the establishment
of rules for making 'fair' samples, and making 'fair' judgements
on the basis of these. But it is with his revolutionary claim that
hypothesis or abduction constitutes a third type of reasoning –
or, to be more explicit, that every hypothesis results from a type
of inference that is subject to its own special rule – that we shall
here be principally concerned. This claim is of importance to us
for two reasons; first because of Peirce's claim that his Pragmatism constitutes 'the whole logic of abduction'; and secondly
because his whole anti-Cartesian conception of inference as the
essential function of the cognitive mind presupposes that the
adoption of a hypothesis is, in all cases, the result of inference.
Indeed, we may say that Peirce's most characteristic criticisms
of the Cartesian doctrine of Intuition depend on precisely this
thesis.

*

It will be useful at the outset to recall a general point from our
previous chapter. We there saw that, although the ordinary
man knows perfectly well how to employ the word 'inference'
in familiar contexts, he has no explicit theory about the nature
of inference. Any proposed definition of the word will, therefore, almost certainly rest upon some *philosophical* theory of the
nature and status of inferences; and any such theory will derive
its plausibility from very wide considerations relating to our
use, not only of the word 'inference', but of other cognitive
words as well. Moreover, any such theory, owing to the complexity of the issues which it embraces, can always reasonably be
questioned: hence no definition of the word 'inference', no
matter how long-established, can claim to be authoritative. If,
then, anyone should urge that ordinary, correct (i.e. traditional
philosophic) usage disproves Peirce's view on this matter, his
argument is of very little value. Now we shall find that Peirce
rejects, for very good reasons, the traditional philosophical conception of the nature of inference; and once the reasons for this

rejection are understood, there is little difficulty in seeing why he maintains that hypothesis should be counted as a third, distinct type of inference.

Most logicians from the seventeenth century onwards have regarded inference as one kind of cognitive or thinking process whose characteristic functions and patterns are *expressed* in those forms of speech we call arguments. A man infers, it would be commonly said, when because of some truth or truths already known, he is induced to consider, and eventually to accept, some further truth not previously known. More precisely, inference on this view consists in a unique kind of passage or movement of thought from a complex state in which we (a) assent to the truth of a certain premiss or premisses, and (b) notice something about the form or arrangement of the premiss or premisses which forces us to assent to a further truth, the conclusion; the whole process being completed when we proceed to assert and employ this conclusion in its own right. The function of an argument, spoken or written, is, therefore, simply to express such a passage of thought; and presumably, on this view, when an argument persuades someone who hears it, it does this by inducing him to experience a movement or passage of thought similar to that experienced by the original 'inferrer'. Let us call this, for brevity, the conception of inference as a mental process. Those who adhere to it agree, to be sure, that the most *important* fact about any such process is that it is subject to logical rules – the inference is valid or invalid, plausible or unplausible; and it is perhaps remarkable that the only other essential feature which adherents of this view ascribe to the process of inference is that what we described as stage (a) above must precede *in time* our knowledge of the inferred conclusion.

Peirce rejects this account of inference almost *in toto*; and the one respect in which he shows agreement with it is the most dubious feature in his own account. His main reason for rejecting it is brought out clearly in the following passage. 'Practically', he writes, 'when a man endeavours to state what the process of his thought has been after the process has come to an end, he first asks himself to what conclusion he has come. That result he formulates in an assertion, which, we will assume, has some sort of likeness – I am inclined to think only a conventionalized one – with the attitude of his thought at the cessation of the motion. That having been ascertained, he next asks himself how he is justified in being so confident of it; and he proceeds to cast about for a sentence expressed in words which shall strike him as resembling some previous attitude of his thought, and which at the same time shall be logically related to the sentence representing his conclusion, in such a way that if the premiss-proposition be true, the conclusion-proposition necessarily or naturally would be true.'* In other words, when we say that we have inferred something we say nothing whatsoever about the *nature of the mental process* that has just taken place; all we are saying is that something which we might have asserted at an earlier phase in our thinking could be used, or is available, to prove or confirm the assertion with which our process of thinking actually terminated. Peirce makes the same point more forcibly when he writes, 'There may, for aught we know or care, be a hundred ways of thinking in passing from a premiss to a conclusion,' † and again, 'Inference ... may be, not to say probably is, of an entirely different construction from the thinking process.' ‡

In sum, just as Peirce uses the word 'inquiry' to stand, not for some describable mental process, but for the fact that certain of our activities have come to be guided by signs and symbols which admit of logical criticism, so he uses the word 'inference' to stand not for any felt (or postulated) 'passage of the mind', but for the fact that usually, when we make an assertion, we are in a position to *give a reason for it*. On this view, clearly, the purpose of an argument is not to express (or reproduce in some hearer's mind) any actual process or movement of our thought. A man employs an argument as a means or device of eliciting a certain kind of agreement from others. He employs a form of speech whose arrangement is such as to show that 'if the premiss-

* 2·27.　　　† 2·54.　　　‡ 2·59, cf. 2·183.

proposition be true, the conclusion-proposition necessarily or naturally would be true.' The whole duty of his argument is to show this, or to remind other people of it: but how it achieves this result – what peculiar mental process different people go through in reading, or getting to see the point of, the argument – is something wholly irrelevant. And equally irrelevant, as it turns out, is the question whether anyone who understands an argument (and thereby infers a conclusion) has previously known the truth of that conclusion. This happens, for example, whenever one employs an 'alternative proof' in mathematics. Obviously, we could not use the new proof as a proof unless we inferred the conclusion from it; and yet that conclusion was one to which we had previously assented.

In the light of this discussion we can now see without much difficulty why Peirce maintains that hypothesis constitutes a third distinctive type of inference; for it would be a very queer – and indeed wholly useless – hypothesis for which we could supply no supporting reasons whatsoever. Possibly, however, it might be suggested that these reasons are not of a unique kind – they might, in all cases, be supplied by inductive arguments, so that a hypothesis would consist, in the application to a special case, of certain aptly selected (and combined) inductive conclusions. As against this suggestion, Peirce retorts that ' ... the conclusions of Hypothetic Inference *cannot be arrived at inductively*, because their truth is not susceptible of direct observation in single cases. Nor *can* the conclusions of Inductions, on account of their generality, *be reached by hypothetic inference*. For instance, any historical fact, as that Napoleon Bonaparte once lived, is a hypothesis; we believe the fact, because its effects – I mean current tradition, the histories, the monuments, etc. – are observed. But no mere generalization of observed facts could ever teach us that Napoleon lived.' * On the other hand, Peirce reminds us that we ' ... inductively infer that every particle of matter gravitates towards every other. Hypothesis might lead to this result for any given pair of particles, but it never could show

* 2·714.

that the law was universal.'* In general, Peirce maintains, the great distinction between induction and hypothesis comes to this: that in the former 'we conclude that facts, similar to observed facts, are true in cases not examined,' whereas in the latter 'we conclude the existence of a fact quite different from anything observed'; † 'the former classifies, and the latter explains.' ‡

What, then, is the peculiar format or arrangement of the kind of argument which justifies an hypothesis? Peirce gives a number of elaborate, and not wholly consistent, answers to the question: but his general view is sufficiently shown by the following simple schema:

(1) The surprising fact, C, is observed;
(2) But if A were true, C would be a matter of course,
(3) Hence, there is reason to suspect that A is true.§

Two features of this schema call for special attention. First, the conclusion (3) is altogether tentative in character: all that is argued or defended is that a certain suggestion or conjecture is *worth considering*. Second, there can be no question but that the schema indicates the kind of consideration in the light of which, in science as in everyday life, we would defend a hypothesis in the sense of showing why it is reasonable or worthwhile. The further question, whether a given hypothesis is justified by the facts, or what proportion of the relevant facts it serves to explain, is, as yet, simply not raised. This further question must wait until the necessary consequences of the hypothesis have been elaborated deductively, ‖ and until the range of its application (assuming that it has been generalized) has been established inductively: all this is a question of applicability and reliability, whereas the initial and indeed peculiar question with regard to any hypothesis is whether it opens up a new line of thought that deserves detailed exploration and testing. Here the peculiar importance of hypothetical inference in Peirce's scheme of ideas becomes clear. It is, according to him, the one form of inference that originates wholly new ideas, that plays a distinctive rôle in the *advancement* of knowledge, as opposed to the re-application

---

* 2·714.   † 2·636.   ‡ 2·636.   § 5·189.
‖ See especially 7·182 and 7·206.

and progressive testing of knowledge already gained.

But we must not make the mistake of thinking that hypothesis, because it fulfils this unique function, is therefore an autonomous or self-dependent form of inference. On the contrary we shall find that Peirce's Pragmatism – when conceived as a logical rule for judging the admissibility of hypotheses – requires that every genuine hypothesis shall be such that there can be *deduced* from it consequences which can be tested *inductively*, i.e. experimentally. Nor, according to Peirce, is such dependence all on one side. As we have seen, he thinks of induction as essentially a method of *testing* conclusions; and these conclusions, he claims, are always suggested in the first instance by hypothetic inference. By induction we generalize and test the consequences that can be deduced from a given hypothesis; so that the mutual dependence of these two forms of inference, and their common dependence on deduction, are equally clear. Moreover we shall find, in Chapter VI below, that Peirce enlarges this conception of the mutual dependence of the different forms of inference to apply to deduction also.

*

We are now in a position to give a first, provisional explanation of Peirce's conception of inference as the essential function of the cognitive mind. Thought at all levels – the perceptual, the inquisitive, the deliberate, the scientific – displays, in Peirce's view, the same fundamental pattern: it is a matter of the mutual interplay, and continuous mutual support, of inferences of the three types we have distinguished. To think in any concrete situation, or to meet any concrete situation intelligently, means that we are in a position to *defend* our attitude to it; say by showing that this attitude embodies an intelligent conjecture (hypothesis) having such and such testable necessary consequences, or that it accords with certain well-established experimental findings. Or, to employ Peirce's language, the life of thought is a matter, at every stage, of the formation and/or exercise of certain *habits of inference*. Fully to appreciate the force of this last conception, however, we must turn for a moment to a second threefold division of inferences which Peirce makes, and which cuts clean across the division to which we have so far been attending.

Peirce distinguishes (a) what we may call Reasonings, that is, inferences which are fully conscious and are – at least in the opinion of the reasoner in question – fully articulated. Such is, for example, the reasoning of a mathematician who sets out, in what seems to him the most illuminating order, all the premisses and, in Peirce's phrase, all the leading principles, which are necessary to his conclusion. Every Reasoning, therefore, involves what Peirce calls 'the side-thought' that it is only one particular instance of a certain class or family of inference, every member of which employs the same leading principle. Broadly we may say that logic has traditionally taken Reasonings in this sense for its subject-matter.* But (b) very few of our inferences in daily life, or for that matter in science, have this fully articulated character. Thus, when we conclude that a given man will some day die, we do not go through the whole business of syllogizing: all men are mortal; this individual is a man; therefore he will some day die. Still less do we always recognize or know how to state the leading principles to which our everyday inferences conform. Now whenever the premisses or leading principles of an inference are not explicitly stated, then that inference is of the kind Peirce calls *a-critical*.† By this he means that it cannot, as it stands, be effectively made subject to logical control; if such an inference should lead us into error, we must 'cast about' to discover those features of it that have misled us. Lastly (c) there are, Peirce claims, 'operations of the mind which are logically exactly *analogous to inference* [our italics] excepting only that they are unconscious and therefore uncontrollable and therefore not subject to logical criticism.'‡ Quite the most important instances of this kind, according to Peirce, are provided by our 'perceptual judgements' – for example our recognizings of the colour or shape of any object we see, or of the number

* 5·440, cf. 2·446, 6·497.   † 5·440.   ‡ 5·108.

and spatial or temporal relations of any small group of objects; and it is, according to Peirce, with hypotheses or abductions that perceptual judgements are 'logically exactly analogous', – apart from the qualification that they are unconscious and therefore uncontrollable, etc.

What this qualification amounts to is that while we are making a perceptual judgement, or whenever we actually recall it in memory, we are psychologically incapable of conceiving that it *might be false*. Now in this respect perceptual judgements stand in striking contrast to explicit hypotheses – especially on Peirce's interpretation of these as inferences which essentially call for critical assessment and inductive confirmation. But Peirce's way of explaining this contrast suggests that it is after all perhaps not fundamental; for, as we shall find, he regards our incapacity to control – or, as it were, to un-do or un-judge – our perceptual judgements as more or less a psychological accident, which leaves the logical analogy between our explicit hypotheses and our perceptual judgements virtually intact. But before turning to this point, let us see where the analogy between them lies.

It is to be found in the fact, already emphasized in our previous chapter, that every perceptual judgement, like every explicit hypothesis, involves necessary consequences. Now some of these consequences will be of a general nature. To give an example of Peirce's, if one judges that an event C appears to be later than an event A, one is thereby committed to maintaining, as a necessary consequence, that any other event standing in this relation of 'apparent subsequence' to C, must stand in the same relation to A also.* But one would be *justified* in making this inference only on the supposition that the perceived event 'C subsequent to A' embodies all the necessary or defining properties of the relation of apparent subsequence; and to suggest that one actually sees this in making a particular perceptual judgement is surely quite absurd. How then are we to explain the fact that every perceptual judgement undoubtedly involves some

* 5·157.

necessary consequences, such as the one we have just instanced? We can explain this, Peirce maintains, only by assuming that certain premisses, which would justify us in drawing these consequences, are in our minds *habitually*;* but, since we are unconscious of, and therefore incapable of controlling, these premisses, we find ourselves prepared to draw the relevant consequences *without knowing how*.† Hence our experience, our undeniable experience, that perceptual judgements are forced upon us, so that we cannot imagine what it would be like to form a perceptual judgement and at the same time to doubt or deny it, is to be explained by the fact that we simply happen to be unable to un-do or un-judge, so as to control and criticize, our perceptual judgements; just as we simply happen to be unable to un-see (physically) what we have actually seen, for all that the total physical activity of seeing an object is one that could, theoretically, be decomposed into simpler elements.

*

We can now better appreciate the signal contribution of Peirce's conception of habits of inference. In the case of any a-critical, and still more obviously in the case of any unconscious nference, the place of an explicit guiding principle and a required premiss is taken by an inarticulate, and most commonly wholly unconscious habit of inference. We infer – or, as we would more naturally say, jump to – a given conclusion without knowing how, or more precisely, without being able to formulate our reasons. But we should notice that in Reasonings also habit plays an all-important part: for unless our use of a certain method of reasoning were habitual – and in particular unless it were reproducible in a form (usually verbal) which is within our control – we should obviously be unable to commend or criticize or correct it. The essential difference therefore between Reasoning and other less explicit forms of inference comes to

* Probably the clearest statement of this position is to be found in Peirce's review of William James's *Principles of Psychology* in the *Nation*, vol. 53 (1891), p. 32. (See *The Philosophy o Peirce*, p. 305.)   † 5·151 .ff., 5·568.

this: that in the former a given habit of inference is subjected to the control of a habit of a higher order, whereas in the latter the relevant habits of inference remain largely, or in some cases totally, beyond all critical control. (Needless to say *any* habit of inference is subject to the ultimate test and control of the facts to which it is applied: an unconscious habit of inference which always led us to false conclusions would never come in for logical criticism but would certainly, sooner or later, be dropped.)

It is this conception of habits of inference – habits that are good or bad, commendable or corrigible inasmuch as they do or do not lead to true, or for the most part true, conclusions – that makes Peirce's theory of knowledge, despite its many-sidedness, in essence a remarkably simple and unified one. It provides the essential link between his criticisms of the doctrine of Intuition, his account of Inquiry and, as we shall see below, his account of Thought-signs. But it might reasonably be objected that Peirce's conception of mental life, as a matter of the formation and exercise of habits of inference, contains one palpable gap: it appears to tell us nothing of the actual occasions – the experiences – in relation to which our habits of inference are formed, exercised, and re-formed. How, on Peirce's view, do the 'hard facts' of experience – the things we see, hear, touch, and react to – enter into our thinking? That they somehow do enter into it, and indeed that they provide most of our thinking with its raw materials and constrain it to conform with them, is perfectly obvious: and yet in Peirce's account of mental life there seems to be no place for such hard, ultimate facts. In logical parlance, Peirce denies the possibility of absolutely first premisses; he maintains that our perceptual judgements (the most obvious candidates for this rôle of absolutely first premisses) are logically analogous to hypothetical inferences, since they depend on prior premisses and leading principles, for all that these, as it happens, exist only habitually and unconsciously in our minds. It appears therefore as if the never-ceasing inferential mill is hopelessly cut off from the raw materials which it is meant to grind.

Peirce's theory of knowledge seems, indeed, to be faced at this point with the following impasse. There are no Intuitions, therefore there can be no first factual premisses; therefore all our knowledge, including our perceptual judgements, must consist in the exercise and/or formation of general habits of inference. But a habit only exists, or gets exercised, in certain actual occasions: habits of inference, therefore, require their own appropriate occasions; and how can these be provided, unless our perceptual judgements are of a wholly non-inferential character? Peirce's way out of this impasse is provided by his conception of *unconscious inferences*. Our perceptual judgements, when carefully analysed, are seen to rest on certain habitual assumptions; therefore they are, in their logical structure, hypotheses and therefore theoretically liable to error. Nevertheless, as we have seen, they are not subject to logical correction and control: they are forced upon us: we find ourselves, for instance, inevitably judging that something *is* red when it seems red to us, irrespective of the fact that it might conceivably not possess all the necessary, or defining, properties of redness. Our perceptual judgements, therefore, although hypotheses in their logical structure, in effect enter our thinking as though they were absolutely first, that is, uninferred premisses. They provide both the initial suggestions for our other inferences (critical or a-critical) and the ultimate tests of these inferences. Moreover, inasmuch as our perceptual judgements are actually forced upon us, we inevitably *re-*act in this process: in particular, when their contents surprise us, we feel ourselves offering a kind of resistance to them. Hence our perceptual judgements bring us face to face with the brute 'there-ness', the obtrusiveness, of external existence. On both these counts, therefore, our perceptual judgements are well suited to serve as the occasions for the formation and exercise of our habits of inference.

The obvious objection to this is that Peirce is here trying to have things both ways. Perceptual judgements are to count as hypotheses (results of unconscious inference), and for this reason they involve necessary consequences which admit of verification: at the same time they are to count as absolutely first premises, forced upon us, not subject to logical correction – in a word, indubitable. Now it is true that Peirce wants to have things both these ways; but is there any reason why he should not have them so? For it is one thing to say that a judgement is *in fact indubitable* because it is forced upon us and beyond our power to criticize and control, quite another thing to say that such a judgement is self-evident, wholly non-inferential, essentially indubitable, and so on. What *cannot* be doubted evidently is not doubted: but what cannot be doubted need not possess any of the essential – and logically objectionable – features of Cartesian Intuition.

But would not the acceptance of Peirce's account of perceptual judgement involve us in an untenable sceptical position? If it is possible (theoretically) for us to misjudge the character of an object we actually see – to think we see a red object, say, in a case where the testimony of others or our own later experience suggests that the object we saw must really have been brown, or to think we see three objects where, for the same sort of reason, we later admit we ought to have counted four – then, since perceptual judgements provide the initial suggestions for, and are necessary to the inductive confirmation of, all our more general beliefs, must not the achievement of absolute certainty be for ever beyond us? This is a conclusion which Peirce was perfectly willing to accept; but he would have denied that it implies scepticism in the pejorative sense of that word, or that it is in any way incompatible with our daily usages and beliefs. For we all know, as a matter of daily experience, that surprising and often quite unaccountable slips in observation do occur. Our intellectual faculties are as frail and fallible as our physical faculties: indeed, if we want machine-like reliability of response, we should look for it in machines rather than in men. On the other hand, the fact that no particular perceptual judgement can be accounted wholly infallible, is no reason why we should lapse into a general scepticism; for in deciding that a given perceptual judgement must have been erroneous, we inevitably ground our decision on other perceptual judgements, as often as not relating to the same object. Thus there is no inconsistency in maintaining that our perceptual judgements on the whole are reliable – not just, as they are in fact, severally indubitable – while at the same time admitting, as a general proposition, that in any particular case we may perhaps have judged erroneously.

Nor should it be thought that, in thus admitting the possibility of perceptual error, we are thereby representing perceptual judgement as, after all, subject to logical correction. A particular perceptual judgement *never* gets corrected; it is just not the kind of thing that *can* get corrected. We see something in front of us, and judge, say, that its colour is red, and later we infer that we must have misjudged its colour. But our original perceptual judgement is not thereby corrected. What happens, rather, is that we correct or inhibit the tendency to act, think, and speak as that particular perception prompts us to do.* In a somewhat similar way we might decide, after the event, that a particular slip in observation was occasioned by some well-known cause of error, and this decision might teach us to be more wary of similar slips in the future. But as we have already seen, we just don't know how to un-do or un-judge and thus self-correctingly to *re*-judge the particular perceptual judgement in which we went wrong. The best we can do is to shrug it out of existence, with apologies to anyone who may have been affected by our error and with the determination to be on guard against slips of this kind in future, but for the rest trusting our perceptual judgements as before.

Peirce's conclusion, then, that we may rely on our perceptual judgements as a whole while admitting the theoretical possibility of error in any particular judgement, seems to conform exactly to the facts which we all acknowledge in everyday life. On the positive side, it is the common-sense position that we should trust our faculties; on the negative side Peirce describes it as fallibilism, the recognition that error is always

---

* It is only from the point of view of their general results that scientific procedures are to be preferred to the intuitive responses of animals which, for their own specific purposes, are quite 'inhumanly' reliable and exact.

and everywhere possible. This balance of 'critical common-sensism' and 'contrite fallibilism', to use two of his most expressive phrases, is wholly characteristic of Peirce's theory of knowledge. It is particularly prominent in his account of our perceptual judgements, but it also affects his elucidation of all cognitive words, and hence his elucidation of such words as 'inductive' and 'deductive' which stand, not indeed for any cognitive claims or achievements, but for the peculiar standards by which different claims to knowledge are judged. Thus it is an essential feature of Peirce's 'theory of induction' that the most carefully and accurately selected sample may, quite irrespective of possible slips in observation or calculation, lead to an altogether erroneous conclusion *in any particular case*. On the other hand, this admission does not, in Peirce's view, indicate anything fundamentally unreliable or objectionable in the inductive method as such. Induction, as Peirce sees it, is an essentially fallible method, but also an essentially self-correcting, and therefore logically self-justifying, method. Similarly Peirce maintains that the most carefully and accurately presented deductive proof may, as a matter of fact, be invalid. What it declares to follow necessarily from certain axioms or suppositions may in fact not follow from these alone: other axioms and suppositions, existing 'habitually' in our minds but not made explicit in the proof, may in fact be necessary to the conclusion we draw. This is *always* possible, as the history of mathematics makes clear; and to be alive to this possibility – without being lunatically haunted by it – is no doubt one of the hall-marks of mathematical genius. On the other hand, this gives us no grounds for doubting that in the great majority of 'established mathematical truths' we are presented with examples of absolutely water-tight deductions. To doubt this in practice would be as absurd as to doubt the general reliability of our perceptual judgements, and to philosophize on the basis of such doubt would be as absurd as to philosophize on the basis of Cartesian doubt with regard to the reliability of the general run of our perceptions. Peirce's fallibilism, therefore, is certainly no brand of scepticism. It is one side of his profound insight into the nature of inquiry, and it has the effect of reconciling the paradox that error is a necessary element in the attainment of truth with the common-sense position that truth is always there to be found in any field in which we *know how to inquire.*

Peirce's account of inference largely explains his paradoxical view of truth in that basic sense in which truth is correlative with reality. That truth means 'the correspondence of a sign with its object' Peirce does not deny; and for purely formal purposes this definition suffices. But a more adequate account of truth will show how it functions as thought's ideal end. Thus Peirce writes: 'Now thought is of the nature of a sign' and therefore 'if we can find out the right method of thinking – the right method of transforming signs – the truth can be nothing more than the last result to which ... this method would ultimately lead us.'* Here truth is presented as the result of the right method. But elsewhere Peirce emphasises that rightness in thinking must be relative to what we conceive to be thought's 'full expression' – a notion which he equates with his claim that thought is only genuine while it is 'living and growing in incessant new and higher translations'.† Now this *essential developability* of thought must presuppose an ideal end, viz. that towards which (it is the scientist's faith) thought will be led, so long as it develops in conformity with logic's rules conceived as a species of self-criticism and self-control. Perhaps this could be restated in homelier language as follows. If we are to understand what it means to be a truth-seeking animal, we must first understand what kind of sign-using animal could conceivably have a use for the notion of ultimate truth. And the answer is: one whose uses of signs admit of ideal development because they obtain effective – which involves both public and private – correction and control. Here we have the beginnings of an explanation of Peirce's strange claim that truth means the opinion to which inquiry ultimately leads us and in which 'the community settles down'.

* 5·553.   † 5·594.

CHAPTER FIVE

PEIRCE'S THEORY OF KNOWLEDGE

III. *The Doctrine of Thought-Signs*

*

T HE conception of Inquiry as a theoretically endless activity, no actual results of which can properly be considered closed or final, and the conception of Inference as the essential function of the cognitive mind, provide all the background that is strictly necessary to an appraisal of Peirce's Pragmatism. Starting from these conceptions, we might therefore proceed at once to a more detailed account of hypothesis as one distinctive type of inference, and of Pragmatism as the logical rule which determines whether any particular hypothesis is admissible or not. But, if we were to do this, we should be leaving undeveloped one of the most interesting by-products of Peirce's theory of knowledge as so far outlined. This is his thesis, that 'we have no power of thinking without signs'* or that 'all thought is in signs', a thesis which he was to develop into the far more drastic claim that 'all thought whatsoever is a sign, and is mostly of the nature of language',† and that *all we mean* by thought or intelligence or mind is 'a sign developing in accordance with the laws of inference'.‡ It is with this latter claim, his doctrine of 'Thought-signs', that we shall be concerned in this chapter.

Apart from its intrinsic interest, this doctrine demands our attention for three main reasons. First, although it is not strictly necessary to an appraisal of his Pragmatism, it helps us to see why Peirce presented his Pragmatism *both* as a method of definition ('a method of ascertaining the meanings of hard words and abstract conceptions') *and* as a rule of Inference ('a rule as to the admissibility of hypotheses to act as hypotheses'). Second, the doctrine of Thought-signs has the effect of forestalling or under-

---

* 5·285, cf. 5·253. † 5·420. ‡ 5·313.

cutting the most familiar and natural objection to Peirce's Pragmatism; viz. that to equate the meaning of a conception with its effects or consequences is senseless, or at least circular, since these effects cannot be determined until the meaning of the conception itself is known. Third, the doctrine is of importance since it serves to introduce us to certain conceptions which reappear – somewhat strangely transfigured to be sure – in Peirce's metaphysics, and which, unless their origin in his doctrine of Thought-signs is appreciated, are likely to remain hopelessly obscure.

*

Peirce's efforts to formulate an adequate definition of the general notion of a sign, and his work on the detailed classification of signs, are undoubtedly among his most impressive contributions to philosophy; they provide striking evidence of his capacity to carry through in detail unusually difficult work in a field in which there had been few previous explorers. On the other hand, it must be admitted that his work in this field does not make easy reading. It abounds in strange – and perhaps to some ears monstrous – coinages, e.g. 'Qualisign', 'Sinsign', 'Legisign', and, when we enter the complexities of his classification, such terrifying combinations as 'Rhematic Indexical Legisign'. Expressions such as these are, however, quite as necessary for any detailed analysis and classification of signs as are the unfamiliar verbal, alphabetical, and numerical symbols employed by chemists for the purposes of chemical analysis and classification. The fact is that Peirce's quaint coinages stand for combinations of ideas for which ordinary English has no names, and which indeed could not be described in ordinary English, short of abominable prolixity. It is not only terminological difficulties, however, which make this part of Peirce's work difficult reading. His successive attempts to initiate a scientific study of signs are almost certain to strike the general reader as unnecessarily tortuous and oblique. This impression is very largely due to the fact, already mentioned, that Peirce's habits of thought are, for a philosopher, of a surprisingly strictly

scientific character. He thinks and writes, now as a mathematician or formalist seeking to give his ideas the most exact
definitive or demonstrative character possible, now as an experimentalist trying out some idea, seeking to evaluate it by its
effects, by the way it assists in the solution of a variety of
problems. These characteristics of Peirce's work on signs certainly make it exciting; we see in it the first movements of a
broad shift in philosophical interests and methods, the full effects
of which can scarcely today be foreseen. On the other hand, the
general reader may well complain that before we can appreciate
such excitements – a great mind and a great new line of philosophical activity on the move or in the making – we should be
given, what Peirce nowhere gives us, namely a simple outline of
why he came to embrace his doctrine of Thought-signs, and a
clear systematic statement of what he took its main implications
to be. Such an outline can perhaps best be given in the form of
answers to the following questions:

1. What does Peirce mean by a formal doctrine or theory of
   signs?
2. Why does he maintain that all sign-action is necessarily
   and irreducibly triadic (three-term) in structure?
3. Why does he maintain that every sign requires another
   sign to interpret it?
4. Why does he maintain that every sign is essentially capable
   of evoking an endless series of further 'interpretant' signs?
5. Why does he assert the identity of what we would
   ordinarily distinguish as on the one hand a sign, and on the
   other hand the thought or intention which that sign expresses?
6. Of what nature – roughly, mechanical or teleological –
   does Peirce conceive the action of signs to be?

1. *What does Peirce mean by a formal doctrine or theory of signs?*

One main cause of the difficulty of understanding Peirce's writings on signs is the unusually wide sense which he gives to the word 'sign'. Even if we waive his wildest metaphysical extensions of its ordinary meaning, we find him using the word to cover a very wide range of cases, from the simplest acts of communication in the animal (and perhaps even in the vegetable)* world, to those highly sophisticated uses of conventional signs or symbols which are required for scientific discourse. This width of view accounts for the importance of many of the things which Peirce has to say about signs; but it also serves to cloak certain confusions, or at least certain divided purposes, in his thinking. On the one hand, as a formalist – as well as a most daring metaphysical speculator – he is continually seeking to define that peculiar property which will distinguish any sign-situation from any situation in which no element of sign-activity is present. On the other hand, as a logician or analyst of scientific thought, he usually has at the front of his mind those highly complex uses of signs and symbols which the practice of science, and indeed of all strict reasoning, requires. The result is that Peirce seems often to be attributing to *all* signs certain properties which should perhaps only be ascribed to such signs as must be used by 'a scientific intelligence, that is to say by an intelligence capable of learning by experience';† certainly he often fails to indicate what qualifications must be made to his detailed analyses of signs of this latter class, if his results are to be applied to other more elementary forms of sign-activity.‡

Bearing this difficulty in mind, let us try to see what Peirce

---

* 2·274.   † 2·231.

‡ It is only in his later writing that Peirce distinguishes clearly between signs used for informative and scientific purposes and signs used for the purposes of immediate action or to meet the needs of some immediate state of feeling (in his own queer language the distinction between 'logical', 'energetic', and 'emotional' interpretants of a sign). What he has to say about this distinction is, however, of the first importance. See e.g. 4·488 ff.

meant by a formal or 'quasi-necessary' doctrine of signs. He believed that, by reflecting on the signs with which we are familiar, we can come to see what are the *necessary* characters or properties of any sign-system which could be used by a 'scientific intelligence'. His claim here, it should be noted, is that certain properties appear to be necessary to any intelligent use of signs, not that this necessity can be strictly or completely demonstrated: on the contrary, he emphasizes that his own suggestions in this regard must be taken as 'eminently fallible'. This does not prevent him, however, from persistently attempting to set out his own suggestions in deductive or semi-deductive form, i.e. as results of applying certain very general principles, assumed to be necessary to all signs, to the particular signs we know. Central among these principles is one which, Peirce believed, suffices to *distinguish* any type of sign-action whatsoever from any type of action into which the notion of a sign in no way enters. In other words, the property which this principle attributes as necessary to all sign-action gives us, in Peirce's opinion, the proper formal definition of a sign. Two warnings must be issued at this point. Peirce nowhere claims that the possession of this property suffices to *constitute* a given sign; and he nowhere suggests that it is by means of, or in terms of, this distinguishing property that we ordinarily recognize or claim that this or that particular action or happening is a sign. What Peirce does claim for his property is, first, as we have said, that it provides the logical differentia of all sign-action (or at least of the action of all such signs as might be used by a scientific intelligence); and secondly – and this is a vaguer claim – that it is an important ordering property, i.e. a property such that once we see what the possession of it implies, we thereby come to see the interconnection of many other properties which are necessary to sign-action.

Evidently this whole method of procedure presupposes that there is some very general or abstract property common to all sign-situations, or, in other words, that there is one fundamental sense of the word 'meaning', for all that there may be an immense variety of specific ways in which different types of signs mean what they do. This may seem a reasonable enough assumption; but it is well to notice that it is open to the following line of criticism. To explain the meaning of this or that particular word or sentence or other sign is to disclose the peculiar way in which this, that, or the other sign is properly used. To do this calls for very different methods, devices, illustrations, exercises – some simple and familiar, others perhaps immensely complex – according to the different distinctive purposes of the different signs. The attempt to find some property which is common to each and every sign-situation and which at the same time will really help us to understand the function of each, is to indulge in a wholly unwarranted assumption: viz. that every general word or term stands for a common property, and that the word 'sign' in particular stands for what we have called an important ordering property. But there are many general words, e.g. the words 'king', 'beauty', 'play', with regard to which this assumption is almost certainly invalid. For example, not every king (at any rate as this word is used in literary English) is a ruler, a supreme executive; nor are (or have been) the functions of all kings political or military. Suppose we were to say, then, that at least a king is always male. Here, maybe, we do reach a property common to all kings, but quite clearly it is not an ordering property which will help us towards deciding about the kinghood of this or that individual in some doubtful case, or towards deciding what other properties this, that, or the other individual is likely, in virtue of his being a king, to possess. Now in view of the obviously very wide range of contexts in which we find the word sign and its equivalents employed, is it not rash to *assume* that it is one of those general words which stand for a genuine common property, and more, for an important ordering property, in the way that Peirce supposes? *A fortiori*, is it not rash to assume that language-in-use, living speech, is the kind of subject-matter with regard to which a general theory, centred on some one or more formal definitions or principles, can possibly be devised?

Various answers might be made to this objection; but for our purposes it is sufficient to point out that again and again in the history of science highly abstract ordering properties have been discovered by men of genius in fields long familiar to others less gifted, and then to ask why this should not be so in the field of signs. Peirce claimed to have found an important property common to all sign-situations; and when such a claim is made by a reputable author, it surely deserves a fair hearing. To dismiss it on the grounds which we have just mentioned would be to 'block the road of Inquiry' with a vengeance! Moreover, whether or not he was right to make this claim, in doing so Peirce was certainly not neglecting the obvious differences in complexity and function of different types of sign. No other logician has ever attempted such careful analyses and classifications of signs as Peirce made. In his best-known treatment of this subject he distinguishes ten main classes of signs, one of which is the obviously very wide class of propositions or informative signs; and later, working on a more elaborate principle of division, he claimed that we ought to recognize sixty-six fundamental classes of signs. It seems fairly clear, therefore, that Peirce did not lightly or lazily presume that to the common noun 'sign' there must correspond some distinctive general property.

2. Why does Peirce maintain that all sign-action is necessarily and irreducibly triadic in structure?

The characteristic property which Peirce claims to find in every sign-situation is that it is essentially triadic; sign (first term) standing for object (second term) to interpretant (third term). This property obtains, according to Peirce, whether the sign be of the nature of a proposition (or informative sign), an argument (an in greater or less degree self-justifying or self-explanatory sign) or of either of two relatively incomplete or indefinite types of sign – the type which logicians refer to as a Term, e.g. a common noun considered without reference to its function in a complete sentence, and the kind of bare indication of an object which is given by an act of pointing.

As a first step to establishing this thesis Peirce found it necessary, since most previous logicians had entirely ignored the
existence of triadic relations, to show that some of these are
irreducible – that they cannot be decomposed into two parts,
two ordinary dyadic relations sharing a term in common. For
example, no fact of the form 'A gives B to C' can be decomposed
into the two facts 'A parts with B' and 'C comes into possession
of B'; for such a sheer conjunction of dyadic facts would lack
the characteristic unity of intention which distinguishes an act
of giving from an accidental exchange of property. Very similar
considerations apply to facts of the forms 'A indicates B to C',
'A suggests B to C', and more generally 'A signifies B to C'.
The irreducible triadicity of the sign-relation is liable to be
obscured by the fact that we also employ dyadic forms of speech
such as 'A means B' and 'C interprets A'. But expressions of
these latter sorts are almost certainly elliptical; A could not
mean B except to some interpretant C; nor could C interpret A
except as standing for some object B.

This conclusion might be defended in more detail as follows.
Peirce is willing to admit that for certain purposes it is legitimate
to abstract from a sign's relation to its interpretant and concentrate exclusively on its relation to the second term in the
sign-situation, i.e. the object signified. When regarded in this
way signs fall, according to Peirce, into three main classes –
Indexes, Icons, and Symbols. An Index is a sign whose peculiar
mode of signification depends on an actual dynamic relation
between it and its object: for example, a weather-vane which
indicates the direction of the wind as a result of the wind's
action upon it. An Icon is a sign whose peculiar mode of signifying depends on some likeness, qualitative or structural, holding
between it and its object: thus a soap bubble is naturally, or one
might say accidentally, suited to serve as an Icon of an air-
balloon; or again, so long as the likeness is not *intended*, or is not
imposed by some process such as photography, a picture may be
said to be an Icon of any object which it resembles. Finally, a

Symbol is any artificial or conventional sign which has something like the effect of indicating or 'iconizing' an object, despite the fact that it has *neither* any direct dynamical connection with, nor any significant resemblance to, that object. Almost all words and sentences in European languages are Symbols in this sense. But now, neither an Index nor an Icon nor a Symbol can actually function as a sign unless or until it is interpreted. Taken by itself, the weather-vane's veering with the wind *means* nothing: it is just one event – or as Peirce likes to say, one brute fact – among others. Similarly, taken by itself, or in so far as it simply happens to resemble some object or other, a picture means nothing; and quite obviously a Symbol means nothing unless and until it is interpreted. In general it seems that, no matter how well suited by its character or its actual relations anything may be to serve as a sign, it cannot actually function as a sign simply in virtue of its own intrinsic character or its own actual dynamic (two-term) relation to something else.

Peirce's initial contention, then, that there are some irreducibly triadic relations and that the sign–relation is one of these, is at least highly plausible. We should notice in passing, however, that, in the course of his many ingenious arguments to this end, Peirce became convinced that the sign–relation is in some way involved in all other irreducibly triadic relations. This suggestion is of great importance; and it is pretty clearly justified when applied, for example, to the relation of giving. He who makes a gift signifies by his action a certain future property of that which he gives, namely that it shall henceforth be considered as belonging to the person who receives it. It is greatly to be regretted, however, that Peirce did not work out this suggestion in examples drawn from other fields; for instance in connection with the geometrical relation 'between'.*

* Peirce believed that all four-term, five-term, and other higher multi-relational complexes can be analysed into combinations of three-term and two-term relations. The essence of his teaching on the logic of relations is, therefore, that two-term relations cannot be analysed into combinations of one-term (subject-predicate) facts, and that genuine three-term relations cannot be analysed into combinations of two-term relations.

3. Why does Peirce maintain that every sign requires another sign to interpret it?

What we have said so far about the essential triadicity of all sign-action would naturally suggest that the third term, the interpretant, must be some person or mind. And a number of Peirce's statements seem at first to accord with this suggestion; for example, 'A sign ... is something which stands to somebody for something else in some respect or capacity,'* and again, 'A *Sign* is a Representamen' (Peirce's technical name for the first term in any triadic complex) 'with a mental interpretant.' † But when these statements are considered in their context, and still more when they are considered in relation to the main drift of Peirce's teaching, this impression is seen to be misleading. For instance, the first of the sentences just quoted is followed up by: 'It (the sign) addresses somebody, that is, creates in the mind of that person an equivalent sign, or perhaps a more developed sign. That sign which it creates I call the *interpretant* of the first sign.' In general, when Peirce writes of some particular interpretant of a given sign – as opposed to what he refers to as a sign's 'entire intended general interpretant' ‡ – he means some *further* sign of the object of that given sign. This is a very strange usage: and although, as we shall soon see, it serves to express one of Peirce's most profound and original philosophical insights, it easily gives rise to misunderstandings.

Why should we not say simply that the interpretant of a sign is somebody, some person or mind? For everyday purposes, it would of course be perfectly natural and proper to do so. Somehow or other a sign is made, and whether or not the making of that sign involves some person or mind, it seems clear that there is need of some person or mind to respond to, or understand, or interpret it. But for the purposes of obtaining a definition of the general notion of a sign and of building up a formal theory of sign-action, this familiar way of thinking proves inadequate. In the first place, there are, almost certainly, sign-processes which

* 2·228.   † 2·231.   ‡ 5·179.

do not involve the action of minds or persons in any ordinary sense; e.g. communication-processes among the bees and other termites. The presence of a foreign body in a hive seems to be communicated by the bees which first encounter it to other members of the hive, so that these latter, without actually encountering the body, proceed to take suitable organized action with regard to it. The suggestion that communication of this sort involves minds in any ordinary sense of the word seems to be wholly unwarranted; and this is a consideration which weighed greatly with Peirce, for reasons which will become clear in Chapters VIII and IX.

But there is a second consideration which, for all that Peirce himself nowhere mentions it explicitly, is even more pertinent here. Suppose that in any particular case we are in doubt whether some sign made by an individual A has been interpreted or understood by a second individual B. How should we set about trying to settle this question? Should we somehow or other try to discover directly what B's 'mental reaction' has been? It seems quite certain that we have no means whatever of doing this. What we should do, surely, is to try to discover whether B has made some overt response such as A's sign would justify, or such as A's sign is ordinarily used to evoke. Alternatively, if no overt response could be detected, we should try to discover indirectly – say by questioning B – whether he is prepared or disposed to make some suitable response in view of A's sign. In general, the fact seems to be that we recognize or infer the action and existence of a mind on the evidence of its use of and response to signs, we don't recognize that a sign has been interpreted by observing some mental action. If, therefore, we were to say that every sign requires an interpretant in the form of some interpreting mind, this would be either patently incomplete or else utterly uninformative: we should always have to add that the mind in question interpreted the sign in some particular way or other, i.e. that it made or was prepared to make some appropriate response to the sign in question.

To give an example. If in the course of a country walk one

individual A stops short and points at the ground, this gesture would most naturally be interpreted, in the sense which Peirce gives to the word, by some action on the part of his companion B, for instance B's turning quickly to look in the direction pointed at. Now such an action on B's part can quite properly be considered as at least potentially a sign of the same object as A's gesture signified. Thus, a third individual, C, might well call out in the situation imagined, 'What are you both looking at?' Central to all Peirce's thinking on signs is this insight, that any appropriate response to a sign is, in virtue of its very appropriateness, capable of itself serving as a sign of the object originally signified.

Much the same retort could be made if, in place of the suggestion that every sign stands for its object to some mind, we were to say that at the very least every sign must stand for its object to *some body*, i.e. some organism. For, if this suggestion were made, we should still have to refer more specifically to those parts of the organism's behaviour in virtue of which we are entitled to say that it makes a response – an appropriate response – to the sign in question. And whatever part of its behaviour was specified, it would again have to possess the property of being in some way directed on to the object of the original sign, and for this reason it would at least be capable of serving as a sign of the object originally signified.

To make this point clear, let us employ the following illustrative scheme. First let us write:

(i) A sign stands for (ii) an object by (iii) stimulating some organism or person to (iv) some appropriate response which is (v) itself capable of signifying the object of the original sign.

Now let us eliminate stages (iii) and (iv) as – according to Peirce – not essential to the distinctive character of sign-action. We shall then be left with

(i) A sign stands for (ii) an object by (iii) evoking some further sign of the original object. Or, to give one of

Peirce's own formal definitions, 'A *Sign* ... is a First which stands in such a genuine triadic relation to a Second, called its *Object*, as to be capable of determining a Third, called its *Interpretant*, to assume the same triadic relation to its Object in which it stands itself to the same Object.'*

Clearly the usefulness of this definition depends entirely upon the justifiability of eliminating stages (iii) and (iv) above. Now we must emphasize that Peirce never wished to maintain that signs can exist and act on one another as it were *in vacuo*, or that communication could ever possibly take place if there were not minds, or at least organisms, to do the communicating. The point of the above elimination is this: in order to bring out what is distinctive or peculiar to sign-action, as opposed to other types of interaction between organisms, there is no need to refer, for example, to the ways in which signs may act on the senses of different organisms, or to the specific ways in which such sensory action may give rise to later motor action or response, or even to the ways in which responses so caused may prove to be of benefit to the creature in question or to its species. All we have to mention, according to Peirce, is the way in which *what* the sign signifies depends on the occurrence of an appropriate response: such a response being necessary both to show *what* the sign signifies and indeed to show *that* it signifies anything at all.

To bring the point at issue down from these very abstract heights, let us concentrate attention on one particular use of signs, namely dialogue or discussion. Before people can begin to discuss any question they must of course have a great many general things in common – fairly similar sensory equipment, a common language to whose conventional meanings and rules they at least try to conform, certain broad common purposes, and so on. But what they actually discuss is always some particular problem. To settle or get light on this they proceed to ask questions, make statements, devise arguments, criticize and

* 2·242.

reformulate these, apply them to parallel cases, etc. Now let us ask: What appears to be the distinctive property of signs as used in dialogue or discussion? One plausible answer would seem to be that every sign used in discussion requires, and indeed is aimed at eliciting, *an answer*. Such an answer may of course be the merest nod of assent or dissent, or an indication of interest or puzzlement; but an answer of some kind seems to be required by every sign – up to the point where the discussion is actually broken off, say on the words 'That's settled'. So true is this that we could quite properly say that unless a sign used in course of dialogue receives an answer, it is, for the distinctive purpose of the dialogue, not only useless, but meaningless. Why is this? Broadly because, the purpose of dialogue being to achieve a common decision on some point at issue, what really matters in it is not what a particular participant, A, says in the course of it, but the way in which what A says gets taken up by what B, C, and D say in return. For the distinctive purposes of dialogue, therefore, it is only the *answered* – i.e. the questioned, criticized, accepted, or rejected – statements that matter. In other words, a sign works in dialogue only in so far as it obtains a response in the form of *some other sign*.

Here, then, we seem to have one – if not the only – distinguishing feature of that use of signs which we call dialogue or discussion. But does this feature really distinguish dialogue from other uses of signs? Peirce is unable to accept this conclusion, largely, if not wholly, because he maintains that all uses of signs – including the use of signs in private thinking – are essentially, even if not obviously, dialogic in character. (Every thought, as he quaintly puts it, 'addresses itself to another thought', as well as being interpreted in it.) What he does, therefore, in effect, is to generalize our conclusion in the preceding paragraph and to maintain that the use of any and every sign requires something very like an answer in the form of some other sign; moreover he maintains that this follows as a necessary consequence from his general definition of signhood. This is a most important and interesting claim, but before we go on to examine it, we should notice a prior problem which the case of dialogue raises in a particularly illuminating way, and which a little reflection on our everyday experience of dialogue should enable us to answer.

Consider the following imaginary snippet of conversation:

A:'Today is Tuesday, isn't it?'
B: 'Yes ... yes, of course it is.'
A: 'Of course – it was Sunday the day before yesterday.'
B: 'So what?'
A: 'Well there was something we had to do this Tuesday.'
B: 'Where's the diary?'
A: 'No good. I never make notes of anything except bills.'

This snippet of conversation makes sense, for all that, like almost all everyday conversation, it is highly elliptical and allusive. It makes sense, for all that its successive stages lack any obvious *verbal* interconnection, and it compares unfavourably in this respect with the following snippet of nonsense conversation:

A: 'Today is Tuesday.'
B: 'So is π an irrational number.'
A: 'Agreed, but that's irrelevant.'
B: ' "That", on the contrary, is a relative pronoun.'
A: 'Oh rats to you. ...'
B: 'What are rats to me?'
A: 'Oh give up.'
B:'What?'

Now what distinguishes our first sensible conversation from this latter piece of nonsense? Suppose that we were to say that in the first case every statement, question, or what-not after A's initial 'Today is Tuesday ...' interprets that sign in the sense, required by Peirce's definition, of standing for the object of the original sign. Everything said in the first of our conversations has to do in some way or other with the fact, or supposed fact, that today is Tuesday. By contrast, despite the puns, associations, and other superficial linkages between its different stages, there is no object common to the various signs which make up the nonsense conversation. We can bring out the force of this suggestion by expanding our first conversation somewhat pedantically as follows:

A (*aloud*): 'Today is Tuesday, (*sotto voce*) but is it in fact Tuesday? (*Again aloud*) Isn't it?'

B (*sotto voce*): 'He says "Today is Tuesday", but is clearly thinking after the reason why it should be. But, apart from the fact that the calendar shows Tuesday, it was certainly Sunday the day before yesterday, and therefore must be Tuesday now. (*Aloud*) Yes. ... Of course it is.'

A (*sotto voce*): 'He agrees that it is Tuesday, and from his tone he clearly knows *why* it must be. Now among possible reasons would be ... (*Aloud*) Of course ... it was Sunday the day before yesterday.'

B (*sotto voce*): 'Now he has thought of a reason why it must be Tuesday, but still there must be some reason for his bothering about it at all. (*Aloud*) So what? ...'

Thus expanded, the conversation shows fairly clearly the different ways in which its different stages all refer to the same common object, i.e. how every later sign stands in some sense for the object of the initial sign. Some of them do this by simply reiterating or duplicating it; but others go further, they in some sense develop it; they take it up and combine it with further signs for the purpose of inference. Now Peirce uses the word 'interpretant' to stand for any such development of a given sign, so long as reference to the object of that original sign is retained. Simply to reiterate or duplicate a given sign is not to interpret it; but to accept, reject, question or qualify, combine or apply it along with further signs, *is* to interpret it.

In this very broad sense of 'interpret', it is clear that any given sign admits of *alternative* interpretations; it can be developed, in combination with different groups of further signs, in many different ways. (There is a virtually endless number of possible proofs of, and consequences of, today's being Tuesday.) If, then, every sign requires an interpretant in the form of some·

further sign, and admits of such interpretation in a virtually endless number of alternative possible ways, it follows that there can be no such thing as *the* (one and only) sign of a given object, and no such thing as *the* (one and only) interpretant of a given sign. The belief – still all too prevalent among philosophers – that a sign can stand in a simple two-term relation, called its meaning, to its object, is thus seen to rest on a radical misconception of the kind of thing a sign is and of the way in which it functions. The truth is that a sign can function only as an element in a working system of signs: it means what it does only in virtue of the fact that *other* signs belonging to the same system mean the slightly – or immensely – different things that *they* do.

Peirce was the first philosopher to recognize the importance of this conclusion for the philosophy of language and indeed for the general philosophy of mind. And whatever may be said against his definition of the general notion of a sign, at least this must be said for it, that it definitely implies and is intended to suggest this conclusion. He might, to be sure, have reached this conclusion by other more obvious means. To illustrate one of these, let us ask: What distinguishes the simplest act of pointing from a mere meaningless movement of the arm? Surely, that the person who points can say or show in a variety of ways *what* he is pointing at: he has, as it were, up his sleeve, a variety of possible interpretants of his original sign. He can, for instance, go on to describe the object at which he points; or he may make clear what he has pointed at by correcting the response of someone who has looked in slightly the wrong direction. Pointing, therefore, involves knowing what one has, and therefore also what one has not, pointed at; or, in other words, to indicate one thing by one sign involves being able to discriminate other things from it by other related signs. In a somewhat similar way, to describe a thing in terms of its positive qualities is also, implicitly, to distinguish it from other things which lack those qualities. It would therefore appear that to use any given sign is to display, in some particular way, one's mastery – or at least partial mastery – of the sign-system to which that sign belongs; i.e. to say or show anything involves at least the *capacity* to say or show certain other related things. Now this is not very far removed from Peirce's claim that every sign requires something akin to an answer or comment from some further sign if it is to stand for or signify its object.

4. *Why does Peirce maintain that every sign is essentially capable of evoking an endless series of further interpretant signs?*

If it can be granted that every sign requires to be interpreted, in Peirce's sense, by some further sign, what further consequences follow from this? An immediate and at first sight highly paradoxical consequence follows: namely that, since the interpretant of any given sign is itself at least capable of acting as a sign, it requires, in virtue of that capacity, some further interpretant which must itself be capable of acting as a sign and must therefore require some further interpretant... and so on indefinitely.*

No part of Peirce's teaching on signs has given rise to more bewilderment and misunderstanding than this. But in fact there is nothing so very queer about it, once we grasp what Peirce himself emphasizes repeatedly, that this endless series is essentially a *potential* one. His point is that any actual interpretant of a given sign *can* theoretically be interpreted in some further sign, and that in another without any necessary end being reached: *not* that such a series must, *per impossibile*, be realized in fact before any given sign can actually signify at all. On the contrary, as Peirce frequently points out, the exigencies of practical life inevitably cut short such potentially endless development. Moreover, and this is an even more important point, any merely random succession of a sign's potential interpretants would be, logically, most uneconomic. For, if Peirce is right, we could theoretically go on talking for ever on any given subject, go on exemplifying, qualifying, expanding, re-applying what we have said without reaching any necessarily final statement or

* 1·541, 2·92, 2·242.

logical full stop. Such a discussion, however, would evidently lack what we ordinarily refer to as direction, point, and purpose. Why then, it may be asked, should Peirce have laid so much emphasis on this capacity of every sign for theoretically endless development? Why, besides stressing that every sign allows a number of alternative possible interpretants, should he have actually chosen to define a sign so that its capacity for endless development through a succession of further possible signs is made to stand out as its most important necessary characteristic? Why does he insist so strongly on the at first sight somewhat trivial fact that we can always go on talking, that there is no statement which does not admit of question, comment, or correction; and that in general every sign is a phase in a conversation to which there can be no necessarily last term?

Peirce insists on these facts because he wants us to appreciate by means of them – by our recognition of the essential incompleteness of every sign – the further fact that our competent use or our understanding of any given sign is always a matter of degree. Not only can a sign be interpreted in a number of alternative possible ways, some of these are evidently more adequate, more logically commendable, than others. A child, a housekeeper, a fruit-farmer, and a botanist all know the meaning of the word 'apple'. But the child interprets the word, most likely, by thinking of or mentioning the apple's shape, colour, and sweetness, and the housekeeper by thinking of its cost, dietetic properties, and place in the larder; by contrast, the fruit-farmer thinks of apples in terms at once wider and more exact, and the botanist in terms which are yet wider and which are systematically connected with other botanical terms. What any given person means by the word 'apple', therefore, depends upon the amount of his general information and on the degree to which he has systematized that information, – whether in the form of scientific theory, or of practical competence and skill. At the same time, the meaning of a word remains, at any stage of information and skill, something essentially developable. We can easily imagine, for instance, a piece of nursery conversation in and through which we could almost literally observe a child's understanding of a word being made more adequate – more general, more flexible, more exact in relation to the meanings of other words. But something rather like this is true of all of us all the time. Because every sign that we use is essentially incomplete, we can always, theoretically, come to use and understand it better than we actually do.

What interpretant, or succession of interpretants or line of interpretation, a given sign receives, will depend, then, as a rule, on the exigencies of practical life and the peculiar interests of its users; nevertheless we are all familiar with situations in which it is natural to say that, as a result of certain logically commendable lines of interpretation, the meaning of a word or other sign has been rendered clearer, if never completely or ideally clear. Thus the way in which a botanist uses or interprets the word 'apple' succeeds in netting or collecting together in systematic fashion all – or almost all – the various possible interpretants of that word which the rest of us might supply, but in entirely unsystematic, higgledy-piggledy fashion. We might therefore say that the botanist possesses, in contrast to the rest of us, 'the entire general intended interpretant'* of the word, or that interpretation of it which gives us its 'very meaning'† (subject always to the qualification that *his* interpretation also remains inherently something developable). Possession of such an interpretant clearly ministers to what Peirce calls 'the economy of endeavour'; it gives command of a whole range of a sign's possible interpretations which we should otherwise have to traverse in blind, wasteful fashion before hitting upon that particular interpretant of it which is peculiarly relevant to the problem in hand. The scientist stands in contrast to the rest of us in this respect: he is able to make use – and make sense – quickly and confidently of a range of signs which to the rest of us display no obvious or familiar mutual relations, and thus his scientific practice embodies in a high degree what Peirce calls 'concrete reasonableness'.‡

* 5·179.   † 5·427.   ‡ 5·3.

But in making this contrast between the 'entire general intended interpretant' of a sign on the one hand, and each and any of its alternative possible interpretants on the other hand, we must not forget that the two belong to one common root: they are equally results of the fact that every sign is essentially incomplete and therefore essentially developable. In giving to the word 'apple' any one of its possible interpretants we are, however unwittingly, opening up a certain possible line of interpretation which, if appropriately pursued, could lead us towards the entire general intended interpretant of that word; we are, willy-nilly, taking the first step towards that interpretation of it which approximates most closely, at any given stage of information and intelligence, to its *very* meaning. The question which faces us therefore is how, in Peirce's view, *certain* lines of interpretation of a given sign lead us with peculiar directness and efficiency towards this result, for all that any permissible interpretant of that sign is in the nature of a contribution towards 'the development of concrete reasonableness'.

To answer this question, it will be useful to introduce here a second terminology which Peirce sometimes employs to describe the facts which we have so far explained in terms of a sign's capacity for endless development in other (interpretant) signs. The meaning of a sign, Peirce tells us in one passage, is best described in terms of 'the habit which it is calculated to produce'. Peirce uses the word 'habit' in a very wide sense, to cover what we would ordinarily refer to as general capacities and dispositions, whether acquired or innate; and he uses his habit-terminology in connection with signs to reinforce his thesis that the meaning of a sign is something 'altogether virtual',* something which any one of a number of alternative possible interpretants can disclose. A habit or disposition or capacity is essentially something general, not simply in the sense that it is a pattern of actions to which no definite time-limits are set (a man might truly be described as a habitual drunkard, even though he should die before he gets his next drink), but in the

* 5·289.

further sense that it allows, in greater or less degree, of alternative ways and means of achieving its characteristic results; for example, a man's habitual courtesy could be shown equally well in a variety of ways in one and the same social situation; and similarly, as we have recently argued, with what one (habitually) means by a given word or sentence or other sign.

How, then, does this new terminology help us to distinguish those of a sign's possible interpretants, or lines of interpretation, which are logically useful and commendable from those which are not? In ordinary life we develop the meaning of any sign that is addressed to us by means of its most familiar or most obviously – practically – relevant interpretants: we combine sign p with sign q to permit the further interpretant 'therefore r', because that is what we usually do in the circumstances, or because r stands for the one fact or need that particularly interests us at the moment. Now the habit of interpretation thus displayed *may* in fact conform to logical standards and requirements, but it is not deliberately guided and controlled by attention to such standards: to apply Peirce's habit-terminology, it is not an exercise of habit which is itself continually kept subject to a logical habit of higher order, such as is most naturally displayed in the appropriate use of the questions 'Why?', 'On what evidence?', 'So what?', and 'To what end?' By contrast, when we think or speak or engage in discussion with the express purpose of finding something out, we tend to interpret the signs that we use or that are addressed to us in such a way – in such a deliberately chosen form and order – as almost inevitably evokes or suggests the above-mentioned logical questions. In particular we interpret scientific statements in terms of those of their logical consequences which will falsify or confirm them. Now, if we accept Peirce's principle of fallibilism, this process of 'verification' can in strictness never be completed, for every logical consequence of a scientific statement must itself admit of being questioned and tested. At the same time, scientific discourse is distinguished by the fact that it is subject to logical habits which render it progressively more exact, more generalized and more manageable.

Thus, starting from the conception of the essential incompleteness and developability of every sign, we are led to the conclusion that it is only in a sign's logically controlled uses in purposive thinking about general problems that we reach its 'very meaning'.* We can only get the meaning of a sign clear, or at least clearer, on the basis of our actual uses of it in the course of Inquiry. This conclusion recalls our first provisional account of the doctrine of Pragmatism in Chapter I. It also helps us to see why clarity, which has proved to be a will-o'-the-wisp in philosophy, is a naturally accepted by-product of all successful work in science.†

5. *Why does Peirce assert the identity of what we would ordinarily distinguish as on the one hand a sign, and on the other hand the thought or intention which that sign expresses?*

In his earliest published paper Peirce endeavoured to demonstrate that all thinking involves the use of signs, a thesis whose immediate converse is the denial of the possibility of absolutely first premisses or Cartesian Intuitions. How did he pass from this to the much more revolutionary view that 'all thinking whatsoever is a sign and mostly of the nature of language,' and that all we mean by an intelligent mind is 'a sign developing in accordance with the laws of inference'?

A number of considerations seem to have weighed with him on this issue. First, there is the fairly obvious fact that children communicate before they reason in any strict sense of the word, and the fact that animals of many species communicate, although no one would dream of attributing thought, still less reasoning, to them. At the same time, when adult humans reason they invariably make use of signs or symbols which they also use for purposes of communication; and further, they can always communicate the results of their reasonings. This naturally suggests that thought or reasoning is one rather peculiar form of communication, namely a kind of internalization of the speech and gesture habits which we learn first through actually com-

* 5·427.   † 8·118.

municating with our fellows; or, more simply, that thought is, as Plato said, 'the soul communicating with herself.'

This evolutionary consideration can be supported by another. From the biological standpoint thought and communication are both of them *adaptive* characters; their special function is disclosed, not through any subjective feelings that may attend or clothe their occurrences, but by the fact that whenever a creature acts with thought, or communicates by means of signs, it thereby adjusts the behaviour of itself or of other creatures to a common environment. Let us concentrate on *thought* as an adaptive character. Regarded in this way, a thought works when it enables the thinker to adjust his real or potential reactions in a biologically useful way; but further, this adjustment must be of a kind that we call 'conscious', i.e. it must be a response to something *noticed* or interpreted. But this again suggests that the action of the thought is the action of a sign – which only acts of course by being noticed or interpreted. Thus we again reach the suggestion that what a man thinks to himself is what, in some form or another, he says or shows to himself.

This conclusion can be reinforced from the side of logic. Logical canons, as set out in textbooks and as utilized in life, apply in the first instance not to thoughts – if these can be radically distinguished from the signs that express them – but to arguments, i.e. complex symbols of certain kinds. The critical logician pins down our *words*: he shows us, for instance, that if we or anyone else use certain words in one particular way, then certain other uses of these words cannot be permitted. But there is also a second reason why critical logic has no concern with thoughts as opposed to words: as we saw in the previous chapter, strictly speaking it is only habits, not individual acts of thought, that can be criticized and corrected. The concern of logic therefore is with any habitual use – anyone's habitual use, yours or mine, at any time – of signs in argument: it therefore has no interest whatsoever in anything that may 'lie behind' my actual use of certain signs now or your use of them tomorrow, relevant and interesting though such hidden accompaniments of the use of signs may well be to the psychologist. Now this strongly suggests that in so far as our interest is in *thought*, as opposed to other aspects of human activity, we can get along perfectly well by fixing our attention on the signs by which, as we would ordinarily say, our thoughts are expressed.

But for Peirce all these considerations require to be related to that general property by means of which he wishes to define sign-action, i.e. its irreducible triadicity, and the consequent capacity of every sign to be developed in some (alternative possible) further sign, and that in some further sign, and so on indefinitely. Can this property, or some clear analogue of it, be shown to hold of our thoughts? If it can be, then, as it seemed to Peirce, the identification of thoughts and signs could be regarded as proved.

Peirce is evidently trying to suggest such an analogy when he writes that 'every thought addresses itself to another'* and is interpreted in another. This suggests, on the one hand, the essential incompleteness of every sign, its need of another sign to interpret it; and, on the other hand, the fact that all thinking rests on prior assumptions, and for this reason involves appreciation of consequences which can always in theory be questioned. Now it is perhaps stretching words a long way to say that whenever one thinks or takes an object to be, say, an apple, one thereby 'addresses' that thought to some potential future thought – such as might justify or correct it; yet in taking an object to be an apple, one is certainly preparing oneself to accept certain consequences, and to resist or react in surprise to certain others. Perhaps, indeed, the main logical difference which has been emphasized by the traditional distinction between a given 'thought-situation' and the sign- or communication-situation corresponding to it, is that in the latter one anticipates an immediate response to one's sign, whereas in the former one's attitude is somewhat vaguer; one assumes that the future course of one's experience will justify one's use of, say, the word 'apple' in a certain context, but at the same time one is ready, should

* 5·284.

some future experience throw doubt on this, to reply or come back at one's former judgement, perhaps by qualifying it, perhaps by rejecting it outright. (We might compare the difference between a chairman's 'Any questions?' and a student's 'Keep this point in mind in future reading.') This difference, however, leaves intact an important identity. 'Here is an apple', whether actually spoken or judged in the course of private thinking, has a meaning only in so far as certain future statements or thoughts *might* confirm, qualify, or correct it. The meaning of the statement, or the judgement, depends upon the possibility of its obtaining some come-back or reply in the course of future experience. That every thought addresses itself to another, helps, therefore, to explain why it is that 'thought cannot happen in an instant, but requires a time,'* i.e. is something that takes a time to reveal the thing that it is, i.e. is essentially a 'would-be', never something given in the immediate present, complete, self-dependent, self-justifying.

This analogy between what we ordinarily distinguish as a thought-process on the one hand and a sign- or communication-process on the other, seems to have been the main consideration that influenced Peirce on the present issue; and, quite apart from its surprising posthumous up-to-dateness, it is perhaps one of those rare cases of philosophical insight that deserve the name of discoveries.

6. *Of what nature – roughly, mechanical or teleological – does Peirce conceive the action of signs to be?*

Whether we think of a sign as evoking a habit (which, so to say, covers all or most of the ways in which appropriate, intelligible responses to it might be made) or think of it as capable of giving rise to an endless series of further interpretants, the following important fact emerges: namely, that any given sign is capable of discharging its function in a variety of ways, so that we can properly say of it, that it *works* in any given situation,

* 5·253.

irrespective of the particular character of the succeeding signs through which it works.

Now this is, at first sight, a very strange sense of 'works' or 'acts'. It is not at all the sense in which we speak usually of the action of a cause, i.e. of an efficient cause. When, for instance, a force is added to a given system of forces, the immediate consequence (in classical and in rule-of-thumb mechanics) is regarded as strictly determinate: there is one, and only one, way in which the force can be shown to have acted. But, as we have seen, there is an indefinite number of ways in which a sign, in any given context, may discharge its function as a sign. To bring out this point in another way, when we say the sign has been interpreted, we are not saying anything about – or claiming to know or assuming anything about – the particular means or mechanism of its action; on the contrary, our claim is based simply on the fact that the interpretation of the response is of a sort which the sign would *justify*. An object is signified to be of such a character that ... well, that any one of a number of further signs or responses are applicable to it: one of these was in fact made: therefore, in a sense still to be determined, the sign's occurrence caused or was responsible for or explains this further sign or response.

According to Peirce, this means that every sign acts in virtue of a final cause, since in his view all that is necessary to final or teleological causation is that, given certain initial conditions, a result of a certain general description tends to come about, 'irrespective of any compulsion that it should come about in this or that particular way': * or, more simply, 'final causation does not determine in what particular way it is to be brought about, but only that the result shall have a certain general character'. † Whether this suffices to distinguish final causation, as traditionally conceived, from other forms of causation, may very well be doubted. Action in accordance with a final cause is usually conceived as action towards some *envisaged* end; and as the history of philosophy clearly shows, there are enormous

* 1·211.   † 1·211.

difficulties in extending the notion of final cause to cover forms of action whose end cannot be said to be actually envisaged. What is certainly true, however, is that we do commonly distinguish many kinds of activity by means of Peirce's criterion, i.e. by reference to general results, such as may be achieved in a number of alternative ways, and not by reference to their strictly determined effects or their strictly determining causes. Sign-activity provides one instance of this kind: others could be found in most if not all forms of co-operative activity in the human and animal world and in such long-term tendencies, whether in animate or in inanimate nature, whose specific *directions* we cannot account for in terms of efficient causes.

In calling attention to this fairly obvious truth, Peirce was providing a much-needed correction to the main drift of modern philosophy and showing his kinship with certain Aristotelian and medieval habits of thought. But of course Peirce does more than call attention to the existence of non-mechanical forms of activity: he throws an entirely new light on them by suggesting that their prototype, or most illuminating and important instance, is afforded by the action of signs. Let us therefore ask what Peirce takes to be the distinguishing goal of sign-activity.

Our natural inclination would be to say that of course sign-activity has many different ends: on this occasion it subserves one biological need, on that another; in yet other cases it serves to advance rational projects or to spread information as to matter of fact. But many biological needs which are met by means of sign-activity might quite conceivably have been met by specific physical adaptations; therefore the fact that sign-activity subserves such needs tells us nothing of its peculiar or distinctive character. On this question Peirce's view is clear: what is peculiar to sign-activity is its inherent, even if for the most part largely unrealized, capacity for development *towards* what he calls the sign's 'entire general intended interpretant'. Man is essentially a sign-using animal, but essential to his uses of signs is his capacity to criticize and correct them in the light of certain logical ideals. More simply, communication is something which can only be done at all because it can always be done better than it ever actually is done. Like the activity of Inquiry, of which it is the most obvious and important expression, sign-activity is essentially directed towards a goal which, in any particular case, it cannot be said ever to have fully and finally achieved.

*

In this introductory discussion of Peirce's doctrine of Thought-signs we have been concerned with what seemed to him to be the necessary and distinctive features of any and every case of sign-activity, or, in other words, with certain very general conditions to which any and every instance of sign-activity must conform. We must now repeat our earlier warning that it is not by means of these highly abstract features that we ordinarily recognize a sign as a sign. On the contrary, we ordinarily do this only after we recognize the distinctive meaning of this or that particular sign; and recognition of *this* requires attention to other aspects of sign-activity which we have so far only mentioned in passing, notably the capacities of different signs to indicate, to 'iconize', and to symbolize in their own distinctive ways. Peirce's Pragmatism takes over from his formal doctrine of signs by asking what distinguishes the meaning of this or that particular sign – a question which, we shall see, calls for essentially the same answer whether it be asked with regard to Terms, Propositions, or Arguments. What his Pragmatism derives or inherits from his doctrine of signs is that the meaning of any sign – the way it stands for its object – can be understood only in virtue of the ways certain other related signs point to, represent, or more generally bear on, the object of that original sign. In other words, the meaning of a Term, Proposition, or Argument is not something that can be fully grasped or established before or unless its 'consequences' are appreciated; on the contrary, appreciation of its consequences determines in a quite crucial way what any sign is used or taken to mean.

CHAPTER SIX

PRAGMATISM AS A PRINCIPLE OF LOGIC

★

IN Chapter I we introduced Pragmatism as a method of clarifying the meaning both of 'intellectual concepts' and of 'hard words', including scientific terms and formulae. Our discussion in the previous chapter helps to explain this dual usage; for, if Peirce's doctrine of Thought-signs be accepted, a conception or thought possesses meaning in exactly the same ways or under exactly the same conditions as does the word or sentence which expresses it. But in the course of Chapter IV we had occasion to anticipate another shift in Peirce's usage, viz. his claim that Pragmatism is 'the whole logic of abduction', i.e. of hypothesis. How is this further description of Pragmatism to be reconciled with the account which we gave of it in Chapter I?

In our discussion of the meaning of the word 'lithium' we saw that a chemist has live knowledge of the meaning of that word, because, unlike the rest of us, he knows how to apply tests for the identification of lithium, i.e. because he knows, in Peirce's words, what he is to do in order to gain a perceptual acquaintance with the object of the word. Now it would not be true to say that, whenever the word 'lithium' figures in a chemist's thought, it is accompanied consciously by something like Peirce's precept for obtaining perceptual acquaintance – or operational contact – with a specimen of lithium: it is much more likely to figure in some such sequence of thought or statements as the following:

(i) This piece of metal has the effect of liberating hydrogen in water;

(ii) But if the metal were lithium, then that reaction would be a matter of course;

(iii) Therefore there are grounds for supposing that this *is* a specimen of lithium.

But the point which we should notice about this inference is that the chemist, in making it, *presupposes* his own knowledge of how to get and operate upon standard specimens of lithium, so that he can whenever necessary point to certain effects of these and compare them with the effects of the piece of metal which he is merely surmising or supposing to be lithium. In other words, the chemist's conclusion is one whose consequences admit of experimental verification.

This suggests one way, and in many respects the best way, of explaining the function of Peirce's Pragmatist teaching. 'Pragmatism', he writes, 'proposes a certain maxim which, if sound, must render needless any further rule as to the admissibility of hypotheses to rank as hypotheses, that is to say, as explanations of phenomena held as hopeful suggestions; and, furthermore, this is *all* the maxim of Pragmatism really pretends to do. ... For the maxim of Pragmatism is that a conception can have no logical effect or import differing from that of a second conception except so far as, taken in connection with other conceptions and intentions, it might conceivably modify our practical conduct differently from that second conception.' *

Let us try to see as clearly as possible the logical parallelism between this account of Pragmatism and that which we outlined in Chapter I. The former account was applied to what logicians call Terms, viz. abstract words or conceptions; the present account is applied to one form of Inference or Argument, viz. the hypothetic; we might therefore expect to find mediating between these, what Peirce in fact sometimes gives us, namely an account of Pragmatism which applies to informative statements or Propositions.† Now Terms, Propositions, and Arguments are one and all signs, but they are signs at different levels of explicitness. Any given Term suggests a possibility of information; e.g. the abstract noun 'redness' suggests

* 5:196.   † 5·13.

the possibility of any statement of the form '*x* is red'. A Proposition, on the other hand, claims to *give* us information about some state of affairs. But Propositions do not arise and do not function *in vacuo*: there are, we may recall from Chapter IV, no absolutely first premisses or Cartesian Intuitions; real information is always in the nature of a conjecture or supposition, based on other information provisionally accepted as true, and therefore essentially open to confirmation and correction. This, we may recall, was Peirce's main reason for regarding all informative statements as hypotheses – as 'explanations of phenomena held as hopeful suggestions'; but it also explains why in his most sustained treatment of the subject (his Harvard Lectures of 1903) he prefers to treat Pragmatism as a rule of inference – that which determines the admissibility of the conclusion of any hypothetic inference – rather than as a rule of definition or as a criterion of the meaningfulness of statements. For if we neglect the inferential or quasi-inferential ancestry of any given statement, we are also likely to neglect its inferential progeny – those of its possible interpretants, its necessary experimental consequences, which, according to Pragmatism, serve to articulate its distinctive meaning. To make the same point from a slightly different angle: it is not difficult to admit that the meaning of a given Term can be disclosed only through the completed statements in which it – or one of its cognate forms – functions as subject or predicate; it is perhaps more difficult – but also more important – to recognize that the meaning of any given Proposition or informative statement is disclosed only through certain of the ways in which it can function, in combination with other statements, as a premiss for inference, i.e. through the practical or experimental consequences to which, when it is combined with other statements, it necessarily gives rise.

To sum up this part of our discussion, Peirce's Pragmatism has the effect *both* of disclosing an important identity of function as between Term, Proposition, and Argument, viz. that signs of any of these types contribute to or yield information only in so far as distinctive practical or experimental consequences can be

derived from them, *and* at the same time of emphasizing that it is through one class of Arguments, viz. the hypothetic, that this informative function is most fully and unmistakably disclosed.*
Hence, while it is sometimes convenient to discuss Peirce's Pragmatism in terms of words, symbols, sentences, and so on, it is advisable, whenever important questions arise, to recall that the meaning of any isolated symbol can only be articulated in what Peirce calls 'the living inferential metaboly of symbols'†
and that his Pragmatism is primarily a rule of inference, a rule as to the 'admissibility of hypotheses to rank as hypotheses.'

To have shown that questions as to the distinctive meaning (if any) of this or that word or conception, as to the meaningfulness (or lack of meaning) of this or that proposition or statement, and as to the reasonableness (in the sense of worthwhileness) of this or that conjecture or hypothesis, are all questions of the same basic sort, since considerations of the same kind – whether they be labelled 'effects having practical bearings' or 'empirical verifications' or 'experimental fruitfulness' – serve in the end to answer questions of all three types, is a considerable logical achievement. But it may all too easily be regarded as, in Schopenhauer's phrase, a purely professorial achievement, that is, a mere re-classification of old truths under new names. What does it tell us, the critic may complain, beyond that all informative signs, at whatever level of complexity and explicitness, derive their peculiar force in the end from *things*, or from differences in things that can be pointed at or indicated? What, if any,

---

* We may usefully notice in this connection that different languages have radically different rules of sentence-structure and division; so that our own familiar divisions of intelligent discourse into name-units and statement-units may easily give rise to unwarranted generalization. On the other hand, the ways in which we distinguish the logical phases of any piece of intelligent discourse – a hypothesis here, an induction there, now a further hypothesis, now its full deductive development – have nothing arbitrary or conventional about them: the pattern of an argument remains, irrespective of the different languages in which it can be expressed, and of the different statement-units or terms-units into which we choose to divide it. This is most obvious when an argument is developed mathematically, through a succession of equations.

† 5·402, note.

is the peculiar virtue of Peirce's Pragmatist teaching – whether it be regarded as a theory of definition, or as a test of empirical meaningfulness, or as a rule of inference – over and above this quite familiar burden of modern Empiricism?

In answer to this criticism we may point out first, that, as formulated by Peirce, Pragmatism provides us with a most useful, because flexible, tool of criticism, which can be directed with equal effect at the key terms, the pronouncements and the arguments (or seeming arguments), of any piece of discourse. When it is applied to the conceptions or hypotheses of metaphysics or theology, the emphasis is no doubt usually on the question: Has this conception or hypothesis any genuine meaning at all? When, on the other hand, it is applied to the 'hard' conceptions or hypotheses of mathematics and the developed natural sciences, the emphasis will no doubt usually be on the question: What is the distinctive meaning of this conception as against some other closely related conception? But in fact these two uses of Pragmatism are inseparable. Mathematicians and metaphysicians alike are liable, just because of the highly abstract character of the questions they pursue, to fall into highly sophisticated confusions, with the result that in certain contexts they use expressions which in fact lack the distinctive meaning which they would claim for them. And exactly the same thing is liable to happen in the more theoretical development of the so-called 'empirical' sciences: physics, chemistry, biology, psychology – all have ghosts or skeletons in their cupboards, phrases or formulae which long seemed to possess genuine empirical meanings, but which in fact contributed in no way to the established truths of any of these sciences.

But Peirce's Pragmatism is more than an instrument of criticism and polemic. It embodies a positive thesis of the first importance, which other empiricist thinkers to be sure have advocated, but which few if any have developed as carefully and illuminatingly as does Peirce. Probably the simplest way of stating this thesis is to say that, for Peirce, the command 'Experiment!' ranks as a principle of logic, conformity to which, or at least a readiness to conform to which, is a necessary condition of the use of any hypothesis or the understanding of any allegedly informative statement. Put more moderately, and perhaps more persuasively, it amounts to saying that, in order to understand an informative statement or appreciate the peculiar force of a hypothesis, one must be in a position to say, or show how, evidence for or against it could be obtained, that is, obtained by deliberate intention and not, so to say, stumbled upon by mere good fortune. Unless this condition is fulfilled, a hypothesis or a piece of alleged information just isn't what it claims to be or appears to be: it is as logically inadmissible as a conclusion allegedly derived from two negative premises or as a generalization from instances which we have no reason for considering a fair sample of the kind or collection that is being examined.

It is of course just this exclusion of the possibility both of information that is accidentally gained and of information that is accidentally confirmed, that makes Peirce's experimentalist thesis at first sight so very queer and indeed unplausible. To take the first of these points. It seems perfectly natural to say that a man in delirium, or even a parrot, is capable of making suggestive or informative utterances; but in fact the suggestive and informative value of such utterances is due to what *other* intelligent people can make of them and do with them. In general, the giving of information means the informing of some person or mind with certain habits of sign-interpretation; and to be informed is to be rendered capable of doing certain things either with or on the basis of certain signs, irrespective or whether these have been made by an intelligent person or by some inanimate object such as a weather-vane. Information, then, may be accidentally given, it cannot be accidentally appreciated or understood; and unless a conjecture, a hypothesis, or a statement be interpreted as relevant to a particular problem, and unless it is used to supplement other information already accepted as relevant to that problem, it is altogether wanting in informative value.

To turn now to the second point: viz. that Peirce's Pragmatism appears to exclude the possibility (or should we not say, appears to deny the obvious fact?) that a hypothesis may sometimes be confirmed by what it is natural to describe as a lucky accident. Now although, as we shall see in the next chapter, Peirce is not as clear or as consistent on this point as we could wish, yet the main purpose of his Pragmatism is not to deny this possibility, but rather to affirm that *some at least* of the relevant evidence for or against a given hypothesis must be obtainable as a result of deliberate action such as anyone, who really understands that hypothesis, must know how to take. Unless some evidence is in this sense obtainable, then the alleged hypothesis is the idlest supposition without any explanatory value; it is simply one of the innumerable propositions that appear to be compatible with the state of affairs to be explained. This explains why Peirce regards this command 'Experiment!' as a principle of logic; for an experiment *is* an action expressly planned so that evidence for or against a particular hypothesis shall result from it. Other philosophers besides Peirce have noticed that there is an experiment-like phase or moment in all purposive thinking: but few, if any, have appreciated this fact in its full import, i.e. have recognized that conformity to the command 'Experiment!' is part of that apparatus of self-criticism and self-control which serves to distinguish purposive thinking or Inquiry from mere passive acquiescence in habitual unquestioned belief.

Peirce stands apart from most philosophers who would admit the experiment-like character of thinking – that is to say, its practical character or what the Benthamites and later the Marxists have called 'the unity of theory and practice' – on a second and much more surprising score: namely, his insistence that any experimentalist theory of meaning, such as the one which his Pragmatism embodies, presupposes that there are real general tendencies, or general laws that are really operative, in Nature. Indeed, Peirce goes so far on this score as to claim that *his* form of Pragmatism could hardly have entered a head that was not already convinced of the truth of this, his own – indeed very much his own – version of 'scholastic realism'.* What is the explanation of this peculiarity in Peirce's thought? What is the importance of his resistance to that tide of Nominalism which appears to have carried all before it in philosophy since the Renaissance? In attempting to answer these questions it will assist us to revert for a few paragraphs to the comparison which we introduced in Chapter I between the Pragmatism of Peirce and the Pragmatism of James; for on this particular issue James may be taken as a very fair representative of the main stream of modern empiricism.

*

James, as we said in Chapter I, was an analytical or descriptive rather than an experimental psychologist; as such his main interest was to explain – or, where this was impossible, at least to throw useful light on – various aspects or phases of the mental life of any (standard) individual by relating these aspects or phases to others in the mental life of the same individual. This does not mean that the analytical psychologist has no interest whatsoever in the results of experiments on the sense-organs and the brains of men and animals. Certainly James showed an intelligent appreciation of the results, or prospective results, of such experiments; nevertheless his main interest was always in the 'stream of consciousness', in the inner biographies of individuals in so far as these admit of fruitful comparison and contrast, and ultimately perhaps – though on this issue James showed a wise scepticism – of explanation by means of established causal laws.

Now within the continuous flow of any individual's experience, certain phases stand out as having a special intensity or importance from the point of view of that individual: for example, those sensations which directly satisfy some basic organic need, or again those sensations which initiate a succession of experiences which lead to or terminate in some direct satisfaction. It is in terms of such processes of 'leading', such transitions from one focal point in the flow of experience to

* 5·503.

another, that James seeks to elucidate the meaning of a thought or of a sign. James recognized, to be sure, that a transition which *could* lead from one focal point of experience to another might in fact *not* be followed through: in which case the meaning of this thought – its linkage with other parts of experience – would remain, to apply Peirce's words, 'something altogether virtual'. But the point to be emphasized is that, on James's view, any transition which could lead from one part of experience to another is itself something intrinsically experienceable; and that any actual transition can only lead from one concrete experience (however complex) towards (even if it should fail in fact to connect with it) another equally concrete experience.

This 'naturalistic' approach to the theory of knowledge, James tells us, implies that 'whenever we intellectualize a relatively pure experience, we ought to do so for the sake of redescending to the pure or more concrete level again; and that if an intellect stays aloft among its abstract terms and generalized relations, and does not reinsert itself with its conclusions into some particular point of the immediate stream of life, it fails to carry out its function and leaves its normal race unrun.'* And he makes the same point, with specific reference to his Pragmatism, when he asserts that 'the meaning of any philosophic proposition can always be brought down to some particular consequence, in our future practical experience, whether active or passive; the point lying rather in the fact that the experience must be particular, than in the fact that it must be active.'†

Now there is one important point of agreement between these statements of James and all the versions of Peirce's Pragmatism which we have so far examined. Peirce's Pragmatism requires, as much as James's does, that among the necessary consequences of any hypothesis, or of any informative symbol, there shall be some which are particular in the sense that they could actually be indicated – that they might act on us and cause us to react to them in turn – in certain specifiable circum-

---

* *Essays in Radical Empiricism*, p. 97.
† *Collected Essays and Reviews*, p. 412.

stances. And thus far Peirce would be altogether with James in maintaining that every thought, or at any rate every informative sign, must 're-insert itself ... into some particular point of the immediate stream of life.' But now comes the point of difference; namely that, for Peirce, among the necessary consequences of any hypothesis or informative symbol are some *which are general but which nevertheless have real practical value.* Indeed, we shall find Peirce maintaining that appreciation of such general consequences is necessary if we are to do what Pragmatism says we must do in using any hypothesis, viz. take deliberate action of a kind that will afford evidence for or against that hypothesis.

To see the force of this claim, which provides the basis of Peirce's scholastic realism, let us proceed step by step, and ask first why every proposition, of whatever form, involves some consequences of a general character. Consider our earlier example: from the statement 'The event B appears to be later than the event A' it follows that *any* event x standing in this relation of apparent subsequence to B will inevitably stand in this relation to A also. Similarly from the statement 'Here is bread' it follows that any man, or almost any man, can here find nourishment. Now why do these general conclusions follow from statements which are evidently about *particular* events or states of affairs? The traditional answer would be: because every statement contains one irreducibly general element, commonly called its predicate, and because any consequences drawn from a given statement must contain either this same predicate or some logically permissible development of it. Philosophers who favour logical realism commonly urge that there is nothing surprising or mysterious about these irreducibly general elements in our thinking; and to be sure, it is difficult to see how without them any statement or other sign could mean the same thing to different people or indeed to one and the same person on different occasions. Nevertheless, there is much to be said for the Nominalist objection to admitting the reality of anything which cannot ultimately be pointed at or reacted against; and it will therefore be useful to give an alternative statement of the grounds of Peirce's scholastic Realism in terms derived from our previous discussion of his doctrine of Thought-signs.

The meaning of 'Here is bread' is evidently not fully displayed in *any particular one* of its conceivable practical consequences; on the contrary, its meaning is shown or suggested, however partially, through the mention or thought of *any of all* its practical consequences. It is therefore something 'altogether virtual', as Peirce says: something that cannot be pointed at since it involves an indefinite range of occasions in which, in various ways, its nature can be displayed. But to say this is to say the main thing – certainly the most defensible thing – which philosophers of realist sympathies are getting at when they assert that every statement or informative sign must include one irreducibly general element.

The same conclusion can be established and developed a stage further if we start from Peirce's conception of a sign as that which evokes a *habit* of interpretation. Habits are commonly judged good or bad, useful or harmful; but because a habit necessarily involves, in some degree, alternative ways and means of realizing its characteristic result, it must be judged good or bad, not with reference to this or that particular situation in which it is exercised, but with reference to any situation of an appropriate general kind, irrespective of the differences in detail which different instances of that general kind will almost certainly show. This, however, is only another way of saying that a sign works by (*inter alia*) habituating or adapting our conduct to certain general features or tendencies of the world around us; or that the irreducibly general element in any informative sign in some way corresponds, if the sign is reliable, to an irreducibly general element in the world within and about which we make our signs.*

To press this argument yet one stage further. We have seen that, in strictness, it is only habits or dispositions that can be well or ill adapted – just as we saw in Chapter IV that it is only habits

* 5·431.

or dispositions, as opposed to particular actions, that can be criticized and corrected. Now the difference between successful and unsuccessful adaptation in any sphere of life is a real fact having pretty obvious 'practical bearings'. Yet we have seen that each pole, so to speak, of any process of adaptation is of an essentially general character – the tendency on the part of an organism to act in such and such a variable manner being well or ill adapted to the general or variable character of the relevant parts of its environment. If, then, we think of the action of signs or thoughts as being in any sense adaptive, we must attach as much importance to their general as to their particular, indictable effects.

It was his 'naturalistic approach to the theory of knowledge' – in reality the subjectivist approach of the analytical psychologist – that concealed from James the importance of considerations such as these. Himself the most sociable and socially sensitive of men, he was surprisingly inattentive to the general and social aspects of thinking and meaning. Just as a physiologist's training and interest confine him, naturally and rightly, to processes that occur *within* the nervous systems of men and animals, so James's 'psychologism' confined his attention to processes, transitions, etc., that fall within the inner life-history of any standard individual. General terms, general consequences, general tendencies of thought or behaviour, seemed to him mere shorthand descriptions of the realities which constitute the living stream of our thought: that is, our salient sensations and satisfactions, and those intrinsically experienceable transitions in virtue of which one salient phase of experience is said to 'mean' another. No doubt we are forced to *speak* in general terms; and it must be confessed that we appear also to *think* in general terms. Yet general terms are essentially 'conceptual short-cuts'; their function, as James sees it, is simply to guide us from one particular experience to another. Admittedly, James did at times pay lip-service to a form of 'logical realism', and suggested that we should consider abstract concepts as forming 'a realm of reality' co-ordinate with that of our particular perceptions and feelings. But the natural tenor of James's thought – of what is important and strong, even if erroneous in it – is altogether in the opposite direction: as he himself admitted when he emphasized the close affinity of his own Pragmatism to Nominalism, in virtue of its 'constant appeal to particulars'. And in fact the difference between the Pragmatism of Peirce and the Pragmatism of James rests, essentially, on the different attitudes of the two thinkers towards the age-old Realist-Nominalist dispute: do general terms, general statements, and general arguments stand for natures, facts, and laws which, irrespective of the way we happen to think of them, are really general; or, contrariwise, does reality, irrespective of our thoughts and representations of it, consist solely of individual existences?

*

The dispute between the Realists and the Nominalists is one of the three grand themes in the history of western philosophy; and yet it is, in the eyes of the world – and for that matter in the eyes of most contemporary men of science and of most historians – the perfect *reductio ad absurdum* of all philosophical disputation; the supreme instance of the folly of philosophers, of the futility of their non-factual, non-experimental researches: in a word, of their scholasticism. So much ingenuity, so much energy, such patience and such passion (for there were ages when men drew on the arguments of the two camps to support different theses and claims in jurisprudence, in politics, in natural science even) – and all expended on an issue in which not one single question of fact is involved. For the facts remain unaffected (or so it is commonly supposed), whether we accept the arguments of Plato or of Aristotle or of the Epicureans, of the Scholastic Realists or of Ockhamists, of Berkeley or of Hegel; and undisturbed by the dust and din of the scholastic battle, men of genuine learning, historians and scientists, have gone on observing, classifying, thinking, writing – advancing human knowledge.

But when it is resumed in terms of Pragmatism, or rather in

terms of the two Pragmatisms of Peirce and of James – of the greatest logician and of the greatest psychologist in the nineteenth century – the ancient dispute seems less obviously vain and vacuous. Perhaps, after all, it has a meaning and an importance even for the modern world of experimental science and fact-reverencing history. We have just considered James's naturalistic, psychologistic, approach to the question of the meaning of any conception or sign or hypothesis. His fundamental assumption, which precisely parallels the fundamental assumption of all nineteenth-century positivistic philosophies of science, is that any term which possesses genuine meaning must stand, directly or indirectly, for something that is experienceable, something that is, theoretically, describable. What is a thought? It is something real, something that happens, something experienceable, describable. What then is the object of a thought, that which the thought is 'of' or 'about'? Evidently the same answer must apply, if the thought in question is a genuine thought. How then does this thought connect with or mean its object? Evidently by means of something, some process or transition, which is, at the very least, experience-*able* and theoretically describ*able*. Underlying this view (as underlying the positivist philosophy of physics which stems from Comte and Mill, Kirchhoff and Mach) is the Nominalist assumption that, irrespective of our thoughts and representations, our symbols and hypotheses, reality consists solely of individual existences, of particulars that could be experienced. Whenever we are tempted to think in terms of real types or classifications or lines of cleavage in nature, or to speak of general laws actually operative, or of broad tendencies disclosed in nature, we are being deceived: types and classes, laws and tendencies are nothing real – they are hypostases, i.e. parts of the symbolic shorthand by which we represent the world of real individual existences and which we mistakenly 'read' into reality itself.

Let us now try to see how Peirce, by contrast, envisages the Nominalist-Realist dispute. 'The question', he writes, 'was whether all properties, laws of nature, and predicates of more

than an actually existing subject are, without exception, mere figments or not.'* And he adds, as illustration of the realist answer to this question: 'Anybody may happen to opine that "the" is a real English word; but that will not constitute him a Realist. But if he thinks that, whether the word "hard" itself be real or not, the property, the character, the predicate, *hardness*, is not invented by men, as the word is, but is really and truly in the hard things and is one in all of them, as a description of *habit, disposition, or behaviour* [our italics], *then* he *is* a Realist.'†
Nominalists, on the other hand – and under this title Peirce brackets almost every philosopher since Descartes – 'recognize but one mode of being, the being of an individual thing or fact, the being which consists in the object's crowding out a place for itself in the universe, so to speak, and reacting by brute force of fact, against all other things.'‡ This exclusively *individual* mode of being, Peirce himself prefers to call *existence*.

As against this Nominalists' claim, Peirce urges that there is a mode of being which consists in the fact that events tend to take on, or conform to, a determinate general character. 'Five minutes of our waking life will hardly pass without our making some kind of prediction; and in the majority of cases these predictions are fulfilled in the event. Yet a prediction is essentially of a general nature, and cannot ever be completely fulfilled. To say that a prediction has a decided tendency to be fulfilled, is to say that the future events are in a measure really governed by a law. If a pair of dice turns up sixes five times running, that is mere uniformity. The dice might happen fortuitously to turn up sixes a thousand times running. But that would not afford the slightest security for a prediction that they would turn up sixes the next time. If the prediction has a tendency to be fulfilled, it must be that future events have a tendency to conform to a general rule. "Oh," but say the Nominalists, "this general rule is nothing but a mere word or couple of words!" I reply, "Nobody ever dreamed of denying that what is general is of the nature of a general sign; but the question is whether future

★ 1·27.   † 1·27, note.   ‡ 1·21.

events will conform to it or not. If they will, your adjective 'mere' seems to be ill-placed. A rule to which future events have a tendency to conform is *ipso facto* an important thing, an important element in the happening of those events." [*] Such a rule, Peirce claims, is as important a fact, as *good* a fact, as that this, that, or the other individual thing is existing, is actually reacting, actually manifesting some particular characteristic here and now, or was doing so there and then. Realism, for Peirce, means acceptance of the fact that the laws of nature are as real, and as much matters that we take account of practically, as any or every particular configuration or succession of individual existents.

*

Here we reach the most important development which Realism receives at Peirce's hands. The Realists of the ancient world and of the Middle Ages had argued chiefly in defence of the reality of abstract properties – hardness, straightness, health, manhood, justice, goodness, and the like. They had maintained, to be sure, that such properties could be grouped in hierarchical systems: but they had regarded the most supremely general properties – those standing at the head of any hierarchy – as self-explanatory, or intelligible 'in themselves'. Peirce's long apprenticeship in the school of 'exact logic' saved him from this error. It enabled him to see that 'to think of a given property' means in fact to pay special but never exclusive attention to *one* term in some general proposition or law – in particular, to pay attention to a term that is *common* to a number of different general propositions or laws. What, for example, should we understand by the property *weight* – save in relation to (the law of) gravity? What should we understand by *force* – save in relation to the laws in accordance with which accelerations are compounded? What should we understand by *hardness*, unless that a given (hard) substance will not be scratched or penetrated by many other substances? To Peirce it seemed that this relational character of all properties, or the fact that every property

* 1·26.

is essentially a term in some law and unintelligible save in the context of some law, was the most important logical lesson that modern science has to teach: and neglect of this fact seemed to him largely to explain why Nominalism had been accepted by most scientists and philosophers at the very time when our knowledge of general truths was being increased, with such astonishing speed, through the development of the physical sciences. The thought of the philosophers of antiquity and of the Middle Ages had been centred on the value men should put on particular existing things rather than on the operations which men can perform upon them or with their assistance. They therefore tended to think of the world as composed of more or less self-intelligible substances. This being so, it was almost inevitable that they should assimilate thought about abstract properties and relations to what seemed to them to be direct perceptions, or intuitions, of particular things. The development of modern science, or rather the great logical lesson of modern science, viz. that all concepts and properties are essentially relational, leaves us with no excuse for persisting in such 'substantival' interpretations of thought at any level – from the most abstract mathematical thinking to our (apparently) most direct and immediate judgements of perceptions. But this does not mean that the doctrine of scholastic realism should be rejected *in toto*. If modern science has no use for a 'substantival' logical realism, it has even less use, Peirce claims, for the Nominalist view that reality consists exclusively of individual existents. On the contrary, the prodigious increase in our knowledge of general relational truths which we owe to the development of the physical sciences, enables us to see much more clearly the important point which the great medieval realists had to labour so tortuously, because of their inadequate logical apparatus, to express.

That the lawfulness of a thing, the regularity or predictability of its behaviour in general, is part of what we mean by that thing, part of what that thing *is*, should, Peirce holds, have come by now to be regarded as a commonplace. 'The existence of things consists in their regular behaviour. If an atom had no regular attractions and repulsions, if its mass was at one instant nothing, at another a ton, at another a negative quantity, if its motion, instead of being continuous, consisted in a series of leaps from one place to another without passing through any intervening places, and if there were no definite relations between its different positions, velocities, and directions of displacement, if it were at one time in one place and at another time in a dozen, such a disjointed plurality of phenomena would not make up any existing thing. Not only substances, but events too, are constituted by regularities.'*

We should notice, however, that such regularity is not to be confused with, or confined to, observed or observable *actual* sequence of a regular character. Here is a match; and it is an absolutely real fact about it that it *will* light if it is actually struck. But this facet of the match's 'regularity' could be expressed equally well by saying that it *would* light if one *were* to strike it. In general, to apply some of Peirce's most expressive philosophical slang, the regularity of a thing consists in its 'would-be's' and 'would-do's' quite as much as in its 'will-be's' and 'will-do's'. We should think of a thing's properties in a corresponding way: these consist in its *conceivable* effects – that is, effects answering to certain general descriptions – upon, or in relation to, other things. Thus *the lawfulness or regularity* of a thing, and *the reality of its general properties*, are alternative expressions of the same fact about it: both point to the inadequacy of the view that reality consists simply of individual existences; both teach us that 'generality is an essential ingredient of reality.' †

We are now in a position to show the bearing of Peirce's 'scholastic realism' on that other more immediately obvious facet of his Pragmatism, his insistence that every informative sign must possess consequences, such as can, if the sign is true, be *indicated*. To James it seemed sufficient to say simply that any informative sign or any hypothesis must involve sensible, or

* 1·411.   † 5·431.

particular or practical results, whose occurrence the hypothesis either explicitly or implicitly predicts. But this simplicity is obtained at a cost – the cost of slurring over the question, How, in using or understanding a given hypothesis, do we *think of* these presumptive sensible results? In contrast to James and most other Empiricists, Peirce always returns, in his account of Pragmatism, to the point which we expressed in Chapter I, with deliberate vagueness, by saying that in order to understand a sign we must know what to do with it. Thus Peirce tells us that the use of any hypothesis 'turns upon the idea that if one exerts certain *kinds* of volition one will undergo in return certain compulsory perceptions' (our italics).* And this sort of consideration, he continues, 'namely that certain *lines of conduct* will entail certain *kinds* of inevitable experiences [our italics], is what is called a practical consideration.' † These statements may be compared with Peirce's remark that whatever assertion you make to an experimentalist, 'he will ... understand as meaning that if a given *prescription* for an experiment *ever can be* and ever is carried out in act, an experience *of a given description* will result ... ' ‡ (our italics); or with his claim that the simple supposition that a given stone is *hard* involves the general belief that 'no matter how often you try the experiment' (of scratching or penetrating the stone with another substance) 'it will fail every time. That *innumerable series of conditional predictions* is involved in the meaning of the lowly adjective' § (our italics).

In these and numerous similar statements Peirce is labouring to bring out the intimate connection of two theses which, taken together, serve to distinguish his Pragmatism from many contemporary theories of meaning as well as from the Pragmatism of James. The first of these theses is that the particular compulsory perceptions which are necessary to the meaning of a hypothesis must be of such a kind as would result from certain (conceivable) actions on our part, should we deliberately choose to take them; the second is that such compulsory results can be *conceived* only if logical realism of the relational, rather than of

* 5·9.   † 5·9.   ‡ 5·411.   § 1·615.

the scholastic 'substantival' type be true. Thus, from the subjective side, the meaning of a hypothesis depends on *our* dispositions or capacities to act (or imagine ourselves acting) in certain specifiable ways; while, from the objective side, its meaning presupposes the reality of some general law governing the relation of the facts supposed in the hypothesis to certain other *observable* facts which will, in some measure, confirm the hypothesis if it is true. (Alternatively, we might say that these observable facts would necessarily result if the hypothesis corresponded to a state of affairs having a real tendency to develop in certain specifiable ways.) In sum, Peirce's Pragmatism holds that to understand a hypothesis means to know how to produce evidence for or against it, in the form of a proposition whose subject-term (to be indicated as a result of applying certain general procedures) and whose predicate-term (to be conceived as the requirement of some really operative law) *both* presuppose the kind of scholastic realism that is advocated by Peirce.

This elucidation of the conditions under which a hypothesis is admissible may well come to be regarded as one of the great milestones in the history of modern empiricism. Three of its distinctive merits may be mentioned here. (i) From the purely logical standpoint, Peirce's Pragmatist teaching depends on and illustrates his view that the three great forms of inference – deduction, induction, and hypothesis – for all that they fulfil distinct functions, are in their applications never wholly independent one of another. The conclusions of hypothetic inference provide the necessary materials both for pure deduction and for the progressive application of inductive tests; but at the same time a hypothesis is only permissible if it admits of deductive elaborations which can be experimentally – i.e. inductively – tested. In thus emphasizing the mutual dependence of the three forms of inference, Peirce's Pragmatism avoids that besetting sin of logicians, the desire to reduce all forms of inference to one original, or genuinely valid, type. (ii) We should notice that Peirce's Pragmatism does not require that the state of affairs envisaged by a given hypothesis must be *itself* directly verifiable, but only that it should include among its necessary consequences certain 'compulsory perceptions'. It thus allows us to maintain the existence of events or entities which, as common sense finds necessary and obvious, could not *themselves* be observed in any conceivable circumstance. This is obviously the case with regard to past historical events and also with regard to such obscure, but no doubt perfectly real, entities as electrons and genes and unconscious wishes – not to mention such general entities as long-term physical or biological or social trends. As against the view of James and other nineteenth-century positivists that to assume such unobservable entities or events is 'metaphysical' in the pejorative sense of that word, Peirce retorts: 'Students of heat are not deterred by the impossibility of observing molecules from considering and accepting the kinetical theory; students of light do not brand the speculation on the luminiferous ether as metaphysical. ...'* So long as such hypotheses possess 'practical effects', so long as they can be experimentally tested, Pragmatism has nothing against them; and in this respect it concedes more – though it does not concede everything – to that 'literal-mindedness' of common men (and of practising scientists) which most other forms of empiricism are compelled to disown. (iii) Peirce's Pragmatism draws the sting of another question which has proved virtually unanswerable on most empiricist theories of knowledge; namely, how, if every hypothesis must refer to certain compulsory perceptions – which are presumably experiences of individual people – do we nevertheless manage in our thoughts and speech to refer to a common world of public things and processes? Or how, in more dramatic phraseology, do we succeed, in our thoughts, in somehow escaping or transcending the circle of our own individual perceptions? Here Peirce's Pragmatism gives useful support to the common-sense answer that everyday language, by its very nature as a means of communication, inevitably refers to things and happenings in a common world; that as far

---

* Review of Wm. James's *Principles of Psychology*: *Nation*, vol. 53 (1891), p. 15.

as its meanings go it is 'not *my* experience or *your* experience, but *our* experience that is to be thought of.' Pragmatism adds to this the consideration that the meaning of every hypothesis, or the lesson of every experiment, depending as it does on the reality of some general law, is itself of an essentially general or public character. The result or teaching of an experiment – the *experimental phenomenon* – is not some 'particular event that did happen to somebody ... but what *will surely* happen to *everybody* ... who shall fulfil certain conditions. The phenomenon consists in the fact that when an (*sc.* any) experimentalist shall come to act according to a certain scheme that he has in mind, then will something else happen and shatter the doubts of the sceptics, like the celestial fire upon the altar of Elijah.'* This accords exactly with our earlier claim that every scientific *statement* is public, in the sense that the predictions it makes are such as anyone can, theoretically, learn to make and test for himself. Similarly, Peirce claims, the terms in which a scientist *thinks* are essentially public; he is concerned not with this, that, and the next particular perception which contributes in its own peculiar way to his own individual life-history, but with the fact that a particular observation, having been obtained under certain describable (general) conditions, could be reproduced under similar conditions, and would probably be interpreted by all competent investigators in the same way. Alone in his workroom, tinkering with apparatus the purpose of which he may have communicated to no one else, never for a moment 'escaping from the circle of his own perceptions', the scientist nevertheless succeeds, as if miraculously, in concerning himself exclusively with questions and results of essentially public interest. He succeeds in doing this because he perceives only 'what he is adjusted for interpreting', and he interprets what he perceives, not as a particular individual but as a representative of the 'community of scientists'. He sees only what is for *all* to see – once they have learnt how to look for it.

This contrast between the private character of a man's own

* 5·425.

perceptions and the public character of what they mean to him is no doubt particularly striking in the case of scientific knowledge and practice; but it is dangerous to generalize too far from this particular instance. Peirce, unfortunately, seems to have assumed that the public character of our thought depends in all cases on conditions essentially similar to those which obtain in the laboratory. But it is easy to detect at least two features which distinguish the hypotheses of experimental science from those which we employ in, say, historical thinking or in dealing with the practical problems of daily life. It is, for instance, characteristic of the empirical sciences that they are concerned with types or classes of events, not with this or that particular event; and that, as a consequence of this, the result of any laboratory experiment is regarded as a specimen or sample event illustrative of a certain kind of lawful process. But secondly, the 'scheme' in the mind of the laboratory experimenter – the systems of classification which he takes for granted and the range of alternative possible results which he has in mind – is always much more clearly and completely articulated than is the 'scheme' with which, say, a historian or an investigating officer must work in formulating a hypothesis that is to be brought to experimental test. Nevertheless, despite these differences, any hypothesis which a competent detective will form to account for a particular crime will be in a broad sense experimentally verifiable. It would have a meaning for anyone who knows how certain 'compulsory perceptions', which the hypothesis necessarily involves, can be obtained by the exercise of 'certain kinds of volition' (for instance by the method of reconstructing the crime). Peirce's neglect of the fact that a hypothesis may have genuine, that is to say, public meaning, even though it differs in a number of logically important ways from a hypothesis of laboratory science, largely accounts for that crucial weakness – or at the very least crucial ambiguity – in his Pragmatism, which will be the subject of our next chapter.

*

There is, however, another large difficulty in connection with Peirce's Pragmatism which claims our more immediate attention, for all that it is quite beyond the plan of the present volume to include an authoritative treatment of it. Peirce's Pragmatism is, primarily, the logic of hypothesis; its aim is to prescribe and articulate the one essential condition to which every genuine hypothesis must conform; and broadly this condition is that a hypothesis must be verifiable experimentally. This being the case, it would be natural to assume that Pragmatism has a bearing solely on questions of matter of fact, questions about the world which is disclosed to us, ultimately through our sensations. It should therefore have no bearing whatsoever on our purely formal *a priori* knowledge, that is, our knowledge of logical truths and of pure mathematics. But, although Peirce's writings on this issue are distressingly scrappy, there can be no doubt that he did *not* wish the scope of his Pragmatism to be restricted to thoughts, statements, or hypotheses concerning questions of empirical fact. Pragmatism, he maintains, has an important relevance to those parts of our knowledge which are commonly described as purely formal, or apodeictic. He urges, for example, that his Pragmatism *must* affect almost all deduction in some degree since 'anything which... puts a limit upon admissible hypotheses will cut down the *premisses* of deduction, and will thereby render a *reductio ad absurdum* and other equivalent forms of deduction possible which would not otherwise have been possible.'* This consideration leads to the further more general question: How, or in accordance with what principles of 'admissibility', does a pure mathematician select his hypotheses in the first instance? The importance of this question lies in Peirce's (implied) rejection of the view that the only condition to which such hypotheses must conform is that of internal consistency; for it is certainly pertinent to ask how, if this were the only condition in question, one hypothesis or supposable state of affairs is distinguished, in the pure mathematician's thinking, from another.

* 5·196.

Peirce's own answer to this question would undoubtedly have been that different supposed states of affairs can be distinguished, from the point of view of purely deductive treatment as from any other point of view, only by the distinctive operations that can be performed on them *and* the distinctive consequences of these operations. In defence of this answer he maintains that, since Pragmatism makes every conception to consist in its *conceivable* practical effects, it will allow 'any flight of imagination, provided this imagination ultimately alights upon a possible practical effect.'* For instance, 'to imagine that a quadratic equation which has no real root has two imaginary roots...' is to say '... what would be *expectable* if we had to deal with quantities expressing the relation between objects related to one another like the points of the plane of imaginary quantity. So a belief about the incommensurability of the diagonal relates to what is *expectable* for a person dealing with fractions; although it means nothing at all in regard to what could be expected in *physical measurements*, which are, of their very nature, approximate only' † (our italics throughout). This, however, is a line of thought which Peirce never develops very far.

In at least one important passage Peirce admits that, while Pragmatism has thus bearing on the premisses of pure deduction and hence on what we should understand by the phrase 'mathematical thinking', yet it has no bearing whatsoever on the *rationale* or logic of deduction itself. But in a number of other passages he goes far beyond this moderate position, urging that at its every step deductive procedure involves something at least akin to observation and to experimental selection and testing of consequences. One such passage may usefully be quoted at some length. 'Mathematics as a serious science, has, over and above its essential character of being hypothetical, an accidental characteristic peculiarity – a *proprium*, as the Aristotelians used to say, which is of the greatest logical interest. Namely ... it is necessary to set down or to imagine some individual and definite schema, or diagram – in geometry, a figure composed of lines

* 5·196.   † 5·541.

with letters attached; in algebra an array of letters of which some are repeated. This schema is constructed so as to conform to a hypothesis set forth in general terms in the thesis of the theorem. Pains are taken so to construct it that there would be something closely similar in every possible state of things to which the hypothetical description in the thesis would be applicable, and furthermore to construct it so that it shall have no other characters which could influence the reasoning. How it can be that, although the reasoning is based on the study of an individual schema, it is nevertheless necessary, that is, applicable, to all possible cases, is one of the questions we shall have to consider. Just now, I wish to point out that after the schema has been constructed according to the precept virtually contained in the thesis, the assertion of the theorem is not evidently true, even for the individual schema; nor will any amount of hard thinking of the philosophers' corollarial kind ever render it evident. Thinking in general terms is not enough. It is necessary that something should be DONE. In geometry, subsidiary lines are drawn. In algebra permissible transformations are made. Thereupon, the faculty of observation is called into play. Some relation between the parts of the schema is remarked. But would this relation subsist in every possible case? Mere corollarial reasoning will sometimes assure us of this. But, generally speaking, it may be necessary to draw distinct schemata to represent alternative possibilities. Theorematic reasoning invariably depends upon experimentation with individual schemata. ...' *

Many philosophers of mathematics would agree, no doubt, that all Peirce says here is true; but they would add that, as Peirce himself virtually admits, it has nothing to do with the *essence* of mathematical reasoning, viz. its apodeictic character. But if the history of philosophy has one sure lesson to teach us, it is that we should beware of 'essentialist' slogans. No competent philosopher since Leibniz has failed to recognize the defining character of mathematical reasoning – that which distinguishes it from all our reasonings as to questions of fact;

* 4·233.

but very few philosophers have done much to *illuminate* this character, by showing its dependence on such procedures as Peirce describes in the passage just cited. Peirce's belief that his Pragmatism, his rule as to the admissibility of hypotheses, applies to every step and stage of deductive reasoning, may have been confused: certainly, if it is to be maintained, further elucidation of his idea of 'effects that might conceivably have practical bearings' would be required. It is, nevertheless, the belief of a man bent on understanding how mathematical reasoning is possible, and possessing a wellnigh unrivalled equipment, logical and mathematical, for this Herculean task.

CHAPTER SEVEN

AN AMBIGUITY IN PEIRCE'S PRAGMATISM

*

IN the previous chapter we followed Peirce's practice in his Harvard lectures of 1903, by considering Pragmatism primarily as the logic of hypothesis, as the requirement – which Peirce describes in those lectures as 'approximately the doctrine of Pragmatism' – that every genuine hypothesis must have verifiable consequences. If we genuinely understand a given hypothesis, we must know how *some* evidence could be produced for or against it: only in this way can one genuine hypothesis (or conception) be differentiated from a second, and only in this way can it possess genuine, i.e. distinctive, meaning. For our present purpose the important fact to be noticed about this thesis – which we shall call from now on the *wider* form of Peirce's Pragmatism – is that it says nothing about what *constitutes* the meaning of any given hypothesis, or about what that meaning *consists* in. We might say, of course, in the light of Peirce's general account of Thought-signs, that Pragmatism in its wider form assumes that the meaning of any given hypothesis (or sign, or statement, or conception) consists in a certain habit of interpretation; but about that habit of interpretation Pragmatism, in its wider form, has nothing more to say than that it must issue in *some* statements that could be tested experimentally. But this is by no means the whole of Peirce's Pragmatist doctrine, at any rate as he usually expresses it.

In the original maxim of 1878 the *whole* meaning of a conception is said to consist in 'effects that might conceivably have practical bearings'; and the importance of our emphasis on the phrase 'whole meaning' is made clear in a revised formulation of the maxim, dating from 1905, in which Peirce, having again demanded that one should consider 'what practical consequences might conceivably result by the necessity from the truth of (a given) conception,' adds significantly that 'the *sum* of these consequences will constitute the entire meaning of that conception.'* This emphasis is repeated in other writings of the same period, for instance when Peirce urges that 'the *very* meaning of any proposition' must be in a general description of '*all* the experimental phenomena which the assertion of the proposition virtually predicts' † (our italics), or when he states compendiously that the meaning of a term, a proposition, or an argument, lies in its 'entire intended general interpretant'. ‡ Pragmatism, in its *narrower* form, is conceived therefore as a method of articulating the entire meaning of any conception or hypothesis; and it teaches that, in order to articulate this meaning, we must either detail all its necessary practical consequences or else possess what Peirce's expositor Dr Buchler has usefully described as 'a formula for the entire class of the confirmable consequences' of the hypothesis in question.

But do we always possess – or are we always in a position to act *as if* we possessed – such a formula, whenever we put forward or accept a hypothesis with genuine understanding? It will assist us in answering this question to consider some of the conceptions by means of which Peirce illustrates the force of his Pragmatism when thus narrowly interpreted. In his paper of 1878 he considers the three conceptions of *hardness, weight,* and *force,* as these are (or were then) currently employed in physical science; and he has little difficulty in persuading us that a formula for the entire class of the confirmable consequences of each of these conceptions, as it figures in physical experiment, could in fact be provided – even if none of his own suggestions for such formulae can be counted altogether satisfactory. He then turns to certain metaphysical conceptions, and in the first place to the conception of *substance,* underlying and distinct from those properties in terms of which we differentiate, by observation and experiment, one thing or one kind of thing from another. As a live example of this issue he considers, in

* 5·9.   † 5·427.   ‡ 5·179.

highly Humian style, the Roman Catholic doctrine of the transubstantiation of wafers and wine into flesh and blood in the communion service: the crucial point of this doctrine being that what were wafers and wine literally become flesh and blood, although continuing to possess 'all the sensible qualities of wafer cakes and diluted wine. But', Peirce argues, 'we can have no conception of wine except what may enter into a belief, either – (i) that this, that, or the other, is wine; or, (ii) that wine possesses certain properties. Such beliefs are nothing but self-notifications that we should, upon occasion, act in regard to such things as we believe to be wine according to the qualities which we believe wine to possess. The occasion of such action would be some sensible perception, the motive of it to produce some sensible result. Thus our action has exclusive reference to what affects the senses, our habit has the same bearing as our action, our belief the same as our habit, our conception the same as our belief; and we can consequently mean nothing by wine but what has certain effects, direct or indirect, upon our senses; and to talk of something as having all the sensible characters of wine, yet being in reality blood, is senseless jargon.' To this he adds, somewhat ambiguously, 'It is foolish for Catholics and Protestants to fancy themselves in disagreement about the elements of the sacrament, if they agree in regard to all their sensible effects, here and hereafter.' *

The weakness in this very slick piece of argumentation is the way in which Peirce slurs over the questions: Do we or do we not possess a formula for the entire class of the confirmable consequences of a belief that this, that, or the other is wine? And if not, what reason is there for believing that the whole meaning of the word 'wine' lies in certain sensible qualities which *could in fact be listed*, or *could in fact be deduced from some general formula*, by any reasonably informed person who set himself to this task? Undoubtedly, wine manufacturers and wine merchants, customs officers and connoisseurs of wine, have many reliable tests for deciding whether this, that, or the other volume of liquid is

* 5·401.

wine; but to say this is not to say that anyone possesses a complete list or sum of the defining properties of wine. Such a list would presumably have to include some very vague and variable properties – for instance some of those that are suggested by the phrase 'wine that maketh glad the heart of man' and by the common collocation of the words 'wine, women, and song'. But who would venture to say which of these, in traditional logical parlance, make up part of the 'essence' of wine, and which are mere 'accidents'? To this it might be objected that, quite obviously, anything is wine that is a fluid made by the crushing and fermentation of grapes. But this suggestion is inadequate on many different grounds. On the one hand it would allow wine vinegar to be wine; on the other hand it entirely neglects such questions as the nature of the ferments to be used, ingredients other than grape-pulp that may be introduced, the speed, and other physical conditions of fermentation – not to mention the fact that a number of beverages commonly called 'wine' are not made from grapes at all. We may therefore conclude that if Pragmatism, in its narrower form, were to be applied to most of our *everyday*, as opposed to our scientific, conceptions of different kinds of substance, nothing but useless pedantry would result. On the other hand, with regard to our conceptions of the kinds of substance that figure in scientific thought – for instance, the chemical elements and the more stable chemical compounds – the position is very different. With regard to these it is indeed possible to provide, at any given stage of experimental knowledge, lists of their principal or practically defining properties; and even in Peirce's day it was reasonable to believe that general formulae could be found which would enable one to detail 'all the experimental phenomena' which such statements as 'This is a specimen of unmixed silver' virtually predict.

The objection which we have just raised appears in even more striking form when we turn to Peirce's treatment of another fundamental metaphysical issue: his attempt to state the *essential* practical effects of our customary division of Time into Past,

Present, and Future.* On this matter he has many profound and original things to say; but his main suggestion that the *whole* of what we – all of us, irrespective of our different intellectual interests and training and information – mean by the division is that past facts are facts we cannot alter, future facts are facts over which we have some measure of control, and present facts are those we are currently engaged in endeavouring to control, is surely simple-minded to a degree. At any rate, from this account nothing could be inferred as to the nature of those empirical, observable facts by reference to which – though obviously with prodigiously different standards of exactitude – both plain men and advanced students of physics succeeded in attaching a fairly definite meaning to the uni-directional course of Time's arrow.

But perhaps the best way to appreciate the general force of our present objection to Peirce's Pragmatism in its narrower form – at any rate when Pragmatism in this form is put forward as a *general principle of logic*, applying to all genuine hypotheses – is to recall, at this point, our discussion in the previous chapter of those hypotheses that are concerned with particular states of fact, for instance individual human actions. A detective forms the hypothesis that a certain individual, Smith, was murdered by a second individual, Jones. Is it conceivable that the detective, or anyone else, could provide us with a complete list, with the 'sum', of the necessary experimental consequences of this hypothesis? The question has only to be raised, for us to recognize that it is ridiculous. Quite evidently, a murderer's guilt is not *established* by a reproduction of every conceivable experimental effect of his doing the deed: but is it not almost equally evident that the detective *knows what he means* by the hypothesis 'Jones killed Smith' so long as he knows where a sufficient number – just what number no one can say – of its confirmable consequences can be looked for? As to the sum-total of its conceivable experimental consequences, neither the detective, nor any judge or jury, has the slightest use for so altogether 'unpractical' a conception.

* 5·458 ff.

Nor should it be thought that this situation results from any peculiar complexity or obscurity in the character and conceivable effects of human actions. Precisely similar considerations apply whenever we think of a purely physical event, not as a sample result of this or that kind of reproducible process, but as a phase in this actual life-history of this, that, or the other individual thing. A jar containing salt stands on a shelf next to a jar containing alcohol. Here is a perfectly good fact about two specimens of different chemical character, a relationship which they actually undergo, for all that, as far as scientific classification and explanation are concerned, it is something wholly without interest, an irrelevant accident. The statement that these two specimens have stood in this relation continuously for a period of months or years will of course have its necessary consequences, some of which could no doubt be developed in relation to known or discoverable facts about, let us say, the temperature and degree of moisture of the laboratory, the security of the stoppers or lids of the jars, the habits of the charwoman and the lab. boy, etc. But these consequences would be of no scientific interest whatsoever, and would peter out in a haze of vague and frippery conjecture. And in a basically similar way every historical explanation or hypothesis – every attempt to describe how this or that individual event happened to come about, where and when it actually came about – must indeed have certain necessary consequences if it is to rank as a genuine hypothesis; but these consequences will never be of that ordered, ideally systematized and – relative to any given stage of information – complete character which we find in the hypothesis of the best developed natural sciences.

These last remarks suggest the following conclusion to our discussion thus far. Peirce's doctrine of Pragmatism is ambiguous as between two interpretations, one wider, and the other narrower or more logically exact. On the wider interpretation it is a principle of general logic, indeed the 'whole logic of Abduction (hypothesis)', and consists in two requirements: (i) that every admissible hypothesis (or conception) must have some necessary consequences that are experimental in the sense elucidated in our previous chapter, and (ii) that these consequences shall suffice to distinguish the hypothesis in question from any other with which it might conceivably be confused. But on its narrower interpretation Pragmatism would appear to express a maxim of the logic of science, the demand that every scientific hypothesis shall exemplify a certain ideal of systematization. A conception exemplifies this ideal only when we are in a position to state 'the sum of its consequences' or to claim that we have considered 'all the conceivable experimental phenomena which the affirmation or denial of it would imply.' But quite evidently we are not in a position to do this with regard to every conception or hypothesis we entertain; and equally evidently neither of the two requirements which make up the meaning of Pragmatism in its wider sense implies that we are always in a position to do this. But did not Peirce himself recognize this ambiguity? In his papers of 1878 there is not the slightest sign of his doing so, largely because he there works with the unhappily obscuring terminology of *conceptions* rather than *hypotheses*. A few vague hints of such recognition can perhaps be found in his Harvard lectures of 1903; but here, since he works for the most part with the terminology of hypothesis, his tendency is, as one would expect, to lay emphasis on the wider interpretation of his Pragmatism. It is only in his latest papers on Pragmatism (those in which he adopts the hideous coinage 'Pragmaticism' to distinguish his own views from those of James and others) that he *begins* to recognize the ambiguity which our discussion in the present chapter has disclosed. And even then he does not expressly admit it; and his approach to it is made in a most surprisingly round-about way. Roughly, what Peirce does in these late papers is to push his narrower interpretation of his Pragmatism to the limit – to the point at which the impossibility of regarding it as a *general* principle of logic becomes all but obvious. To be sure, he does not or appears not to see this point in all its obviousness; nevertheless, the way he approaches it does credit to his perseverance and self-critical candour, and has the effect of opening up issues of the very first importance for both logic and the philosophy of language.

In these late 'Pragmaticism' papers, Peirce does not merely emphasize this second, narrower interpretation of his Pragmatism, he appears to be urging that the meaningfulness (i.e. on this interpretation, the *entire* meaning) of any and every admissible hypothesis must depend on its possession of certain characteristics – which are in fact *peculiar* to the hypotheses of the most developed sciences. Thus in one passage he appears to equate 'admissible hypotheses', not with those that possess consequences verifiable in some way or other, but with those and only those that can be inductively verified in the precise, statistical manner of the best developed sciences.* Again, there is one passage in which he urges that all statements of particular fact – most of the statements of everyday life and of history, for example – must be taken to be statements of the form 'Here is a sample of such and such a substance' or 'Here is a specimen case of such and such a reaction.' † But, as if semi-consciously Peirce had come to see the untenable character of these claims, his thought moves on from here in an entirely new direction, or rather, harks back to a line of thought which he had left, calling for further development, since 1878: this is the contrast which he had then drawn so suggestively between Belief, as the *natural*, self-satisfied condition of the intelligent mind, and the essentially questioning and *self*-questioning activity of Inquiry. The thought to which Peirce returns again and again in his late 'Pragmaticism' papers is that our beliefs, unless and until they are taken up – doubted, questioned, logically rearranged, tested, and systematized – by the activity of Inquiry, are *inherently vague*. By this Peirce means, among other things, that we just cannot say what *all* their necessary experimental consequences are; so that he is in effect confessing that a great number of our beliefs, and hence of the conceptions (everyday, rule-of-thumb

* 5·467.   † 5·429.

conceptions) that figure in them, *cannot*, at the present level – and indeed at any imaginable level – of our information and analytical skill, be fully articulated by applications of Pragmatism in its narrower, exacter form.

Peirce mentions, as broad divisions of inherently vague beliefs, our perceptual judgements, our original general beliefs – as that Nature is in some degree uniform – and our basic moral beliefs. The vagueness of our perceptual judgement is closely connected with the fact, which we discussed in Chapter IV, that they are not subject to logical control and therefore in fact indubitable. We do not know how to un-judge them; we cannot analyse out *all* their necessary components by means of experiment: for instance, we have no possible means of deciding whether what we would ordinarily call *visibly distinguishable* features of a perceived object could, in all cases, be distinguished by an intelligence that was dependent, in its perception of the world, on the sense of sight alone. Hence the impossibility of stating the sum of the distinctive experimental consequences of such judgement as that 'this object is red' or 'that surface looks square'. The vagueness of any original general belief is to be accounted for in much the same way. Admittedly one often *pretends* to have reasons for such a belief – to account for the fact that one *cannot* doubt it. For example, in the case of our belief in the uniformity of Nature, 'one dreams of an inductive proof. One surmises that the belief results from something like an inductive proof that has been forgotten. Very likely it did, in the sense of the term "inductive process" that is so generalized as to include uncontrolled thought.'* But this admission must be accompanied by the emphatic denial that the indubitable belief is inferential, or is 'accepted'. What happens, in fact, is that 'one comes to recognize that one has had the belief-habit as long as one can remember; and to say that no doubt of it has ever arisen is only another way of saying the same thing.' †

But it is in relation to our moral beliefs that Peirce does most to illuminate his conception of 'inherent vagueness'. Why, he

* 5·516.   † 5·516.

asks, do almost all human beings believe that incest is wrong? Because of certain observed or imagined consequences? To some extent, no doubt. But this does not mean that we are in a position to define the sum of their consequences, or even to begin an elementary classification of them. And the reason for this is not simply that our belief in this wrongness of incest is a matter of sheer feeling, a quasi-instinctive repugnance to it, powerfully though such feeling colours our belief; the essential fact is that our moral repugnance to it debars us from examining the consequences of incest, either experimentally or imaginatively, and hence from framing a systematic (scientific) theory about them. Similarly with our belief that cruelty is wrong. If it were suggested, with a considerable parade of learning, that a course of highly specialized cruelty to young children would eventually produce beneficial results to humanity as a whole (including, perhaps, the children selected for the experiment), would we engage in this course of cruelty? Emphatically not. In general, it is characteristic of our moral nature that it forbids us to experiment with – and therefore in any serious sense to theorize about – the feelings, and the bodily and spiritual welfare, of our fellows. This explains why, as Peirce saw very clearly, we are all of us, in moral matters, to a large extent 'sentimental conservatives', in the sense that we have no wish to experiment or to 'carry consequences to their extremes' * so as to obtain logically elegant and watertight theories. Science, indeed, is the one possible field for that 'radical spirit which carries consequences to their extremes by experimentation,' † and which theorizes without fear or heed of the tradition and interest which it jettisons or explodes. The degree of vagueness of a belief is thus a sure sign of its relative immunity from the scientific spirit.

*

Peirce re-enforces these conclusions by considering the inherent vagueness of most, if not all, language as currently used. On this score his late Pragmatism papers contain a number of remark-

* 1·148.   † 1·148.

ably penetrating dicta (fragments of a 'logic of vagueness' which he claims to have 'worked out in something like completeness' but which his editors have not been able to discover). He tells us, for instance, that 'every utterance *naturally* [our italics] leaves the right of further exposition to the utterer,'* and hence is inevitably vague to anyone who hears it unless some well-established convention limits and defines its possible developments. Again, he tells us that a sign is objectively vague if it leaves for some further sign or some further experience, which no well-established convention could lead us to expect, the function of delimiting its meaning; consequently, our uses of any 'objectively vague' sign are liable to be self-contradictory.† Lastly Peirce makes the astonishing claim that '*no* concept, not even those of mathematics, is absolutely precise' (*sc.* non-vague);‡ and he suggests that this is due, partly to the fact that 'no man's interpretation of words is based on exactly the same experience as any other man's,' but partly also to the fact that all one's individual private thinking 'is carried on as a dialogue, and ... is subject to almost every imperfection of language.' § The main implications of these pregnant if somewhat cryptic dicta can perhaps be brought out as follows.

It would commonly be said that to use a language correctly involves using it consistently, i.e. in such a way that no inconsistency in our uses of any given expression will occur. But, in so far as a language admits of consistent use, this is neither something 'natural' nor something that has been made possible, for the most part, in conformity to a single design. It is, rather, the result of a piecemeal development in the course of which the 'natural' associations of our predicate or general terms have been sometimes pruned away, and sometimes extended, in the interests of effective communication; and in the course of this development gains in generality have, for the most part, been achieved *pari passu* with gains in consistency and precision. This parallel advance is most obvious where language has been

---

* 5·447.   † 5·505.   ‡ 6·496.   § 5·506.

adapted to the aims and interests of natural science, logic, the law, and other specialisms; but to consider our uses of language in these highly specialized fields as typical of *all* uses of language is a quite unwarranted assumption. Nevertheless we do frequently think in this way, and consequently come to regard vagueness as a kind of regrettable accretion to certain parts, or certain uses, of language: something that results from blameworthy habits of thought and speech, whether on our own part or on the part of our ancestors. As against this false – and from the historical standpoint wholly unimaginative – way of thinking, it would be better to substitute for the question 'Why are some expressions inherently vague?' the question 'Why are certain expressions, to all appearances anyhow, altogether non-vague?'; since it is evidently the non-vague, i.e. scientifically precise and logically self-limiting expressions, which need to be explained, as refinements of the naturally vague and 'unruly' expressions of our everyday speech, and still more of primitive or 'natural' speech. Now it is precisely the substitution of this second of these questions for the first that Peirce's dicta on vagueness have the merit of suggesting.

But how should the second of these questions be answered? Very broadly – for a full treatment of this question would involve the re-creation of that 'logic of vagueness' which Peirce claimed to have worked out – it would seem that an expression can be altogether non-vague, or, better, can be used in an altogether unambiguous way, only when its user could state the sufficient conditions of its correct use in any given context. Thus it would be maintained by some that the correct use of the symbols '2' and ' + ' and '4' in the equation '$2 + 2 = 4$' *could* be established by reference to certain logical axioms which define the correct uses of our familiar arithmetical symbols. Again, it would seem reasonable to say that the correct use in any context of the phrase 'regular cube of uniform density' could be established by referring to the kinds of test which would show that a given object, say a fair die, was of this description; and it seems likely that the correct use of any key concept in the physical sciences could be established, with reference to a given experimental context, in a broadly similar way. Now what this highly compressed and somewhat dogmatic answer to our question suggests is that the familiar distinction between those subjects that are amenable to scientific treatment and those that are not is equivalent to the distinction between those subjects that admit of altogether non-vague descriptions and those the descriptions of which, at any given stage of knowledge and linguistic skill, must remain inherently (but not therefore 'hopelessly' or 'uselessly') vague. And the bearing of this conclusion on the range and value of Pragmatism, in its narrower form, is clear. It explains why it is that Pragmatism in its narrower form, by demanding an account of the *entire* meaning of our conceptions or hypotheses, has the effect of expressing a certain logical ideal, to which every conception or hypothesis of the best developed sciences closely approximates; at the same time it shows why Pragmatism, in this stricter form, cannot possibly be applied to the hypotheses which we employ in history and in the course of practical life. In using such hypotheses we usually mean something genuine, but cannot possibly say, or even suggest, *all* that we mean by them. They possess inevitably a penumbra, or perhaps it would be better to say a nucleus, of vagueness.

Unfortunately, however, this neat explanation of the ambiguity in Peirce's Pragmatism is subject to one snag. For if Peirce is right in claiming that all conceptions, including those of mathematics, are in some degree vague, and if this vagueness is an inevitable result of the dialogic character of our thought and the 'imperfections of language', – then our distinction between those hypotheses (scientific hypotheses) to which the Pragmatism in its narrower form applies and those to which it does not, was, apparently, premature and stands in need of considerable revision. Let us, therefore, try to see what Peirce must have had in mind in referring here to the dialogic character of thinking and the imperfections of language.

A language cannot properly be counted imperfect simply because our actual (and let us assume) correct uses of it lead to unforeseen results. We don't put the blame on 'ordinary language' when an insufficiently precise telephone message leads to a serious railway disaster. A language can be counted imperfect only relatively to certain standards and ideals; for instance, those ideals of generality and precision which are characteristic of physical science. Now, as used and refined for the purposes of science, ordinary language is, as it were, drawn up towards these ideals. But in fact it never reaches them; and it is unthinkable that it should ever do so. It is unthinkable that any set of scientific expressions should ever be held up as an example of perfect, complete, and final generality and precision. And why? Simply because we can never know that a body of scientific knowledge is complete; or, to put the same point in a way that shows us the relevance of the dialogic character of our thinking, because the possibility of someone's questioning a given set of scientific expressions, whether on the score of exactitude, or of complete generality, or of economy, or of internal consistence, is one that can never be precluded. To put the same point in yet another way, it is only by a very arbitrary assumption that we think of a standard scientific statement as being essentially non-vague, i.e. such that the 'sum of its consequences' renders its meaning altogether distinct and therefore, in a sense, complete. This way of thinking presupposes that we can, as it were, draw a line across the course of scientific investigation at any point we choose, and say: 'At this stage in investigation the meaning of the concept, C, is completely expressed in the following experimental results.' But in fact scientific investigation, and the meaning of the formulae and theorems that express its results, require that science really has a *future*, comprised in currently developing procedures, in vaguely formed projects for further experiments and so on; and in relation to these and their as yet impredictable outcomes, any standard scientific expression is vague, i.e. is such that, as actually used in developing investigation, it requires some further experience, whose character cannot as yet be fully predicted, to complete (but then only provisionally) its fully determinate meaning. Now as soon as we look at the matter from this angle, we realize that the vagueness of language, irritating though we may find it, is, among other things, the inexhaustible matrix of every ideal development of language; or, to vary the metaphor, vagueness constitutes that elastic quality in our communication-media to which our thinking owes its resilience, including those occasional wild 'bounces' which it is the task of genius to detect and pursue.

If this elucidation of the last of Peirce's dicta on vagueness be correct, then what he is there saying is something of the first importance for both the philosophy of science and the philosophy of language. But while admitting this, we must nevertheless insist that there is a world of difference between the kind of vagueness that can be attributed to the statements and conceptions of science and the much more obvious, all but self-confessing vagueness that is inherent in the statements and hypotheses of history and of practical life. Consequently, despite the important qualification which we have just made, our previous account of the nature and grounds of the ambiguity of Peirce's Pragmatism can usefully be maintained.

*

The importance of this ambiguity for the logic of history and of our everyday practical inquiries is obvious enough. It is, however, with its bearing on metaphysics, and in particular on the metaphysical statements of Peirce, that we shall be concerned in the remainder of this book. That Pragmatism in its narrower form should be applicable to these statements seems most unlikely. Peirce himself admits the inherent vagueness of his own favoured metaphysical expressions – though urging, with a modesty most uncharacteristic of metaphysicians, that they are more than mere count-words like 'eeny, meeny, miny, mo'. Can Peirce's metaphysical statements, then, be shown to conform to Pragmatism on its broader interpretation? To this question, again, our answer will be a negative one. Or, to speak more naturally, we cannot admit the suggestion that any of

Peirce's metaphysical statements function as genuine hypotheses, possessing consequences that admit of empirical verification. Does this mean, then, that Peirce's metaphysical statements are meaningless? Certainly it means that they are not in any way informative; they tell us nothing; they prepare us for no expectable, practical effects. But this does not mean that they are count-words of the 'eeny, meeny' kind – mere expressions of one man's subjective preference in the arrangement of his general ideas. On the contrary, we shall suggest that the best of Peirce's metaphysical statements fulfil an important function, and indeed provide a most admirable example of the function of worth-while speculative – as opposed to scientific, historical, logical, and ethical – statements. Their function, broadly, is to adumbrate or direct our attention towards certain new styles of description and explanation of fact, which the actual condition of our empirical knowledge can be shown already to require: or, to risk a somewhat dangerous metaphor, that they are approximations to a new focus which we must obtain if we are to hold the main divisions of our empirical knowledge in a single intellectual vision. On these lines we shall endeavour to show that the kind of metaphysical speculation to which Peirce devoted so much of his energy – and into which, we may suspect, even the most conscientious of positivists find themselves slipping in unguarded hours – may well be accorded a place, an honourable if inevitably subordinate place, among the activities of a 'scientific intelligence'.

Hjalmar Wennerberg, in his book *The Pragmatism of C. S. Peirce*, has criticised my main argument in this chapter; viz. that, contrary to what Pragmatism *in its narrower sense* requires, we cannot possibly say *all* that we mean by any of the hypotheses that we use in everyday life or in historical thinking. To this Wennerberg retorts, citing the authority of G. E. Moore, that we can believe many hypotheses without being able to offer a logical analysis of them. My point, however, is that our incapacity here is not just one of fact: it is *logically impossible* to suggest *all* that we mean by any hypothesis which is *inherently vague*, as Peirce himself came to see. Mr Wennerberg's criticism, in fact, neglects my distinction between the wider and narrower interpretations which Peirce's Pragmatism admits. Its interest lies in the contrast which it suggests between Moore's conception of logical analysis and Peirce's conception of Pragmatism as, on its wider interpretation, a rule as to the admissibility of hypotheses.

CHAPTER EIGHT

PEIRCE'S METAPHYSICS

1. *The Universal Categories*

*

PEIRCE's metaphysical writings fall into three main groups. First, there is a mass of notes on traditional metaphysical questions, along with which may be classed the many passages in which Peirce refers to metaphysical questions in the course of illustrating his own logical teachings. Secondly, in a set of articles contributed to *The Monist* between 1891 and 1893 and in a long fragment of the same period entitled *A Guess at the Riddle*, Peirce has given us the main outlines of his cosmology or world-picture, and in particular of his cosmogony – his theory of the coming-to-be and the continuing-to-develop of the universe disclosed by the natural sciences. Thirdly, underlying the writings that belong to both the above groups and giving them their peculiarly Peircian quality, there is his doctrine of the Universal Categories. Peirce's most satisfactory statement of this doctrine is to be found in his Harvard lectures on Pragmatism of 1903; but briefer and often illuminating descriptions and applications of it are to be found in almost every main division of the *Collected Papers*. It is this doctrine, notoriously difficult but unquestionably a major contribution to philosophy, that we shall try to elucidate in the present chapter. In our final chapter we shall see how Peirce applies this doctrine in what he himself regards as his 'scientific' cosmology. The question of the utility or worthwhileness of Peirce's metaphysics, and of its consistency with his Pragmatism, will be raised in a number of slightly different forms at different stages of our exposition.

*

Peirce's accounts of the nature and logical status of meta-physics are by no means easily unified or rendered consistent one with another. On the one hand we find such statements as:

(1) 'Metaphysics seeks to give an account of the universe of mind and matter ... it rests on phenomenology and on norma-tive science' (i.e. virtually, on logic).*

(2) 'Its attitude towards the universe is nearly that of the special sciences from which it is distinguished by confining itself to such parts of physics and of psychics as can be established without special means of observation. But these are very peculiar parts, extremely unlike the rest.'†

(3) 'Metaphysics, even bad metaphysics, really rests on observations, whether consciously or not; and the only reason that this is not universally recognized is that it rests upon kinds of phenomena with which every man's experience is so satur-ated that he usually pays no particular attention to them.'‡

What is important in these statements is obviously their em-phasis on observation, experience, phenomena, etc.

On the other hand we find:

(4) 'Metaphysical conceptions ... are merely adapted from those of formal logic, and therefore can only be apprehended in the light of a minutely accurate and thorough-going system of formal logic.'§

(5) 'Metaphysical conceptions are primarily ... thoughts about words or thoughts about thoughts.' ||

(6) 'The list of categories ... or "*philosophical arrangements*" is a table of conceptions drawn from the logical analysis of thought and regarded as applicable to being.'¶ This line of thought is more fully developed in

(7) 'Three conceptions are perpetually turning up at every point in every theory of logic. ... They are conceptions so very broad and consequently indefinite that they are hard to seize and may be easily overlooked. I call them the conceptions of First, Second, Third. First is the conception of being or existing

---

* 1·186.   † 1·282.   ‡ 6·2.
§ 1·625. || 5·294.   ¶ 1·300.

independent of anything else. Second is the conception of being relative to, the conception of reaction with something else. Third is the conception of mediation, whereby a first and second are brought into relation.'*

What is important in this second group of statements is their emphasis on the logical derivation of the Universal Categories (First, Second, and Third). And these statements seem on this score to stand in open conflict with statements (1) to (3) above. A possibility of reconciling these two views of metaphysics is suggested, however, in Peirce's admission that metaphysics, even when conceived as observational, nevertheless rests on phenomenology and normative science (sc. logic). Now by phenomenology Peirce means a method of examining any experience you please with a view to abstracting from it its most general and, as he claims, its absolutely necessary characteristics. Here, then, is one way of reaching the Universal Categories. But these could equally well be derived, Peirce claims, from reflections on logical procedures, especially the procedures of 'the logic of relations'. Without examining the validity of either of these claims in detail, let us try to see what kind of reconciliation between the above apparently conflicting views of metaphysics they might possibly enable us to achieve. The first view, we might say, emphasizes the 'matter' of metaphysical thinking, those 'phenomena with which every man's experience is so saturated that he usually pays no particular attention to them.' These phenomena *exemplify* Peirce's doctrine of categories. The second view emphasizes the 'form' of metaphysical thinking; it shows how the categorial doctrine is adapted from certain logical reflections. The 'phenomena' emphasized in the first view cannot, however, be said to verify the doctrine of Universal Categories; for if these categories *are* universal – if they are really displayed without exception in our every experience – then evidently the act of articulating them cannot provide us with *new* knowledge in the way that a hypothesis or theory in science does. Here, therefore, at the outset we find a conclusive

* 6·32.

reason why metaphysics, as conceived and practised by Peirce, cannot be expected to conform to his Pragmatist criterion of meaning or of the 'admissibility of hypotheses to rank as hypotheses'. The most that can be expected is that his metaphysics will enable us to regard what we already know in a (somehow) more satisfactory way; but precisely what this more satisfactory way amounts to is something that we have still to discover.

Waiving this difficulty for the moment, let us try to obtain a firmer, if still far from perfect, grasp of what Peirce means by his three Universal Categories. Presumably, they correspond in some way to the familiar division of facts (and propositions) into one-term (subject-predicate) and two- and three-term relational facts and propositions. But that this suggestion is only a first step requiring drastic qualification, is evident as soon as we recall that, for Peirce, no proposition of the subject-predicate or two-term relational forms is as simple, logically, as we are inclined to think; since to apply an apparently simple predicate to a subject or a relational predicate to two subjects involves some appreciation of the necessary consequences of such predication. Similarly, for Peirce, no three-term proposition is as simple or as self-sufficient as we might be inclined to think; since any three-term fact (assuming all such facts must be assimilated to the action of signs) can be understood only as a phase in a potentially endless series of suitably related three-term facts. In general, Peirce maintains, the *fact* to which any true proposition – be it of one-term, two-term, or three-term character – is said to conform, cannot be equated with a snippet of the 'objective history of the universe' possessing, in itself, a one-term, two-term, or three-term structure. It would therefore be a fundamental error to think of the world which verifies true propositions as consisting in a congeries of facts, some of one-term, some of two-term, some of three-term structure, in the way in which, for instance, a ballet might be made up of some solo dancers and some couples and trios of dancers. On the contrary, Peirce would maintain, just because his three categories are universal, every snippet of the 'objective history of the universe'* must exemplify *each* of them, must be, from one point of view, of a one-term or monadic character, but from other points of view of dyadic and triadic character. And this makes it clear that, so far from corresponding to the above familiar division, Peirce's doctrine of the Universal Categories in fact involves a radical criticism of our traditional logical categories of Quality and Relation, whether dyadic or triadic.

It is scarcely necessary to point out that such criticism is attended by enormous difficulties. Broadly speaking, Peirce has to employ ordinary language, and in particular the traditional terminology of logic, to criticize and purify both ordinary language and in particular the traditional terminology of logic: in other words, he has to use ordinary language to show relations and distinctions which it is in no way suited to show. Peirce's difficulty, in his account of his First and Second categories, is that ordinary language inevitably says too much; he has therefore to resort to the strangest devices in order to make his points, pure from unwanted accretions. His difficulty in connection with his Third category is the exactly opposite one: in this case ordinary language can scarcely be made to say enough, and Peirce has to strain it wellnigh to breaking-point to suggest connections of ideas, which, although (as he claims) they are necessary to all our thinking, have nevertheless been left entirely unexpressed in our everyday language and in the technical vocabulary of philosophers. In the face of these difficulties Peirce displays great courage and considerable literary skill. At times he analyses most penetratingly, with effective reiteration of his key words, some feature of the most familiar experience; at other times he virtually 'pelts' us with a succession of phrases or statements, often as not of the most diverse logical types or levels, in the attempt to bring to our notice some hitherto neglected, but in his belief all-important, connection between different fields of fact. To be sure, not all his efforts in this vein are equally successful; and when he writes of work in

* 6·67.

this field as 'one of those functions of growth which every man, perhaps, in some fashion exercises once, some even twice, but which it would be next to a miracle to perform a third time', * it is difficult not to feel the weight of the experience that lies behind his words. Nevertheless, whatever its obscurities and however dubious its claim to completeness, Peirce's categorical doctrine is an impressive statement of certain tendencies of thought which were certainly dominant in Peirce himself, and which, if he predicted rightly, point us the 'general line of growth' of the cardinal ideas of nineteenth-century science.

*

We can now consider in turn Peirce's separate account of his three categories. As we move from the First to the Second category the underlying aim of the categorial doctrine as a whole will grow clearer; but as a first indication of its main burden the following sentences may be useful. 'A man cannot conceive of a one-subject fact otherwise than as more or less analogous to a feeling of his own. He cannot conceive of a two-subject fact otherwise than as analogous to an action of his own. A three-subject fact is comprehensible and is analogous to an utterance, a speech, a thought.' † Anthropomorphism indeed! the positivistically-minded reader may complain. Peirce was perfectly aware that this complaint would be made; but he was not the kind of man to be frightened by the fashionable pejorative use of a word.

The First Category

Peirce's accounts of his First category have two main aims. In the first place, they seek to bring into prominence one all-pervasive feature of our experience, a feature which helps to explain why we employ statements of the monadic ('a has the quality Q') form, as well as statements about relationships between two or more subjects. But in the second place they may be regarded as so many attempts to distinguish this First cate-

* 1·280.   † 6·323.

gory from the traditional logical category of Quality, conceived
as that which corresponds to the predicate or general element in
a proposition of the '*a* has the quality Q' form. Let us start from
this latter standpoint.

'If', Peirce writes, 'a man is blind to the *red* and *violet* elements
of light and only sees the *green* element, then all things appear of
one colour to him. ... Yet since all things look alike in this
respect, it never attracts his attention in the least. ... For the very
reason that it is his own kind of sensation, he will only be the
more entirely oblivious of its *quale* (Latin: "particular suchness"). Yet for all that, that is the way things look to him.'*
The purpose of this example is to emphasize that the *quale* or
particular suchness of the man's visual experience is something
which he does not and cannot think of as being of a certain
quality or kind. In order that he should do this, he would have
to think of it as one of a class of *qualia* (*similar* particular such-
nesses), certain members of this class being manifested in *some* of
his experiences but being entirely absent from others; and he
would have, in addition, to appreciate some of the logical relations of this class to other classes of *qualia*. But, by hypothesis,
Peirce's colour-blind man can do none of these things. Here,
then, we have an experience of which we might say, applying
the Aristotelian distinction, that its *matter* is qualitative (in the
traditional sense of quality) all right, but that its thinkable or
intelligible *form* is not. If only Peirce's colour-blind man could
come to appreciate other colours, then he would at once be in a
position to think of his previous visual experiences as having
been of a certain colorific quality or kind; but by hypothesis
this possibility is ruled out. Hence, in order to bring out the
peculiar status of the man's colour-experience, Peirce has to
devise expressions which, by traditional standards, seem self-
contradictory, e.g. 'a particular suchness' or a 'suchness *sui
generis*' – something that can be appreciated only if we conform
to the rule 'There is to be no comparison.'†

Now why do these expressions seem self-contradictory? Or,

* 6·222.   † 1·303.

to show the force of this question, why have almost all philosophers assumed that what is directly present in sensation is, in itself, an instance of some quality or 'universal'? Chiefly, it would seem, because we are usually able, by means of comparison and contrast, to classify any experience or any facet of our experience as having this or that quality, or being of this or that kind. But the above example shows that there is no necessity why we should always be in this position with regard to a given experience – why we should always be able to classify, describe, and, in general, to interpret it; and Peirce's First category consists in a number of theses with regard to any experience irrespective of any interpretation we might properly or naturally put upon it, and irrespective of any reaction that we, or anything else, might make to it. ('First is the conception of being or existence independent of anything else.')

It should be emphasized, however, that in thus 'prescinding', as he says, the Firstness of any experience from the interpretations that we would naturally put on it, Peirce is not suggesting that such interpretations, whether classificatory or relational, are in any way subjective or unreal. On the contrary, most of the classifications we make are, or correspond to, something perfectly real; only the classifiability of a particular experience – or, in Peirce's categorial language, its Thirdness – is essentially a matter of its relations, not of what it is 'independent of anything else'. (We may recall from Chapter VI that Peirce's 'scholastic realism' is of the *relational*, not of the substantival kind.) At the same time, this fact helps to underline the immense difficulty of expressing or suggesting the Firstness of things, since ordinary language is designed to express and suggest, not simply their Firstness, but their Secondness (their dyadic relations and reactions) and their Thirdness (their classifiability, general properties, and regularities) as well. The following passage shows Peirce trying to overcome this difficulty and to give expression to one of the main theses of his First category.

'When anything is present to the mind, what is the very first and simplest character to be noted in it, in every case, no matter how little elevated the object may be? Certainly, its *presentness*. ... The present, being such as it is while utterly ignoring everything else, is *positively* such as it is. Imagine, if you please, a consciousness in which there is no comparison, no relation, no recognized multiplicity (since parts would be other than the whole), no change, no imagination of any modification of what is positively there, no reflexion – nothing but a simple positive character. Such a consciousness might be just an odour, say a smell of attar; or it might be one infinite dead ache; it might be the hearing of a piercing eternal whistle. In short, any simple and positive quality of feeling would be something which our description fits that it is such as it is quite regardless of anything else. The quality of feeling is the true psychical representative of the first category of the immediate as it is in its immediacy, of the present in its direct positive presentness. Qualities of feeling show myriad-fold variety, far beyond what the psychologists admit. This variety, however, is in them only in so far as they are compared and gathered into collections. But as they are in their presentness, each is sole and unique.' *

The last three sentences in this passage serve to bring out what is perhaps the most interesting thing about Peirce's First category. On the one hand, Peirce is continually emphasizing the monadic or single character of every *quale*, or 'particular suchness'; and this, whilst it distinguishes Peirce's First category from the logical category of quality, also serves to explain why it is that we tend to describe certain situations – those in which Firstness is prominent – by propositions of the '*a* has the quality Q' form. But while stressing this monadic feature in our experience Peirce insists that the same '*quale* element, which appears upon the inside as unity, when seen from the outside is variety',† and, as other passages make clear, 'measureless variety and multiplicity'.‡ It is possible, as we have seen, to conceive of an experience consisting simply in the manifestation of a single *quale*. But in fact our experience displays a vast number of

* 5·44.   † 6·231.   ‡ 1·302.

qualia. Their number might have been unity; in fact it is not. And in strictness we should not speak of 'their number' at all; for since *qualia* are essentially prior to all logical comparison and analysis, there is strictly no possibility of so ordering them that we can conceive of a limit to their number. Thus Peirce's First category is intended to suggest that all-pervasive feature of our experience which is unsayable not only because of its essential (and therefore unthinkable) simplicity, but because of its literally indefinite variety and multiplicity. On both these scores, therefore, Peirce's First category suggests a kind of limit to thought or intelligibility; on the one hand the limit of the absolutely simple and therefore undefinable, on the other hand the limit of the indefinitely various.

The suggestion of such a thought-limiting aspect of experience stands in complete contrast to the traditional conception of a quality or universal. Qualities, as traditionally conceived, function as ordering principles in our thought; in applying them we show our predominant interest in whatever is classifiable, orderable, manageable. But the purpose of Pierce's First category is to emphasize what is, in itself, unclassifiable, unorderable, unmanageable. It is, as he says, 'prominent in the ideas of freshness, life, spontaneity, freedom.' * 'What the world was to Adam on the day he opened his eyes to it, before he had drawn any distinctions, or had become conscious of his own experience – that is *first*, present, immediate, fresh, new, initiative, original, spontaneous, free, vivid, conscious, and evanescent. Only, remember that every description of it must be false to it.' † And again, 'The endless variety of the world has not been created by law. ... When we gaze upon the multifariousness of nature we are looking straight into the face of a living spontaneity. A day's ramble in the country ought to bring that home to us.' ‡

Here, then, we have the first positive thesis contained in Peirce's account of his First category: the same *quale*-element which 'from the inside' is unity, uniqueness, spontaneity, self-

---

* 1·302.   † 1·357.   ‡ 6·553, cf. 2·85.

sufficiency, is 'from the outside' measureless variety and multiplicity. Hence, the main purpose of Peirce's First category is to encourage us to *take seriously* what we commonly refer to as 'the infinite variety of nature', and to face seriously the question: Why *should* the variety of nature be in any way limited? As such we must agree that it fulfils an important suggestive service; and indeed it is difficult to resist Peirce's own conclusion that we must accept infinite (potential) variety as something ultimate, something that itself admits of no possible explanation, but which we must somehow do justice to in all explanations of phenomena that we attempt.

Our account of Peirce's First category is, however, not yet complete; for we have so far made no mention of his often repeated claim that the 'particular suchness' of any object is, essentially, *not* something existent, but a mere 'possibility of existence'. This thesis, on the face of it so irritatingly obscure – for, at first blush, what can be more obviously existent than what is simply *present*? – turns out, once its main purpose is understood, to provide us with a useful bridge from Peirce's First to his Second category. Broadly, what Peirce has in mind is this. In so far as a '*quale*' or 'particular suchness' is *actually* realized, it inevitably is *not* 'such as it is independent of anything else': for its realization here and now or then and there inevitably means its realization *in relation to other things*. A particular existing thing has a particular 'look' of its own; and that 'look' exists or occurs here and now, in certain relations to other looks, sounds, shoves, etc. But its particular location or existence here and now, in virtue of which it acts on us in the way it does and in virtue of which we can react to and indicate it, does not contribute anything to 'the way it looks'. This is as it is, quite irrespective of any possible reactions we may make to it and, *a fortiori*, of any possible interpretations we may put upon it: it is, here and now, its own unique self, which it might equally well have been then and there or be in future in some as yet unrealized place and time. In this sense the *quale*-element or particular suchness of any phenomenon can be said to be indifferent to the actual circumstances of its occurrence, which means – or so we shall find Peirce maintaining – indifferent to existence altogether.

The Second Category

'Second is the conception of being relative to, the conception of reaction with, something else.' And further, 'To say that something has a mode of being which lies not in itself but in its being over against a second thing, is to say that that mode of being is the existence which belongs to fact.'* Understanding of Peirce's Second category requires that we succeed in following sympathetically this movement of his thought; but to do this is not at all easy.

Peirce nowhere gives an adequate defence of his equation of relations – he means simple dyadic relations – and reactions, in a broad sense of that word which includes physical resistances. This is not to say that he could not have defended it, had he realized that other people might find it hard to follow this part of his thinking. It might well be that if we were to analyse closely all our uses of words and phrases and sentences which appear to stand for facts of two-term relational character, we would be led to the conclusion that in the great majority of such uses we are not referring in any way to two-term facts at all. As early as 1867 Peirce had shown that this is the case, for example, with all facts, at first sight simple two-term facts, of resemblance.† Two individual objects can resemble one another in certain respects only; so that what will count as a resemblance for one purpose, or when judged by one standard, will not count as a resemblance for all purposes. Hence, in strictness, statements of the form 'A resembles B' require to be expanded into statements of the form 'A resembles B, when regarded or interpreted in a certain way, or by a certain interpretant, C.' Here, then, we have one example of apparently simple two-term relational facts which turn out to involve the essentially three-term relation of signhood. And quite possibly a somewhat

* 1·432.   † 1·545 ff.

similar result would be obtained from the analysis of all apparently two-term relations save those of reaction and resistance between pairs of actual existents. But although this may be the case, Peirce nowhere proves it, or indeed attempts to prove it.

Assuming, however, that this first position can be granted, Peirce has still to show that the ideas of reaction and of existence are equivalent at any rate in certain specifiable – and for philosophical purposes peculiarly important – contexts. On this issue what contemporary logicians describe as the 'systematic ambiguity' of such verbs as 'to exist' and 'to occur' has to be considered. We speak, for instance, of the existence of sensations and sense-qualities, of numbers, laws, and regularities, as well as, more familiarly, of the existence of concrete things and the occurrence of actual events; and it is perfectly clear that when applied to these different cases the words 'exist' and 'occur' are used with different, although doubtless related, meanings. A number does not exist, a regularity does not occur, in the way that a house exists or a cloud-burst occurs. Now Peirce, although he possessed a keen native sense for differences of this kind, had not developed the necessary logical apparatus for coping with them satisfactorily; hence he often appears to confuse different senses of existence, or, when putting forward his own view of what is common to these different senses, to be shirking some of the most important difficulties. Nevertheless, despite his lack of adequate logical technique, Peirce does at least argue, resolutely and skilfully, in defence of his thesis that existence (or concrete fact) and reaction are equivalent terms.

He begins by calling our attention to certain classes of fact which, at any rate when they are considered in isolation, contain no suggestion of lawfulness or regularity; and he suggests that in these the idiosyncratic element of brute fact or sheer existence should be particularly obvious or prominent. Such, for instance, are facts of the kind we call coincidences, 'a name which implies that our attention is called in them to the coming together of *two* things'* (our italics). Again, '*Three* dots may be placed in a

* 1·429.

straight line, which is a kind of regularity. ... But *two* dots cannot be placed in any particularly regular way. ...' * And again, as a third suggestive example, 'Suppose I have long ago determined how and when I will act. It still remains to perform the act. That element of the whole operation is purely brute execution. Now observe that I cannot exert strength all alone. I can only exert my strength if there be something to resist me. Again duality is prominent, and this time in a more obtrusively dual way than before. ...' † Guided by such examples as these, Peirce sets out to try and prove that an element of duality is to be found in all concrete facts or facts of existence. To this end he draws up a list of cardinal 'features of fact' and endeavours to show that all these features presuppose a single fundamental dyadic relation between pairs of subjects. His argument is extremely complicated and includes some very dubious assertions as to the relation of *identity*; but this is one of those cases where the detailed steps of a philosopher's reasoning are far less important than the broad illumination which he imparts on the way. And, unquestionably, Peirce succeeds in the course of his argument in bringing out with great force and persuasiveness the central thesis of his Second category. To illustrate: 'No law determines any atom to exist. Existence is presence in some experiential universe. ... And this presence implies that each existing thing is in dynamical reaction with every other in that universe. Existence, therefore, is dyadic. ...' ‡ 'We find Secondness in occurrence, because an occurrence is something whose existence consists in our knocking up against it. A hard fact is something of the same sort; that is to say, it is something which is there, and which I cannot think away, but am forced to acknowledge as an object or *second* [our italics] beside myself, the subject or number one, and which forms material for the exercise of my will.' § 'Existence is that mode of being which lies in opposition to another. To say that a table exists is to say that it is hard, heavy, opaque, resonant, that is, produces immediate effects upon the senses, and also that it produces purely

* 1·429.   † 1·429.   ‡ 1·329.   § 1·358.

physical effects, attracts the earth (that is, is heavy), dynamically reacts against other things (that is, has inertia), resists pressure (that is, is elastic), has a definite capacity for heat, etc. To say that there is a phantom table by the side of it incapable of affecting any senses or of producing any physical effects whatever, is to speak of an imaginary table. A thing without oppositions *ipso facto* does not exist.' * And again, at a higher level of generality, 'The fact fights its way into existence; for it exists by virtue of the oppositions which it involves. It does not exist, like a quality, by anything essential, by anything that a mere definition could express.... The fact "takes place". It has its here and now; and into that place it must crowd its way. For just as we can only know facts by their acting upon us, and resisting our brute will ... so we can only conceive a fact as gaining reality by actions against other realities. ... It is not time and space which produce this character. It is rather this character which for its realization calls for something like time and space.' †

Peirce supports such passages as these by some remarkable analyses of those experiences in which, as he claims, his Second category is particularly prominent – our experiences of physical effort and resistance, and of shock, surprise and sudden change, as when a light is suddenly switched on in a dark room. Such experiences contain what Peirce calls a 'sense of *saltus*' (Latin, 'jump'), 'of there being two sides to that instant'; or, alternatively, he suggests that 'a consciousness of polarity would be a tolerably good phrase to describe what occurs.' ‡ Here is one of his analyses of surprise, through which, he maintains, all lessons of experience, all new truths as to hard fact, are obtained. 'Your mind was filled with an imaginary object that was expected. At the moment when it was expected the vividness of the representation is exalted, and suddenly, when it should come, something quite different comes instead. I ask you whether at that instant of surprise there is not a double consciousness, on the one hand of an Ego which is simply the expected idea suddenly broken off, on the other hand of the

* 1·457. † 1·423. ‡ 1·380.

Non-Ego, which is the strange intruder in his abrupt entrance.'*

Peirce is aware that his account of a 'consciousness of polarity' will meet with the objection that what makes such consciousness seem to be of a unique type is that there is a regular and therefore expected connection between, say, certain muscular sensations and certain subsequent movements of physical bodies including our own limbs. The allegedly unique polarity can be analysed away, therefore, in terms of simple sensations and observed regularities – objects which fall under Peirce's First and Third categories respectively. But to this objection Peirce's reply is that polar consciousness, in which his Second category is prominent, has nothing to do with expectation or predictability of results. On the contrary, the *shock* of reaction and resistance in polar consciousness is most prominent when it is least expected.†

*

Perhaps the most striking common feature of Peirce's first two categories is their emphasis on the irreducible plurality and variety of things – both of what might conceivably and of what does actually exist. The initial plurality and variety of any system, Peirce repeatedly insists, is something which no law can explain – all that laws can explain is the occurrence of *subsequent* uniformities within a given system; and *a fortiori* no law or set of laws can explain apparent *increases* in the variety actually displayed in nature. We might make what is essentially the same point by saying that Peirce's first two categories serve at once to distinguish and to relate in a wholly original way what seemed to him to be two distinguishable aspects of the idea of contingency – where this is given a positive meaning and is not taken simply as a reflection of our own ignorance of the laws of nature. What is contingent, in Peirce's view, is the actual outcome of any situation we care to mention. This is never contained in or completely determined by the prior situation, in the way in which the conclusion of a valid syllogism may be said to be contained in or completely validated by its premisses.

* 5·53.   † 5·48 ff.

But there are two sides to contingency – that which no definition can capture, and that which no law can ever bring into (or might we not say, can ever explain into?) existence. On the one hand, there is the contingent happening's immediate quality of presentness, its own unique way of being; on the other hand, there is the complex of its actual dynamic relations with other actual events. Now there is a sense in which, if Peirce's categorial doctrine can be accepted, neither of these things can be explained at all. To ask, for example, 'Why should *anything* ever be or ever have been blue?' is – unlike asking 'Why should any surface appear blue under such and such determinate conditions?' – a meaningless, because wholly unanswerable, question: and similarly with 'Why should this particular situation exist in the completely determinate way in which it does?' – as opposed to the perfectly sensible question, 'Why should this particular situation manifest such and such (mentioned) properties in the degree that it does?' In this sense, pure potentiality of being, and what actually is, are alike in that they can never be reduced to the status of mere instances of a definition or consequences of a law. On the contrary, they are ways of being – categories – which the conceptions of law, definition, class, and quality presuppose.

Now let us try to see how Peirce's emphasis on the infinite potential variety of nature (his First category) colours his accounts of fact, existence, reaction (his Second category). The latter, we may say, are so many attempts to illuminate our everyday uses of the words 'exist', 'occur', 'react', etc. by means of the metaphysically simpler notion of the infinite potential variety of nature; and the result is Peirce's conception of existence as competitive, as struggle – each fact fighting its way into life. This explains why his Second category includes, first, 'that which the logicians call the *contingent*, that is, the accidentally actual, and second, whatever involves an unconditional necessity, that is, force without reason or law, *brute* force.'*

* 1·427.

The Third Category

This part of Peirce's categorial doctrine presents great difficulties. Two of its basic tenets – those derived from his scholastic Realism and his doctrine of Thought-signs – are intelligible enough; but the way in which Peirce combines them with other tenets equally essential to his Third category is lamentably obscure. Moreover, his most characteristic uses and illustrations of this category, without some reference to which his more abstract accounts of it are scarcely intelligible, are to be found in his cosmology, full treatment of which must wait till our final chapter.

'Third is the conception of mediation, whereby a first and a second are brought into relation.' Here by relation Peirce means *intelligible* relation; and his main aim in all his accounts of his Third category is to show that the ideas of natural or operative law and of continuous development are different facets of one supremely general form of mediation, whose prototype is the action of a sign mediating between its object and its interpretant. It is also essential to his general categorial doctrine that this form of mediation – the Third category – shall be manifested in some degree in every experience that we enjoy. But the suggestion that we can detect in our every experience something at once so complex and so vague as this by 'phenomenological' observation and analysis is most unplausible; and in fact Peirce usually relies on arguments – some of them by no means models of lucidity – to render this latter thesis at all persuasive.

Let us begin from Peirce's conception of the laws of nature, since here he consistently maintains two quite intelligible positions. The first is that laws are real, are operative and reliable in a sense in which no mere *de facto* regularity can possibly be held to be. A long throw of heads with an evenly weighted coin is a *de facto* regularity, but it indicates nothing as to the results of future throws; on the other hand, we all believe that the laws of nature are something very much more than résumés of observed regularities in the past. In the second place, the operation of natural laws is essentially conditional; every law presupposes the *existence* of certain facts, and is therefore of the form 'If such and such facts take place, then others will, in most or in all cases, take place also.' This explains why the operation or mode of being of a law must be distinguished sharply from active, brute compulsion. Putting these two points together, Peirce proceeds to grope for – rather than reach – the first distinctive tenet of his Third category: viz. that the operation of a law is equivalent to a tendency for certain processes to develop, not only in a regular and predictable fashion, but in a continuous fashion. His thought here seems to be that granted such a tendency – or granted that there are comparatively few jumps or discontinuities in nature – then the reliability which we attribute to the laws of nature will have been very largely explained.*

Now it is worth noticing that if continuity is necessary to all operative laws, then certainly these cannot be equated with any combinations, e.g. *de facto* recurrences, of brute facts; for a law which involves continuity cannot possibly enumerate or describe its instances, it can only express certain general conditions to which its every instance must conform. But do all genuinely operative laws in fact involve the idea of continuity? Consideration of the best-established laws of nature might well suggest this conclusion; and, more generally, whenever phenomena separate in space and time appear to be regularly connected, scientists always look for – or assume – some continuous process intervening between them. Here is the obvious justification of Peirce's principle of *synechism* which 'insists upon the idea of continuity ... and in particular upon the necessity of hypotheses involving true continuity.' † But this principle would appear to be reached by generalizing from certain very peculiar parts of our experience – the procedures and results of the exact sciences – and is not at all obviously suggested by, or illustrated in, every experience that we enjoy.

To establish this further point, which is crucial to his accounts

* 5·104, 6·68, 6·169 ff.   † 6·169.

of his Third category, Peirce relies on one broad line of argument. Every experience, he claims, contains elements of memory and anticipation, and, more generally, elements of interpretation, however *un*prominent these may be; and the kind of interpretation which memory or anticipation or explicit inferences provide requires that mental action shall be continuous in character. Unless, for example, our every experience contained, as an essential part or feature of itself, the power to continue acting on or actively to overlap with some of the experiences which succeed it, memory – which involves that what *has been* still in some sense *is* – would be utterly impossible.* More generally, just as every experience which we would ordinarily count as a thought or a sign *means* something in virtue of its capacity to determine a theoretically endless series of interpretants, and is itself in some degree determined by logically prior thoughts or signs, so *every* experience may be said to have meaning, in a very extended sense, in so far as it serves to mediate continuously between some of the experiences that went before it and some that will succeed it. An experience counts as First in virtue of what it immediately is; as Second in virtue of what it immediately or actually does to other things; as Third in virtue of its 'would-be' and 'would-do' – its capacity to influence *any* of a describable set of later experiences by developing, with reference to such later experiences, the 'would-be's' and 'would-do's' of certain experiences which preceded it. In sum, Peirce maintains that our every experience possesses in some degree what every sign possesses in eminent degree, a *virtual* character, and that the possession of this character requires that some elements in our experience are continuous, or are developed continuously, from phase to phase. Hence, irrespective of whether we can formulate it or not, there is evidently some law, operative in our every experience, which accounts for its possession of this character. We thus reach Peirce's central contention, that we must assimilate the idea of operative law to that of the action of a sign. †

* 4·641, 5·289, 6·131.   † 5·106 ff.

Now a sign acts by calling out – by developing or exercising – such a habit of interpretation as is capable of contributing to the ideal end of 'concrete reasonableness'. In parallel fashion, Peirce maintains, a law operates whenever an action, by taking place, contributes to the development of, or sustains once there has been developed, a certain uniformity in the actual course of nature. The laws of nature should therefore be conceived as tendencies to uniformity, as habits in the making, or in some cases as habits of action so firmly established that they admit of not the slightest aberrances from them. We shall consider Peirce's most characteristic uses of this conception in our discussion of his cosmology; but we had better face at once the most obvious and general objection that will be made to it. This is, that it is a useless piece of anthropomorphism, throwing no light whatsoever on the genuinely important question of the status of natural laws, or of the derivation, use, and logical force of the formulae which express them.*

Peirce has two answers to this objection. The first, which we shall expand in our final chapter, is broadly that, on any other account than his, the laws of nature are left with the status either of mere *de facto* regularities (like the lucky run of heads) or of the results of some arbitrary *fiat* on the part of a divine creator. To accept either of these positions, Peirce maintains, is to regard the existence of law itself as one brute, unintelligible fact among others; but this is to give way to despair, and to commit the supreme sin against the holy spirit of science – it means blocking the road of inquiry.

Peirce's second answer, which he nowhere succeeds in expressing quite satisfactorily, might be re-phrased for him as follows. It will generally be agreed (by Nominalists especially) that all discussion of the status of the laws of nature must begin from an examination of the ways in which the formulae expressing them actually influence or mould our conduct. Any

---

* There is also of course the subjectivist Kantian view of the most supremely general laws of nature; but this view, as Peirce saw, combines the disadvantages of both the above views with others of its own. See 5·382, note.

given formula means what it does inasmuch as it moulds our conduct in certain distinctive ways – so that all our relevant observations, calculations, etc., take account of, or are made in conformity with, the law which that formula expresses. But what, we may ask, moulded that part of our conduct which was the discovery of the acceptance of the formula in question? The obvious answer is: previous processes of observation and calculation, the disappointment of certain expectations, the provisional use and subsequent elimination of other less accurate versions of the formula, and so on. But all these processes had, as their guiding aim, the disclosure of the one relevant operative law; so that, if we regard them as even approximately successful, we are entitled to say that our conduct *now* is in part moulded by the real operative law as represented, even if imperfectly, by the formula which we employ. The same law which, as disclosed by research and expressed in our formula, tends to mould our conduct in certain ways, likewise tends to impart a uniformity to the relations of the physical facts which are its direct and proper instances. This seems to be the idea which Peirce wants to bring out when he claims that general laws 'may not only be real, they may also be physically efficient,'* for all that he admits that 'what is general is always of the nature of a general sign.'†
Now we know by experience, even if we find it extremely difficult to express, how a word or a formula tends to act on our conduct; and this knowledge, Peirce suggests, provides the only possible analogy whereby we may conceive the action of a law that is operative in the physical world.

One important consequence of this assimilation of operative laws to the action of signs must now be emphasized. The meanings of words and of other signs *grow*. Electricity, for instance, does not mean to us what it meant to scientists of the eighteenth century; it now moulds our conduct in ways that are at once more various, more exact, and at the same time more efficiently co-ordinated. But there is nothing mysterious about the fact that the meaning of a word can grow: what happens is that new

* 5·431.   † 1·26.

and more efficient procedures or habits of action are suggested by new observations and experimental findings, and are added to those habitual procedures which previously embodied the meaning of the word. In like manner, Peirce thinks, a law which expresses some 'would-be' of a physical or biological system will grow or change as new elements are received into that system, or as other systems begin for the first time to affect it. In this way Peirce introduces the idea, so important for his cosmology, that in all probability none of the truly operative laws which we know of 'escapes the great law of evolution'.* Moreover, if laws are liable to change from epoch to epoch, then nothing is more natural than that we should find slight aberrancies from them *within* any given epoch. Here is one main source of Peirce's indeterminism, which he propounds not as a loophole for human freedom in an otherwise apparently determinist universe but as part of his own grandiose conception of operative law as something essentially developable and *therefore* intelligible. For, as a word or sign can be understood only in virtue of its capacity for development through combination with other signs, so, it seemed to Peirce, the fact of lawfulness itself can be understood only on the supposition that all operative laws (a) conform to a supreme, over-all tendency in things towards uniformity and continuity of behaviour, and (b) have developed, in the same general sense in which we speak of habits developing, from a primordial state of affairs which was itself inherently capable of *starting* such development. This way of thinking will of course seem, to use Peirce's own words, 'downright absurd' to anyone who regards the laws of nature as ultimates, incapable of any further explanation; but this is a position which, as we have seen, Peirce rejects – and with some show of reason.

The utility of the doctrine of categories

What is most original and important in Peirce's categorial doctrine can now be summed up as follows: Every experience

* 1·348.

that we care to scrutinize and every state of affairs that we can imagine, displays in some form each of three highly abstract characteristics—Firstness or Presentness, Secondness or Reaction, and Thirdness or Law. In any given experience one of these categories may be more prominent than the other two, but never in such degree as wholly to exclude them. The main lesson to be drawn from consideration of the First category is that no limit can justifiably be set to the potential qualitative variety of nature. This suggests the possibility that altogether new and unpredictable – because discontinuous – ways of being may arise in any part or phase of the universe, despite the reality (expressed by the Third category) of an over-all tendency *towards* continuity and uniformity of action. The most important lesson suggested by the Second category is that we should take seriously so-called *contingent* facts – apparent accidents, coincidences, and the like – since these, whether or not they be wholly fortuitous, display most clearly that character of fact which no law can possibly account for. Facts take place, compel, offer resistance and reaction, here and now; laws do not – their action is essentially that of a tendency showing the eventual outcome of what does take place, compel, etc., here and now. This suggests the main burden of Peirce's Third category, viz. that the operation of natural laws cannot be regarded as something ultimate and unexplainable and therefore, by implication, fixed from eternity to eternity. On the contrary, the operation of natural laws must be conceived by analogy with that of general signs which tend to produce habits of action to be exercised and developed into the indefinite future.

Now these statements, difficult and disputable though they may appear, also appear perfectly intelligible and even, in a very abstract way, informative. But, as we indicated earlier in this chapter, they are statements of a kind which Peirce's Pragmatism, even in its milder form, is designed to exclude and condemn. Broadly, Pragmatism tells us that a statement has a meaning – of the kind that its outward form suggests – if, and only if, some distinctive consequences of an experimental character can be deduced from it. Quite evidently, however, if Peirce's categories *are* universal in the sense he intends, no distinctive consequence can ever result from the assertion that they apply to this or that actual or conceivable state of affairs. Their all-pervasiveness inevitably spells their vacuity – their lack of informative value; and what other value – at any rate of an intellectual kind – can a systematic body of categorical statements possibly possess?

Now there certainly are other uses of language than its purely informative use. For example, we may agree with Vico that before men spoke they sang, and that before they could think in definable concepts they had first to express their embryonic thoughts in logically uncontrolled poetic images. But historically necessary though such forms of speech and thought may have been to the development of informative speech and thought, no one would claim that they possessed any peculiar intellectual value. Nevertheless it is pertinent to our present problem to remember that informative speech *had* an origin, and that its essentially developable character does not consist solely in its capacity to receive piecemeal additions, corrections, and refinements. Among the most important phases in all human history have been those in which some man or body of men has attempted, however fumblingly, to relay the main structural lines of scientific thought and language; and it can plausibly be maintained that this is one of the things, and perhaps the most important thing, that the greatest metaphysical thinkers have tried to or have in effect succeeded in doing. A new great metaphysics, although it may appear in virtue of its categorical statement form to be a system of informative doctrine – a kind of super-scientific theory or hypothesis – is, at any rate in its lasting effects, something very different from this; it might rather be compared to a revolutionary innovation in one of the arts; for instance, the introduction of a new dimension or a new kind of scale. After a great metaphysical doctrine has been assimilated, altogether new kinds of questions come to exercise men's curiosity and sometimes new styles and methods of answering these questions are made possible. Thus Aristotle taught men (of many different schools, in very different ages) to observe and describe the world in terms of material potentiality and formal actualization; while Descartes and Hobbes, in their different ways, taught men of science to banish all mention of potentiality from accurate discourse, and to think of the world as a changing configuration of actual, ultimate, self-intelligible units. To deny that such metaphysical teachings as these have produced important results is simply to show one's ignorance of intellectual history.

But if this way of regarding metaphysics be accepted then we must recognize that, in speaking of the consequences of a metaphysical theory, we are using the word 'consequences' in a noticeably different sense from that in which we speak of the consequences of a scientific hypothesis or theory. Suppose for instance, we were to ask: What are the consequences of accepting a Cartesian, in place of an Aristotelian, metaphysics, or of accepting Peirce's categorial doctrine – with its obvious echoes of Aristotelianism and of scholastic Realism – in place of any of those forms of Nominalism, materialist or idealist, which have dominated western philosophy since the Renaissance? Who, apart from those who would deny any intellectual value to any form of metaphysical doctrine, would be willing to come up with a clear-cut and confident answer? It takes a long time for the distinctive consequences of a great metaphysics to show themselves, whereas the distinctive consequences of a scientific hypothesis must be appreciated here and now if that hypothesis is to have a meaning of the kind which its outward form proclaims it to have. Yet, in its own way, a worth-while metaphysics must have consequences; it must influence men's thinking in such a way as will lead, or will offer a reasonable prospect of leading, to a more efficient arrangement of what truths they already know. Can this much be claimed for Peirce's categorial doctrine? In view of the above discussion it should be evident that no answer to this question can be more than tentative. Nevertheless, we can point to a number of broad probable effects of Peirce's doctrine, which suggest that the ultimate verdict of 'disciplined and candid minds' will be much more favourable to it than current fashions in philosophy might lead us to expect.

In the first place it is instructive to follow Peirce's example and to use his categorial doctrine as a kind of touchstone for appraising other well-known metaphysical positions. Most of these, it then quickly appears, fall short through a virtual blindness to certain aspects of fact which Peirce groups under one or other of his universal categories. For example, a nominalistic materialism such as that of Hobbes succeeds in ignoring almost every consideration that can be comprised under Peirce's First and Third categories. Berkeley's philosophy, on the other hand, is distinguished by its total blindness to the considerations comprised under Peirce's Second category: Berkeley's world consists, roughly, of whatever is or might be sensibly present *plus* the intelligent purposes of God and men. The metaphysics implicit in Hume's writings (and made explicit in some of the writings of Mach and Bertrand Russell) carries this tendency still further; on this view none of the conceptions that fall under Peirce's Second or his Third category corresponds to anything real. And, at the very opposite extreme from this, the Hegelian philosophy admits as real only those aspects of fact that can be comprised under the Third category. The only famous philosophies, Peirce claims, which do anything like justice to all three of his categories, are those of Aristotle and Kant.

At the very least, then, Peirce's categorial doctrine provides an interesting framework for the appraisal and criticism of other metaphysical systems; and this suggests, not only that it does justice to aspects of fact which other systems in their different ways ignore, but that there is something of positive value in the way in which Peirce relates these aspects of fact one with another. We may usefully elaborate this suggestion a little with reference to four problems which have continually exercised and baffled philosophers of the modern period: the problem of our knowledge of the external world, and the problems of causality and freedom of mind, of the relation of mind and body, and of the structure and unity of the individual mind.

1. *The problem of our knowledge of the external world*

Modern philosophy here displays a striking division of opinion. On the one hand, we have those philosophers to whom the external world simply means an ideal or logical construction – a kind of perfected imaginative panorama – suggested and partially confirmed by our successive actual perceptions; and on the other hand, we have those philosophers to whom it means a field of active forces, existing quite independently of our perceptions. Common sense and our everyday usages, when suitably interpreted or doctored, may be said to contain the germ of both these views; and the message of Peirce's categorial doctrine would here seem to be that both parties tell us the truth up to a point, but that both are wrong in thinking that they tell us the whole truth. When we think *of* a particular part of the external world, we inevitably think of it as looking or feeling or sounding in this or that way; we think of how it would sensuously *appear* to us or to any other sensitive being who could communicate his findings to us. But we also think of parts of the external world *as* effects or concomitants of active forces whose sensuous (or any other immediately manifested) characters we either do not bother to think of or else (often) have no possible means of discovering. The physicist is constantly in this latter position, but so is the man who picks himself up after being stunned by a missile which he neither heard nor saw. Philosophers of our first group generalize principally on the basis of the first of the above facts about our knowledge of the external world; they lay exclusive emphasis on those of the relevant facts in which Peirce's First, and to a lesser degree his Third, category are prominent. Philosophers of our second group generalize from those of the relevant facts in which Peirce's Second and Third categories are prominent, to the virtual exclusion of category the First. Peirce is one of the very

few philosophers who have recognized the essential two-
sidedness of our 'idea of the external world'. He is also one of
the very few philosophers who have something useful to say
about the way in which the two sides of this idea are connected.*

2. The problem of causality and freedom of mind

Peirce's categorial doctrine helps us to see the mistaken basis of
this best known of all metaphysical problems. The universality
of each of the three categories requires that there shall be an
element of real spontaneity, an element of brute compulsion,
and an element of meaning or lawfulness in every conceivable
state of affairs. It is therefore a sheer mistake to think of minds
or mental actions as little islands of freedom in a universe that is
otherwise subject to law or blind necessity; indeed the absurdity
of this way of thinking is brought out by the fact that we are
often presented with the almost exactly contrary picture of
human minds as pockets of purposive activity in a universe
which is otherwise an affair of blind chance or chaos. On the
other hand, if the idea of freedom is to have any metaphysical
usefulness, it must contain some suggestion as to how human
minds can be marked off from the rest of nature. Now Peirce
in several places urges that this distinction is to be sought in
terms of different kinds of law – or of the relative predominance
of different kinds of law – not in terms of different kinds of
'stuff'.† More specifically he claims that habits, taken in the
wide sense that he favours, can be regarded both as final and as
efficient causes; the former interpretation being suggested by
the fact that many habits admit the use of a considerable variety
of means towards their proper ends, and the latter by the fact
that the operation of many habits admits of progressively more
and more exact prediction.‡ From this it is a natural step to
suggest that *mental* habits of action are distinguished through
being subject to final causation in an unusually marked degree.
Peirce nowhere develops this idea very far. There are hints

* 1·431, 5·119 ff.   † See 6·101, and 7·366 ff.   ‡ See 6·101.

in many passages* of a doctrine of hierarchy of habits, culminating in habits of self-control with obedience to which Peirce sometimes equates human freedom. There is one passage of very great interest in which he attempts a speculative account of how mental habits have remained in man unusually plastic and never reach a state beyond which they cannot progress in respect of rationally controlled adaptation.† But nowhere are we offered a fully developed account of human freedom. As we have already noticed, Peirce had no wish to present his indeterminist view of the physical world as a kind of loophole for freedom of choice in an otherwise mainly deterministic universe. Indeed, the simple fact of choice, and its apparent freedom, does not seem to have greatly stirred Peirce's philosophical curiosity and imagination. In almost the only passage in which he deals with it, he argues that the familiar belief that we could have acted otherwise than we have acted, should be regarded not as a fact but as a useful way of 'arranging the facts':‡ useful presumably for an efficient development of our powers (or habits) of controlling our particular desires to conform to our long-term ends. All this suggests a typically nineteenth-century attempt to explain ostensibly free human acts as the results or manifestations of highly complex chemical and biological processes.

And yet freedom has a positive and metaphysically very important meaning for Peirce. The word 'freedom' occurs again and again in his highly generalized descriptions or evocations of his First category. He insists that we must start in philosophy from 'something *free* ... neither requiring explanation nor admitting derivation. The free is living; the immediately living is feeling.'§ There can be no question of Peirce's failing to recognize freedom as an essential element, or even dimension, in human experience – an essential spontaneous element in all self-formation and self-direction. What is surprising is that he shows his sensitivity to this element in his descriptions, not of acts of choice, but of intellectual life – the

* See e.g., 5·402 note.   † 7·381.   ‡ 5·403.   § 6·585.

experience of 'learning, of acquiring, mental growth'.* And perhaps the most valuable lesson to be drawn from Peirce's categorial thinking is precisely this: that we should try to begin to think of human freedom, not in terms of individual acts, steps, choices, but always within a context of self-formation, whether intellectual or moral; or that, in Peirce's own fantastic language, freedom is a 'Firstness of a Thirdness', i.e. an element of spontaneous self-direction in certain mental habits and attitudes – not a 'Firstness of a Secondness', i.e. the sheer exemption from law of certain of our choices and actions.

3. The problem of the relation of mind and body

Peirce would undoubtedly have maintained that his analyses of our experiences of effort, resistance, shock, surprise, etc. – experiences which fall under his Second category – suffice to establish the reality of some kind of interaction between mind and body or at least between mind and not-mind. At the same time the universality of each of his three categories requires us to think of mind and body as not wholly distinct or discontinuous in character (he urges, for example, that all our sensations have, in a no doubt somewhat unusual sense, real size or bigness; † and that some processes, which we would ordinarily call physical or material, are almost certainly adaptive in the same general sense as sign-processes are‡). This last point helps us to see that the mind-body problem has traditionally been posed in terms which are in one respect much too general, and yet in another respect far too specific. Philosophers have despaired of understanding how a *motion* could affect a *thought*, and conversely; and behind this question is always the assumption that what has to be understood is some purely mechanical phenomenon in relation to some pure act of volitional or intellectual character or to some purely sensuous state. But in fact such a juxtaposition of generically alien factors could not conceivably be understood *per se*, even by a divine intelligence: it is a sheer or brute

* 1·381.　　　　† 6·133.　　　　‡ 2·274.

Secondness if ever there was one! The only hope of rendering such an occurrence intelligible is through an examination of the context or background within which each item occurs and then through a search for some abstract model which can be applied to both these backgrounds. (Roughly, the way in which originally quite independent branches of physical science came to be unified.) The first point to establish, therefore, with regard to any alleged material cause of a mental reaction is whether that 'cause' is a phase in a material process which, seemingly, admits of complete explanation in terms of efficient (physico-chemical) terms, or whether, on the contrary, the wider process appears to be of an adaptive character or even to show affinities to processes known to admit of some degree of conscious control. Now all plausibly alleged material causes of mental action are changes in parts of our bodies, notably our brains, whose functions are of an evidently adaptive character: – physiologists tell us that the brain functions in literally thousands of ways to achieve the broad ends of adjusting our higher activities to our environment. It therefore seems reasonable to suggest that the question of the *interaction* of mind and body can best be approached through the prior question: How do certain actions of a material character and others of a mental character contribute in complementary fashion to this general end?

This suggestion can be developed equally well from the other side. Any given thought is, among other things, a way of adjusting our potential physical reaction to certain facts that confront us; and we succeed in this process of adjustment largely by envisaging the likely results of certain actions which we might take in relation to these facts. But what no power of internal rehearsal and adjustment – or if it be preferred, no action of a sign or symbol – can do, is to *compel* or *command* a physical action of any kind. Sign-processes or thoughts or mental actions tend beyond all doubt to *affect* our physical actions; but unless those physical actions were already potentially there, irrespective of the action of thought – or, to speak more accurately, unless they were very largely determined by physiological forces beyond our conscious control – thought would evidently have no material to work on, and thus could not discharge its proper function. We are thus again led to think of the mind-body problem as a matter not of a gulf which requires supernatural insight or some leap of faith to bridge it, but rather of the complementary character of different components which are necessary to all controlled intelligent conduct.

4. The problem of the unity of the individual mind

In so far as any experience can be considered as a manifestation of the First and Second categories, that experience contributes nothing to the unity of the mind. The *quale*-element of an experience is as evanescent as Tam o' Shanter's pleasure, and its element of brute reaction as transient as

> ... a step, a blow,
> The motion of a muscle – this way or that –
> 'Tis done; and in the after-vacancy
> We wonder at ourselves like men betrayed. ...

Whatever in an experience contributes to mental unity lies in that experience's capacity to serve as a sign, a mediator, a vehicle of operative law. But what thus gives unity to my mental life or yours is essentially something that might be reproduced in other instances; and in fact the habits of thought and interpretation which unify the mental life of any one individual are, for the most part, very similar to those that unify the mental life of his neighbour, for they are habits of thought inherited from similar sources and applied in a common world. This means that the unity of a mind has very little, if anything, to do with its individuality, its uniqueness: these are mainly a matter of individual feeling-tones, of peculiar circumstances – in particular of physical embodiment and the consequent efficiency or inefficiency of physical reactions. If, therefore, we accept Peirce's categorial doctrine, it is hard for us to adhere consistently to any substantival view of the mind; and perhaps the most important consequence of this is that there is a strong general presumption against the theory of *individual* survival after death.

*

These very brief notes must suffice to suggest the value of Peirce's categorial doctrine when it is applied to separate metaphysical problems. Quite certainly this doctrine is defective in parts; it contains much that is obscure and much that is in all probability confused; possibly the method of phenomenological analysis by which Peirce claimed to reach his results in this part of his philosophy is unsound – besides being ostensibly at variance with his Pragmatist teaching. But despite its defects Peirce's categorial doctrine gives expression to a number of insights of unquestionable originality and suggestive power: the value of these insights remains, even if Peirce's most ambitious applications of his doctrine – in his cosmology – must be judged relatively unsuccessful.

CHAPTER NINE

PEIRCE'S METAPHYSICS

II. *Cosmology*

*

PEIRCE'S main cosmological writings date from that period of his life, 1890–94, in which, on his retirement to Milford, he set about to unify, or at least to present in unified literary form, his own 'system' of philosophy. One aspect of Peirce's failure to realize this aim is that out of his fairly extensive cosmological writings he chose to publish only a handful of articles (contributed to *The Monist*), and that these articles are explicitly tentative and exploratory in character. 'May some future student', he writes at the close of one of them, 'go over this ground again, and have the leisure to give his results to the world.' *

Peirce recognized, then, that his work in this field was imperfect and sketchy; and although he returned occasionally to cosmological speculation in his later years, the fact that he so soon abandoned his efforts to present his thought in unified cosmological form is certainly of more than biographical interest. Nevertheless, it was to his work in cosmology, quite as much as to his Pragmatism and his other logical discoveries, that Peirce owed what little recognition he received from contemporary philosophers. In the previous chapter we saw how Peirce's doctrine of categories enables us to 'rearrange' a number of important traditional metaphysical questions; but such piecemeal applications of a metaphysical doctrine are not likely to win immediate or widespread attention. For a metaphysical doctrine to count with anyone outside a small circle of specialists it must be of a kind that transforms, or claims to transform, some very wide field of speculation or of moral and practical interests.

* 6·34.

Now Peirce's cosmology fully satisfies this condition; for it aims at totally reorientating our ordinary conceptions of the origin and destiny of the universe, of the nature of general laws and their relation to the things or events which conform to them, and at drastically revising – if not obliterating – the familiar divisions between living and non-living, mental and non-mental processes.

Unfortunately, despite – or perhaps we should say because of – this popular appeal, Peirce's cosmology is generally regarded by contemporary philosophers as the black sheep or white elephant of his philosophical progeny. In the first place, its central theses would appear to be, by Pragmatist or indeed almost any other empiricist standards, inherently untestable: either they refer us to a 'never-never land' (never observable, not even conceivable), or else, since they involve the denial of distinctions that are fundamental to everyday thought and practice, it is impossible to say what we could do in an attempt to verify them. In the second place, at least one of these central theses – to the effect that 'chance spontaneity' affords a sufficient explanation of certain actually observable results – appears to rest on logical confusions so radical that they render intelligible expression of it all but impossible; and almost the same might be said of Peirce's conception of a single over-all 'evolutionary law' of which all known natural laws are to be regarded as so many instances. Finally, the sympathetic student of Peirce's own doctrine of categories is likely to see in his cosmology a crude misuse of that doctrine: a virtual denial of its primary tenet, viz. that each of the three categories is universal. Peirce's cosmology seems to stem from the supposition of a primordial state of affairs in which his First category would be so 'prominent' that all trace or suggestion of his Second and Third categories would be lost.

We shall soon find reasons for agreeing that most if not all of these criticisms are only too well justified. What, then, is the value of further examination of Peirce's cosmology? Can it not be forgiven and forgotten as one – and indeed only a temporary – aberration of a brilliantly gifted but, at any rate on this one score, sadly erratic, self-divided, and un-self-critical thinker? There are, however, very strong reasons why we should not lightly adopt this attitude to Peirce's 'aberration'. When we look more closely at each of the main positive tenets of his cosmology, we find that it rests on a more general (and relatively negative) thesis which is of great interest and suggestiveness. Peirce's hypothesis of 'chance spontaneity' may, as positively propounded by him, be downright nonsense; but it rests on his vigorous rejection of two widespread assumptions as to the attitude we should adopt towards the laws of nature; viz. that we should regard them *either* as logical ultimates *or* as in some way the results of a divine *fiat*. Now almost everything that Peirce has to say against *both* these ways of thinking is as valuable today as when he published his cosmological essays in the 1890s; and, as we shall try to show, his conception of a single evolutionary law, and even his pan-psychism, can be, if not defended, at least sympathetically appraised in the light of broadly similar considerations.

In the first of his *Monist* articles of 1891, *The Architecture of Theories*, Peirce discusses the main materials out of which 'a philosophical theory ought to be built, in order to represent the state of knowledge to which the nineteenth century has brought us.'* He begins with a short discussion of the dynamical ideas of Galileo, which for certain broad purposes will remain for ever a model of scientific procedure; but he adds that there are experiments which give us strong reason for doubting whether the fundamental laws of mechanics hold good for single atoms, and that it is thoroughly illogical to look for explanations of biological evolution on mechanical principles. On the latter score he points out that the law of conservation of energy 'is equivalent to the proposition that all operations governed by mechanical laws are reversible; so that an immediate corollary from it is that growth is not explicable by those laws, even if they be not violated in the process of growth.' The question therefore arises: What should be the regulative principle, corre-

* 6.32.

sponding to Galileo's presumption in favour of *simple* laws in the early days of dynamics, which will fruitfully direct and if possible unify our inquiries into the minute structure of matter, and into the phenomena of growth and life and mind? Peirce answers that we must look for such guidance in a 'natural history of the laws of nature',* which will show us what kind of laws we have to expect, so that we can answer such questions as: 'Can we with reasonable prospect of not wasting time, try the supposition that atoms attract one another inversely as the seventh power of their distances?' And he continues: 'To suppose universal laws of nature capable of being apprehended by the mind and yet having no reason for their special forms, but standing inexplicable and irrational, is hardly a justifiable position. Uniformities are precisely the sort of facts that need to be accounted for. That a pitched coin should sometimes turn up heads and sometimes tails calls for no particular explanation; but if it shows heads every time, we wish to know how this result has been brought about. Law is *par excellence* the thing that wants a reason.' †

After mentioning some of the scientific conceptions that are likely to prove useful in this task of devising the 'natural' (or perhaps we should say the 'intelligible') history of natural laws, and emphasizing in particular the ideas of absolute chance and mathematical continuity, Peirce proceeds to the following brief sketch of a thorough-going evolutionary cosmology. 'It would suppose that in the beginning, – infinitely remote, – there was a chaos of unpersonalized feeling, which being without connection or regularity would properly be without existence. This feeling, sporting here and there in pure arbitrariness, would have started the germ of a generalizing tendency. Its other sportings would be evanescent, but this would have a growing virtue. Thus, the tendency to habit would be started; and from this with the other principles of evolution all the regularities of the universe would be evolved. At any time, however, an element of pure chance survives and will remain until

* 6·12.   † 6·12.

the world becomes an absolutely perfect, rational, and symmetrical system, in which mind is at last crystallized in the infinitely distant future.'*

This highly condensed statement of Peirce's cosmogonic vision is rendered somewhat clearer in the following longer passage from a fragment dated 1890. 'I will begin with this guess. Uniformities in the modes of action of things have come about by their taking habits. At present, the course of events is approximately determined by law. In the past that approximation was less perfect; in the future it will be more perfect. The tendency to obey laws has always been and always will be growing. We look back toward a point in the infinitely distant past when there was no law but mere indeterminacy; we look forward to a point in the infinitely distant future when there will be no indeterminacy or chance but a complete reign of law. But at any assignable date in the past, however early, there was already some tendency towards uniformity; and at any assignable date in the future there will be some slight aberrancy from law. Moreover, all things have a tendency to take habits. For atoms and their parts, molecules and groups of molecules, and in short every conceivable real object, there is a greater probability of acting as on a former like occasion than otherwise. This tendency itself constitutes a regularity, and is continually on the increase. In looking back into the past we are looking towards periods when it was a less and less decided tendency But its own essential nature is to grow. It is a generalizing tendency; it causes actions in the future to follow some generalization of past actions; and this tendency is itself something capable of similar generalizations; and thus, it is self-generative. We have therefore only to suppose the smallest spoor of it in the past, and that germ would have been bound to develop into a mighty and overruling principle, until it supersedes itself by strengthening habits into absolute laws regulating the action of all things in every respect in the indefinite future....' †'... Our conceptions of the first stages of the development, before time

* 6.33. † 1.409.

yet existed, must be as vague and figurative as the expressions of the first chapter of Genesis. Out of the womb of indeterminacy we must say that there would have come something, by the principle of Firstness, which we may call a flash. Then by the principle of habit there would have been a second flash. Though time would not yet have been, this second flash was in some sense after the first, because resulting from it. Then there would have come other successions ever more and more closely connected, the habits and the tendency to take them ever strengthening themselves, until the events would have been bound together into something like a continuous flow. We have no reason to think that even now time is quite perfectly continuous and uniform in its flow. The quasi-flow which would result would, however, differ essentially from time in this respect, that it would not necessarily be in a single stream. Different flashes might start different streams, between which there should be no relations of contemporaneity or succession. So one stream might branch into two, or two might coalesce. But the further result of habit would inevitably be to separate utterly those that were long separated, and to make those which presented frequent common points coalesce into perfect union. Those that were completely separated would be so many different worlds which would know nothing of one another; so that the effect would be just what we actually observe.'*

Before we attempt to criticize this extraordinary résumé of cosmic history, let us notice the broad outlines of that interpretation of 'what we actually observe' to which, in Peirce's belief, his cosmogonic vision or hypothesis should incline us.

On this interpretation what we ordinarily think of as purely material processes are those in connection with which the 'tendency to take habits' has become, in one respect, all but completely realized, but in another respect has become curiously checked or ossified. On the one hand they are such processes as appear to have made their final adjustments to all other processes relevant to them; hence the laws governing their behaviour are

* 1·412.

comparatively easy to find out: but they have thereby lost, or have to all appearances ceased to exercise, their birthright of taking on new habits of adjustment to new factors in their environments. In fact Peirce believed – and claimed that the experience of every practising physicist and astronomer provides support for this belief – that there are occasional 'slight aberrancies from law' in all so-called material processes.* This, however, did not prevent him from maintaining that, in contrast with other types of process, viz. those which we call adaptive and intelligent, material processes stand out as prototypes *both* of manifest regularity *and* of blind or 'brute' compulsion. They are peculiarly predictable, just because in one sense they are utterly unintelligible.

By contrast, all living things, and in particular those which we ordinarily think of as housing minds or intelligences, are in some degree out of equilibrium with the things and processes that surround them. They have not made their final adjustments, nor (apparently) have they reached the limit of their capacity for making new adjustments to their environments. What is peculiar to allegedly 'pure' mental processes is the predominant part played by signs which guide, co-ordinate, and control different – and often temporally quite remote – phases of organic behaviour;† or, to supply a terminology used by John Dewey in this department of Peirce's exegesis, Peirce's idea is that sign-behaviour supervenes on other forms of organic behaviour, and in its own characteristic way intervenes in the course of the latter, rendering it more continuous, more adequate because of larger scope, i.e. in a broad sense, more reasonable.

This interpretation of 'what we actually observe' – of the world disclosed to us in everyday experience and by history and the natural sciences – may now be brought into relation with Peirce's doctrine of categories. The development of 'concrete reasonableness', which is most clearly exemplified in the action of signs, but which is also suggested by the generally adaptive

* 6·46, 6·264. † 4·550 ff.

character of all organic behaviour (and perhaps also by the 'completed adjustments' of so-called purely material processes), corresponds to a gradual increase in 'prominence' of the Third category. 'Coalescence, the becoming continuous, the being governed by general laws, the becoming instinct with general ideas, are all but phases of one and the same process of the growth of reasonableness.'* But this increase in the prominence of the Third category will never lead, at any assignable date, to the elimination of 'arbitrary sporting', 'objective chance', 'pure spontaneity': on the contrary – perhaps too much on the contrary to suit Peirce's general world-picture – this tendency to random variation has been very much in evidence, at any rate among organic species on this planet, during recent millennia. Moreover, the tension between these two ('First' and 'Third') aspects of existence serves to explain this all-pervasiveness of Peirce's Second category – the brute reactions and mutual interferences of things or systems of things which have so far failed to come into conditions of equilibrium one with another.

*

We can now return to the main criticisms which this ambitious if sketchy cosmology seems almost designed to invite; and for our present purpose it will be best to concentrate on its origin, i.e. that cosmogonic principle which Peirce tries to express in the two passages quoted on pages 217 to 219. For it is his use of this principle which distinguishes Peirce's special form of panpsychism or hylozoism from others; and if we can expose the essential weakness of his cosmology here at the source there will be no need to pursue its consequences in further detail.

1. Perhaps the most obvious criticism to be made is that Peirce's cosmogonic principle is couched in such openly – one might almost say shamelessly – anthropomorphic terms. In the first of the passages quoted above he finds the cosmic representative of his First category is 'a chaos of unpersonalized feeling', and the cosmic representative of his Third category is the ideal of a

* 5·4.

perfectly symmetrical system 'in which mind is at last crystallized in the infinitely distant future'. Again in the second longer
passage he writes without apology – perhaps biomorphically
rather than anthropomorphically – of 'germs' or 'spoors' of a
'generalizing tendency', meaning the tendency of random
events to fall into a roughly continuous temporal series. But
Peirce was quite aware that his ideas would meet with this
criticism; and he rounds on it boldly, in many passages, with the
retort that we can never hope to avoid some degree of anthropomorphism in our explanatory conceptions.* What Peirce has
in mind is something like this. We saw in the previous chapter
that any immediate quality of feeling can be taken as a 'psychic
representation' of the First category; similarly our direct sense
of reaction, effort, and resistance and the peculiar experience of
'learning or mental growth', provide us with psychic representatives of the Second category and the Third respectively.
Now Peirce could quite reasonably urge that no one could
understand his categories, or could attempt to use them as first
principles of existence, unless he could, however indirectly,
point to instances – to approximations to pure instances – of
them within his or her specifically human experience. But the
specific characteristics of such instances do not enter into the
definition, or generalized description, of the universal categories. The specific qualities of our own immediate feelings and
sensations, and the specific effects of our reactions and intellectual advances, are no doubt unique: certainly they are known
to rest on highly complex physical conditions which may be
destined to obtain for only a very short time on the surface of
this very small planet. But this does not mean that other things
or processes may not illustrate, each in its proper way, the universality of Peirce's three categories. When, therefore, Peirce
honours his 'cosmic representatives' of each of his categories
with epithets drawn from the vocabulary of our specifically
human experience, he is simply doing on a larger scale what all
mankind – including men of science – have periodically been

* 1·316, 5·212, 5·536.

compelled to do: he is making use of metaphor, which does not necessarily imply that he is being deceived by all the imperfect analogies which his metaphorical way of speaking might suggest.

But Peirce cannot be let off so lightly on the present score; for it seems clear that he was deceived by some of these imperfect analogies. This can most usefully be illustrated by the way he uses the broad message of his First category in expounding his cosmogonic principle. We may re-state this message in the proposition that whatever exists manifests some immediate quality of its own, and that proper appreciation of any such immediate quality forces us to recognize the primordial potential 'measureless variety and multiplicity' of the world. Now Peirce of course knew perfectly well that the immediate qualities of our sensations and feelings show a high degree of correlation with certain antecedent physical conditions. Not all immediate qualities, therefore, can be taken as manifestations of 'spontaneity', 'freshness', etc. The effect of Peirce's categorical teaching in this connection is rather as follows. There is nothing self-contradictory in the idea of an immediate quality to whose manifestations no fixed (causal) relations can be ascribed; but again there is nothing in this purely formal statement to suggest that there actually *are* such manifestations of immediate qualities. On the other hand, Peirce's conception of the measureless potential variety and multiplicity of the world does in a sense explain why there may well be at any assignable date 'slight aberrancies from law'; and herein lies the main importance of the first part of his categorical teaching. But it is one thing to suggest or argue for some degree of indeterminacy within a general determinist framework; quite another thing to suggest the possibility of 'a point in the infinitely distant past when there was no law but mere indeterminacy,' or in which there was 'a mere chaos of unpersonalized feeling... sporting here and there in pure arbitrariness'. It is important to emphasize that, as ordinarily used, such words as 'spontaneity', 'freshness', 'arbitrariness', 'sporting', etc., presuppose a background of facts or processes which are *not* spontaneous, sportive, or arbitrary, but which are, on the contrary, repetitive, regular, and reliable. This explains why we commonly use the word 'spontaneous' as a word of sympathetic interest or encouragement: a spontaneous effort or gesture is one which may lead, in relation to some relatively stable background and in contrast to merely repetitive or habitual behaviour, to new and more effective forms of regular behaviour. Similarly we tend to think of a biological 'sport' in connection with its chances of survival within a comparatively stable, or at least regularly changing, environment. But such considerations as these can have no place in Peirce's primordial state of mere indeterminacy. The fact is that, despite Peirce's efforts to show that such a primordial state would contain 'the germ of a generalizing tendency', his accounts of it inevitably suggest a 'cosmic representation' of his First category *alone*; that is to say, he is supposing a state of affairs in which neither his Second nor his Third category would be manifested at all.

To sum up, Peirce can quite plausibly rebut the general charge that his cosmogonic principle, and hence his cosmology as a whole, contains anthropomorphic conceptions. But when this objection is pressed more closely in connection with his cosmogonic principle, it is seen to have real force: it brings out the fact that in applying his doctrine of categories in his cosmology Peirce has virtually gone back on its primary thesis, viz. that each of his three categories *is* universal.

2. Peirce writes of a 'generalizing tendency' or 'tendency to habit' arising from 'pure arbitrariness'. This is a picturesque version of what other passages show to have been a fixed belief with Peirce: namely that a 'universe of absolute chance' would include the one chance that some of the characters manifested in it at random or quite fortuitously might become associated, in the sense that, having once occurred in a definite relation, they would thereupon tend to *recur* in that kind of relation.★ This is the assumption on the basis of which Peirce proceeds to sketch out his picture of a universe in which the tendency

★ 6·200 ff.

towards association or regularity will be constantly on the increase.

Quite apart from the difficulty of conceiving how such an assumption could be tested experimentally, there are two quite fatal objections to Peirce's idea of pure chance 'generating' a tendency towards association or regularity or habit from a state of affairs in which there was 'no law but mere indeterminacy'. The first objection, which echoes that which we have already made against Peirce's use of the words 'spontaneous', 'sporting', etc., is that, as ordinarily employed, the idea of pure chance, or of a purely random distribution of characteristics, presupposes the ideas of (a) a law determining how the purely random character of the distribution shall be ensured, and (b) certain actual physical conditions whose persistence (predictably regular persistence) will ensure the applicability of the law that determines the randomness of the distribution. At least, without these conditions the idea of pure chance has no experimental basis whatever. The truth seems to be that pure chance or randomness is not an isolable conception; on the contrary, it seems inevitably to involve its complementary opposite, the idea of regularity.* But how in that case can the idea of pure chance be applied, with any definite meaning, to Peirce's supposed primordial state of sheer indeterminacy?

The second objection is even simpler and more obviously fatal. If it can be given any determinate meaning (which may be doubted), the phrase 'a universe of absolute chance' must mean a collection of objects or characters such that it would be false to say of any two or more of them that they show *any* tendency towards regular connection one with another. But if this is so, then the conception of such a universe giving rise to a 'tendency to habit' is as meaningless as the conception of a round square.

* Oddly enough, Peirce himself gives many excellent expressions of this point of view, notably at 6·406, where he concludes, 'We may, therefore, say that a world of chance is simply our actual world viewed from the standpoint of an animal at the very vanishing-point of intelligence. The actual world is almost a chance-medley to the mind of a polyp.'

How could Peirce fail to see these objections to the centra principles of his cosmology? Some light on this question is no doubt thrown by the fact that Peirce was deeply – and rightly – impressed by the use of the notion of chance in two of the greatest achievements of nineteenth-century science, Darwin's theory of selection (whose virtually statistical character Peirce alone of his contemporaries had the merit of recognizing) and the kinetic theory of gases. As early as 1878 Peirce had written, 'Mr Darwin proposed to apply the statistical method to Biology. The same thing has been done in a widely different branch of science, the theory of gases. Though unable to say what the movement of any particular molecule of gas would be on a certain hypothesis regarding the constitution of this class of bodies, Clausius and Maxwell were yet able, by the application of the doctrine of probabilities, to predict that in the long run such and such a proportion of the molecules would, *under given circumstances* [our italics], acquire such and such velocities; that there would take place, every second, such and such a number of collisions, etc.; and from these propositions they were able to deduce certain properties of gases, especially in regard to their heat-relations. In like manner, Darwin, while unable to say what the operation of variation *and natural selection* [our italics] in every individual case will be, demonstrates that in the long run they will adapt animals to their circumstances.'* But that these important applications of the idea of probability differ fundamentally from the use which Peirce claims to make of it in his cosmogonic principles is sufficiently indicated by the phrases which we have italicized in the above passage. Maxwell applied the notions of chance and probability to motions of molecules under circumstances of relatively determinate physical character, e.g. a sealed jar of definite dimensions capable of being heated up to certain degrees of temperature; but it is evident that in a universe of absolute chance no such constant or controllable factors can be assumed. Similarly in the case of Darwin's hypothesis, it is as the effect of random variations within

* 5.364.

an otherwise relatively stable or at least regularly changing environment, and in conjunction with the regular operation of natural selection, that the survival or non-survival of particular breeding-groups is explained.

It might be suggested, however, that there are other uses of the calculus of probabilities in science, which help us to appreciate, if not wholly to justify, this part of Peirce's thought. Physicists and biologists write of 'drift phenomena', i.e. changes of motions or of heritable characters whose direction can be accounted for on the assumption of chance variation, without any reference to particular features of their physical or biological environments; and in a number of passages Peirce shows a marked interest in, or anticipation of, phenomena of this kind.* Now it is perhaps natural to say that such phenomena can be explained simply by means of certain probability theories; as, for example, the most likely direction of the 'drunkard's stagger' can be calculated from the theory of random errors. But in fact, in applying the calculus of probabilities to drift phenomena, scientists always presuppose certain broad regularities in the world in which these phenomena occur – at the very least the continuity of their spatial and temporal relations or the continuous operation, relative to them, of certain fundamental physical constants. But, on Peirce's own admission, not even the broadest regularities, not even anything approximating to a continuous temporal series, can be assumed in a universe of absolute chance. Consequently, if he thought that the statistical explanation of drift phenomena gives any real support to his cosmogonic hypothesis of chance spontaneity, he was again mistaken.

3. One of the chief motives that led Peirce to advance his cosmogonic principle was undoubtedly his belief that 'among the regular facts that have to be explained is law or regularity itself', and, even more emphatically, that – in contrast to 'indeterminacy or pure firstness' and 'haecceity or pure secondness' – 'facts of a general or orderly nature' essentially require or

* 1·396–9, 6·15.

call for explanation. Peirce's hypothesis of a world of absolute chance, capable of giving rise to a tendency to habit or order, represents one attempt, albeit a bankrupt one, to supply the required explanation of law or regularity itself. A second step to the same end is his suggestion that the effect of a 'generalizing tendency ... causing actions in the future to follow some generalization of past actions' would be to 'separate utterly' those streams of existence that had already been long separated, and 'to make those which presented frequent common points coalesce into perfect union'; consequently since 'those which were completely separated would be so many different worlds which know nothing of one another, the effect would be just what we actually observe.'

This last sentence may well arouse the suspicion that Peirce's explanatory principle here is too true to be good. For if its effect is simply to account for what we observe – or, if Peirce would wish it, for all that we actually do or possibly could observe *and nothing else* – then, by Pragmatist principles, it is a worthless hypothesis. A genuine hypothesis is one which explains how or why certain facts are as they are in contradiction from the ways other facts are, or from ways these facts themselves conceivably might have been. But Peirce's hypothesis appears not to be subject to these conditions. It is an explanation, or would-be-explanation, which, to all appearances, could not be falsified. Whatever degree of 'unity', 'regularity', 'symmetry', it may manifest, any state of affairs which we observe will have resulted, on Peirce's view, from that 'self-generative generalizing tendency' which has the effect of eliminating as essentially unknowable, or of making so many different worlds of, any streams of existence which have not contributed to the world which we actually observe. But a hypothesis which will explain *anything* that is observed, in fact explains nothing that is observed. Considered as an explanation of facts, therefore, this part of Peirce's cosmogonic principle is no better and no worse than the explanation 'God makes them so'. All it does is to add an *image* – of a combined (cosmic-scale) threshing and binding apparatus –

to the tautologous statement that what is observable excludes what is not observable. As such it is precisely the kind of hypothesis or explanation which Peirce's Pragmatism is designed to exclude.*

If these criticisms of Peirce's cosmogonic principle are sound, then it may seem idle to consider further the general 'world-picture' which, as he claims, this principle requires us to accept. And indeed Peirce's pan-psychism or hylo-zoism, and his conception of a single supreme evolutionary law governing all observably regular processes, lie open to the same line of criticism as we applied to the previous paragraph. Cosmic scale and explanatory all-inclusiveness, if claimed for any hypothesis, are a sure sign of the practical or experimental vacuity of that hypothesis. On the other hand, as we have seen in connection with Peirce's doctrine of the Universal Categories, it is perfectly possible for a proposition claiming universal application to be of genuine value if it has the effect of 'rearranging' traditional explanatory conceptions which have outlived their usefulness. It therefore seems worth while to ask whether hypotheses approximating in certain respects to any parts of Peirce's cosmogonic principle can be found, or seem likely to occur in the future, in different departments of science.

Now it might be suggested that hypotheses showing an important resemblance to Peirce's 'generative-cum-eliminative' principle of 'habit-taking' are likely to be used (if they are not already in fact used) to explain the origins of relatively closed systems – whether physical, biological, or social – from previous relatively open systems. An interesting example of a problem of this sort is provided by speculation as to the first origins of life on this earth. Here the main difficulty is to conceive *at once* of certain conditions of equilibrium, or of certain periodic 'exchange phenomena', between groups of molecules – conditions approximating in some degree to the phenomena of life – *and* of a

---

* It might be argued that its suggestion of a number of distinct time-series provides a loophole against the above criticism; but this is a suggestion which Peirce, in his published writings, nowhere seeks to elaborate.

chemical environment which, although as yet containing none of the characteristic chemical products of living forms, would nevertheless conduce to the emergence and survival of life. Or, to condense this difficulty in a metaphor, the first emergence of life appears to have been the kind of process that inevitably covers its own tracks and thus conceals – or perhaps destroys – its own immediate antecedents. How this difficulty will be met, only the future of science can show; but it seems clear that any answer to it must contain hypotheses as to forms of action of which no direct or unquestionable effects are ever likely to be observed, and that in this situation we have nothing but analogies – and perhaps only the broadest and shakiest analogies – to assist us.

This example helps us to see Peirce's generative–cum–eliminative cosmogonic principle in a more favourable light; for if it does nothing else of value, Peirce's principle at least draws our attention to the fact that every day before our eyes, as well as in the remoter reaches of time and space, new relatively closed systems are coming into being and are either maintaining themselves or being disrupted. The study of the genesis and survival of such systems may not be the supreme object of science, as acceptance of Peirce's cosmology would seem to require, but it is certainly a cardinal object of science and one in connection with which comparatively little progress has been made. The main reason for this seems to have been as follows. Most scientists since the Renaissance have assumed that the only ultimate variety which the physical world displays – the different configurations of particles in different regions of space at different times – is of a kind that was, so to speak, present from the outset, each of its successive manifestations being exactly calculable from a knowledge of any of its earlier manifestations. The question of the origin and maintenance of new closed systems at once renders this assumption suspect, and Peirce's cosmogonic principle may therefore be considered as a pertinent, if very imperfectly formulated, criticism of it. In order to decide whether this criticism contains anything of positive value, we should try to see whether and how far it enabled Peirce to descry the main new watersheds in nineteenth-century science, its main growing-points, and the main dangers and impasses that awaited it. Let us, therefore, consider in this connection some of his most important insights into the structure of nineteenth-century physics and biology.

Peirce was one of the first, if not *the* first, of philosophers of physics to suggest that the fundamental division in that subject is between laws of reversible and laws of irreversible processes. In the physics of Newton, which was to remain the model of scientific explanation to almost all men of science up to the close of the last century, dynamical laws, which determine the past in the same way as the future and are therefore theoretically reversible, are taken without question to be the paradigm of lawfulness or intelligibility. But as against this, Peirce argues that '... almost all the phenomena of bodies here on earth which attract our attention ... are irreversible. Such, for instance, is birth, growth, life. ... Such is all motion resisted by friction or by the viscosity of fluids, as all terrestrial motion is. Such is the conduction of heat, combustion, capillarity, diffusion of fluids ... in short, substantially everything that ordinary experience reveals, except the motions of the stars.... About the only familiar actions which appear to sense reversible are the motion of a projectile, the bending of a bow or other spring, a freely swinging pendulum, a telephone, a microphone, a galvanic battery, and a dynamo.'* Recent developments in physical theory may have slightly weakened the force of some of Peirce's examples here, but the general aim of his argument is sound. It is to show that in accepting mechanical (reversible) processes as paradigms of lawfulness and intelligibility, scientists have made a gigantic and hardly defensible assumption. The result is, as Peirce points out, that 'people are persuaded that everything that happens in the material universe is a motion completely determined by inviolable laws of dynamics; and that, they think, leaves no room for any other influence. But the

* 6·72.

laws of dynamics stand on quite a different footing from the laws of gravitation, elasticity, electricity, and the like. The laws of dynamics are very much like logical principles, if they are not precisely that. They only say how bodies will move after you have said what the forces are. They permit any forces, and therefore any motions. Only, the principle of the conservation of energy requires us to explain certain kinds of motions by special hypotheses about molecules and the like. Thus, in order that the viscosity of gases should not disobey that law, we have to suppose that gases have a certain molecular constitution. Setting dynamical laws to one side, then, as hardly being positive laws, but rather mere formal principles, we have only the laws of gravitation, elasticity, electricity, and chemistry. Now who will deliberately say that our knowledge of these laws is sufficient to make us reasonably confident that they are absolutely eternal and immutable and that they escape the great law of evolution? Each hereditary character is a law, but it is subject to development and to decay. Each habit of an individual is a law; but these laws are modified so easily by the operation of self-control, that it is one of the most patent of facts that ideals and thought generally have a very great influence on human conduct.'*

This is an immensely impressive statement; worth by itself many volumes by later evolutionary cosmologists. No doubt Peirce generalizes wildly when he suggests that all irreversible processes conform to a single 'great law of evolution', and when he goes on to claim that such processes are intelligible only by reference to the ideas of chance and probability.† But the originality of his insights in this last respect was truly astonishing; and he deserves all the credit that has been bestowed on him for his prophecy that the fundamental laws of physics (and of biology and of the social sciences) may turn out to require a statistical interpretation.‡ It might of course be objected that these insights of Peirce are to be attributed to his intimate acquaintance with physical researches, his logical training, his wide readings in the history of science, and so on; but none of

* 1·348.   † 6·73.   ‡ 6·11, 6·85.

these things suffices to explain why Peirce, almost alone of philosopher-scientists of his age, was able to break away so completely from the restricting influences of the classic Newtonian world-picture. And part of the explanation of this fact would seem to be that Peirce possessed an alternative world-picture of his own: a picture which, whatever its shortcomings, allowed him a remarkably illuminating view of the structure of nineteenth-century physics.

*

Peirce's discussions of the central problems of biology, and in particular of Darwin's hypothesis, are of a far more uneven quality than his writings on nineteenth-century physics, and are of a highly polemical character. The Darwinian theory, it seemed to him, had been put forward within that general framework of ideas which stems from Ockham, Descartes, Hobbes, and Newton, according to which (omitting optional theistic trimmings) the only realities are individual existences acting and moving in accordance with what appear to be immutable laws. But 'in their genuine nature', Peirce affirms, 'no two ideas could be more hostile than the idea of evolution and that individualism upon which Ockham erected his philosophy. ... Evolutionism must eventually restore the rejected idea of reasonableness energizing the world (no matter through what mechanism of natural selection or otherwise) which belonged to the scholastic modifications of it by Aquinas and Scotus.'* Here we are back to that insistence on the reality of final causes which we have met in connection with Peirce's doctrine of Thought-signs and in his accounts of his Third category, and which is given more concrete embodiment in his image of a single process of evolution towards 'a world absolutely perfect, rational and symmetrical, in which mind at last is crystallized in the infinitely distant future'.

But surely, it will be protested, such a conception of evolu-

---

* Unpublished Peirce manuscript, dating from 1901, quoted by Wiener in *Evolution and the Founders of Pragmatism*, p. 91.

tion as this can contribute nothing to the understanding of biological science. And when Peirce proceeds to combine the conception with his own hypothesis of chance-spontaneity and habit-taking, it must be admitted that his speculations seem very far removed from the actual problems, methods, and opportunities of biological researchers. On the other hand, Peirce must be given credit for emphasizing the virtually statistical character of the Darwinian theory – a character which rests on its initial assumption of an inherent tendency to variation in the offspring of every breeding-group. Moreover, Peirce also saw, with unusual clarity, that there are two supreme questions or groups of questions involved – and usually confused – in most discussions of evolution. First, what status does any particular biological theory accord to the fact or 'story' of evolution itself? Second, what are the *causes* which any particular theory ascribes to the fact or story of evolution; and how are we to explain the initial bias, displayed by this or that theorist, in favour of causes of this or that particular sort? In his best writings on evolution Peirce gives us remarkably well-balanced answers to both these questions. As to the first, he is content to affirm that, whatever its mechanisms, evolution is essentially an adaptive process, and as such cannot be appreciated with the Ockham-Descartes-Hobbes-Newton world-picture; and he was no doubt right to insist that this fact is in some way bound up with the inherent tendency to variation postulated by Darwin. As to the second question, Peirce was willing to concede that natural selection is one main cause of evolution, and that we should do well to look for appropriate replicas of it when we apply the idea of evolution to the history of human ideas and institutions. On the other hand he insisted that the biological evidence fully allows for the operation of other causes as well.* Among these he mentions evolution by sporting, without reference to the action of natural selection, and evolution resulting from cataclysmic changes in the physical environment of the forms concerned; and he also tries to rehabilitate, in terms of the ideas of sporting

* 6·298 ff.

and of habit, the kernel of truth 'that lies enwrapped in the theory of Lamarck.'* Rejection of causes of these latter sorts by Darwinians was to be explained, it seemed to Peirce, primarily by the fact that the Ockham-Descartes-Hobbes-Newton world-picture has no place for them.

After the passing of fifty years, it is easy for us to appreciate the sagacity of these judgements and the width and balance of the survey of biological theories upon which they are based. And here again, it seems clear, Peirce was greatly assisted, in his capacity as philosopher of science, by the fact that he possessed a world-picture of his own, which, at the very least, liberated him from an unduly narrow, and indeed a contorting, interpretation of current biological problems and discoveries.

*

How can this more sympathetic appraisal of Peirce's cosmology be reconciled with our earlier criticisms of it? These criticisms showed that his cosmology is a failure, and an inevitable failure: its component hypotheses are to be rejected on grounds supplied by Peirce's own logical doctrine of Pragmatism. But now his cosmology appears to have the real merit of suggesting certain salient weaknesses in its dominant rival – roughly, the world-picture inherited from Newton. As against this latter suggestion, however, it may well be urged that all our previous talk of alternative world-pictures has been a sheer mistake. The different sciences, it may be said, do not make up or in any way contribute to – still less do they presuppose – a total world-picture. The only proper description of a given science is in terms of its characteristic experiments and theorems: these represent the systematic development of certain lines of human interest which are, essentially, as selective as the simplest of our perceptions and reactions. Consequently it is impossible as it were to *add* the results of some branch of physics to those of some branch of biology – or *a fortiori* to those of some branch of economics or sociology: the different items just won't add up.

* 6·299.

Moreover, the same argument goes to show that no total world-picture or picture of reality can underlie, or be presupposed by, the discoveries of the different sciences. Quite apart from the fact that we could no more devise or use a picture of reality as a whole than we could react to reality as a whole, the very idea of such a picture rests on an initial misapprehension; viz. that the different sciences provide us with pictures of different 'parts' of reality. What they in fact do (the present objection maintains) is to give us the power to predict in different ways suited to fundamentally different types of situation: i.e. the different sciences *are* their respective experiments and theorems. Vague talk of alternative world-pictures springs from a failure to recognize this fact and succeeds only in obscuring it.

This is an important objection to our later, more sympathetic appraisal of Peirce's cosmology; but it ignores certain important relevant facts and greatly over-simplifies others. In the first place, a science is *not* simply its experiments and theorems; it is rather the devising and getting to these by certain methods and instruments, applied within an inherited framework of ideas. Further, among those inherited ideas are some which can very properly be described as cosmological; for example, the Hebraic idea of divine creation – or the consequent image of a material world which has been complete in all its essentials since it came into existence at some suitably distant point in time – which certainly influenced the thought of Newton and, if less directly, the thought of almost every leading theorist in the natural sciences up to the middle of the last century. Nor has this influence been confined to preambles and appendices, or to the occasional pious turns of phrase, in the texts of the great scientific masters: on the contrary it does much to explain some of their most important 'subjective preferences' – that of Maxwell for explanations of the dynamical rather than the statistical type, or the presumption, so luckily accepted by the founders of modern chemistry, that the elements will retain their essential properties unchanged when they are absorbed into different chemical compounds.

But if this much be granted, then not only ought we to make every effort to understand how *one* cosmological image has entered into scientific thinking, we should also seek to understand the different ways in which different cosmologies have done or conceivably might do this. Here is the general justification of our discussion of Peirce's cosmology, and of our attempts to compare its actual or likely effects on certain departments of science with those of the Ockham-Descartes-Hobbes-Newton scheme of ideas. This means, however, that we are faced with the following paradox. From the strictly logical standpoint, all cosmologies are so many mistakes, misconceptions, monstrosities even; on the other hand, they somehow discharge a function of the first importance both to the advancement of the sciences and to the historical understanding of them. Any attempt to deal with this paradox in general terms would carry us far beyond the scope of the present study; but, in so far as it relates to Peirce's cosmology in particular, we may perhaps do something to illuminate it – and thus to underline the force of our more positive appraisal of this part of Peirce's work.

It seems reasonable to assume, granted continued scientific progress and intelligent general discussion of scientific results, that in a few decades the kind of distinction made by Peirce between laws governing reversible and laws governing irreversible processes will have been both generalized and clarified to cover what are at present obscure or border-line cases. It would then be possible for us to give a useful statement of the distinction which we all vaguely recognize, between those sciences whose laws are primarily (if not exclusively) of a forecasting or predictive character – sciences which we might describe as 'nomic' – and those sciences whose laws serve primarily, not to make predictions, but to unify or 'thicken' our conceptions of different strands of cosmic or terrestrial or biological or human history – sciences which we might describe as '-gonic' rather than 'nomic'. Should this supposition prove true, then it will be much easier for future students of philosophy than it is for us to appreciate the value of Peirce's cosmology.

At the present juncture it would probably be true to say that those philosophers who insist most strongly on the importance of the above distinction, have done very little to clarify its nature; while those who deny its existence – by maintaining that laws of the predictive type (characteristic of 'nomic' sciences) provide us with the only possible examples of genuine explanation – have at least, by the very starkness of their error, done something to stimulate interest on this important issue. Now Peirce's cosmology certainly looks forward to, and in a sense prophesies, that line of scientific advance which, we have supposed, will ultimately facilitate the required distinction (or an adequate account of the distinction) between sciences of the 'nomic' and sciences of the '-gonic' types; but how usefully it does this is a matter on which it is extraordinarily difficult for us to judge. For what it is worth, the opinion of the present author is that Peirce's cosmological writings, considered in this respect, contain many more suggestions of value – suggestions that startle and stimulate not only by their boldness but by their hard-headed, business-like character – than do the more celebrated evolutionary cosmologies of, for example, Bergson and Whitehead.

As to the spirit in which Peirce advanced his own cosmogonic principle in metaphysics ('Tell us how the laws of nature came about, and we may distinguish in some measure between laws that might and laws that could not have resulted from such a process of development'*), nothing can be more certain in the whole of Peircian exegesis than that he believed this principle to express the interests, and the seriously threatened interests, of the free spirit of science itself. To accept as ultimate – as Ockhamism or Nominalism would have us do – a certain plurality and initial distribution of objects or characters to be explained, and a certain plurality of general laws which explain later distribution of these objects or characters, spelt, for Peirce, nothing more or less than barricading (i.e. restricting) the road of inquiry. Whether Peirce was right or wrong in this belief is a

* 1·408.

question whose answer hinges largely on our previous question as to the relation between laws of a primarily forecasting and laws of a primarily unifying character; but whatever answer may be ultimately returned to it, Peirce's claim here is something that should not be allowed to pass unconsidered. And it is an interesting reflection on the present state of philosophy that this particular claim of Peirce, which is so crucial to his general habits of thought, has met with little or no response, positive or negative, from even those philosophers who most freely admit the greatness of their debt to him.

That Peirce's motives in propounding his cosmogonic principle were genuinely scientific in spirit, deserves all the more emphasis because it has sometimes been suggested that in this part of his work he betrays a sad falling-off from his own boasted standards of scientific impartiality, and a sudden descent into that kind of wishful or hopeful thinking that is all too characteristic of 'tender-minded' philosophers. It is true that in one very late passage Peirce maintains as an 'additional reason' for accepting his own cosmogonic viewpoint and in particular his hypothesis of chance-spontaneity, that the world-picture resulting from it 'satisfies his religious instinct' better than does the dominant Newtonian view of a universe 'completed at the outset'.* But as against this one very late passage there are at least a dozen in the *Collected Papers* which show us Peirce's main reason for recommending his own cosmogony in place of the Newtonian world-picture: viz. that the latter inevitably regards the plurality and variety of things as arbitrarily fixed – at the outset – and thus has the effect, sooner or later, of 'blocking the road of Inquiry'.† This is Peirce's central thought in all his cosmological writings, even if his occasional uses of religious phraseology to express the world-outlook which he recommends may sometimes obscure it. In general, despite the obvious strength of his religious beliefs, Peirce succeeded in 'not

---

* Quoted by Wiener in *Evolution and the Founders of Pragmatism*, p. 95, cf. p. 227 *ibid.*

† 1·137–40, 1·405, 1·406, 6·60.

mixing up religion and philosophy'; and when he does draw comparisons between the attitudes of religion and those of scientific inquiry, the result is usually an effective illustration of the latter rather than a vindication, or attempted vindication, of the former.

This point is well illustrated in the following long, rambling, yet surprisingly eloquent – and to sensitive readers profoundly moving – sentence from a fragment dated 1906. 'If', Peirce there writes, 'a Pragmaticist is asked what he means by "God", he can only say that just as long acquaintance with a man of great character may deeply influence one's whole manner of conduct, so that a glance at his portrait may make a difference, just as almost living with Dr Johnson enabled poor Boswell to write an immortal book and a really sublime book, just as long study of the works of Aristotle may make him an acquaintance, so if contemplation and study of the physico-psychical universe can imbue a man with principles of conduct analogous to the influence of a great man's works or conversation, then that analogue of a mind – for it is impossible to say that *any* human attribute is *literally* applicable – is what he means by "God".'* Considered as an attempt to illuminate the religious consciousness, this is perhaps a somewhat banal statement; but, apart from the light which it throws on Peirce's attitude to his own life and character, it gives remarkable expression to one of his profoundest insights into the 'scientific intelligence'. In this respect the mention of Aristotle as an acquaintance is the key to the whole passage. To the great thinkers of the Middle Ages Aristotle was *the teacher* par excellence; so to Peirce is the physico-psychical universe, before which he has stood so long in the rôle of learner, conscious of his practical and moral inadequacies, his need of a master, but conscious now that from the purely intellectual standpoint his attitude of a learner has been not his weakness but his glory. Nor did Peirce make the mistake of claiming supreme value for this attitude, as other scientifically minded philosophers have done. It is altogether characteristic of

* 6·502.

his breadth and generosity of spirit that he ranked moral above intellectual values, and aesthetic values above moral – though with the characteristically tart comment that this latter belief had not been strengthened or illuminated by his readings in philosophical aesthetics. Indeed by nothing more than this, his admirably humane sense of proportion, was Peirce aided in his task of providing scientific men with the kind of metaphysical 'leads' which their work, today as much as in the nineteenth century, so evidently requires. His mistake lay in hoping that such a metaphysics could itself be, in any usefully exact sense, scientific.

BIBLIOGRAPHICAL NOTES

A. General

An almost complete bibliography of Peirce's writings is given in Vol. VIII of *The Collected Papers*. Further bibliographical material, along with much else of the first importance for the understanding of Peirce's life and thought, is to be expected in Professor Max Fisch's forthcoming intellectual biography of Peirce.

Among the available selections from Peirce's writings, in addition to Professor Buchler's *The Philosophy of Peirce*, the following are recommended: *Chance, Love and Logic*, edited by Morris R. Cohen (Peter Smith, New York, 1949); *Values in a World of Chance*, Selected Writings of Charles S. Peirce, edited by Philip P. Wiener (Stanford University Press, 1958), and *Charles Sanders Peirce: Essays in the Philosophy of Science*, edited by Vincent Tomas (Liberal Arts Press, New York, 1957).

Among general commentaries and critical expositions of Peirce's philosophy the following may be mentioned: *Charles Peirce's Empiricism*, by Justus Buchler (Routledge and Kegan Paul, 1939); *An Introduction to Peirce's Philosophy interpreted as a System*, by J. K. Feibleman (Harpers, 1946); *Evolution and the Founders of Pragmatism*, by P. P. Wiener (Harvard University Press, 1949), especially Ch. IV; *The Thought of C. S. Peirce*, by T. A. Goudge (University of Toronto Press, 1950); *The Pragmatic Philosophy of Peirce*, by Manley Thompson (University of Chicago Press, 1953); and *The Pragmatism of C. S. Peirce*, by Hjalmar Wennerberg (CWK, Gleerup, Lund, 1962).

B. Special Notes to Chapters

CHAPTER ONE. Peirce's most successful statement of his own version of Pragmatism – and a statement made with the express purpose of distinguishing his own Pragmatism from that of James – is to be found in Ch. 17 of *The Philosophy of Peirce*. For the Pragmatism of James, see his *Pragmatism, a New Name for Old Ways of Thinking*, and his *The Meaning of Truth* (Longmans, Green & Co.); and for relevant correspondence between Peirce and James, see *The Thought and Character of William James*, Chs. 75 and 76.

CHAPTER TWO. Pending the publication of Max Fisch's authoritative biography of Peirce, the main source of information about his life and character is the article, supplied by Paul Weiss, in the *Dictionary of American Biography*. Important sidelights are provided in *The Thought and Character of William James*, and in the passages grouped as 'autobiographical' in the Indexes of all the volumes of *The Collected Papers*.

For an authoritative general account of Peirce's contributions to symbolic logic see C. I. Lewis, *Survey of Symbolic Logic*, Ch. V, Section VII. Paul Weiss's *D.A.B.* article is also of great interest on this topic.

CHAPTER THREE. The main argument of this chapter is a summary of the first of Peirce's papers of 1868, 'Concerning Certain Faculties Claimed for Man' (*Collected Papers*, 5·213 ff.). Unfortunately this paper is not reprinted in *The Philosophy of Peirce*, but a summary of its conclusions can be found in Ch. 16, pp. 229–30 of that volume.

CHAPTER FOUR. See Chs. 2, 4, 16, 19, and 20 of *The Philosophy of Peirce*. The advanced student of Peirce is also advised to consult on the relation between Induction and Hypothesis, *The Collected Papers*, 2·619 ff., and, on Peirce's distinction between 'percepts' and 'perceptual judgements', *The Collected Papers*, 1·254, 2·141, 5·54, 5·115 ff., and 5·151–79.

CHAPTER FIVE. A useful background is supplied by Ch. 7 and by Ch. 18, pp. 274–81 of *The Philosophy of Peirce*. But the advanced student must consult the Indexes of all volumes of *The Collected Papers*, under 'Sign' and 'Thought'.

CHAPTERS SIX AND SEVEN. See Chs. 17, 18, and 19 of *The Philosophy of Peirce*, also John Dewey's Supplementary Essay in *Chance, Love and Logic*.

CHAPTER EIGHT. See Chs. 6 and 22 of *The Philosophy of Peirce*.

CHAPTER NINE. See Chs. 22–8 of *The Philosophy of Peirce*, and, for a more sympathetic treatment of Peirce's Cosmology, Morris R. Cohen's Introduction to *Chance, Love and Logic*.

INDEX

B
945
P44
G3
1975

Gallie, W. B. 1912–

Peirce and
    pragmatism

DATE			